W9-CEZ-565

Gabon

WORLD BIBLIOGRAPHICAL SERIES
General Editors:
Robert G. Neville (Executive Editor)
John J. Horton

Robert A. Myers   Ian Wallace
Hans H. Wellisch   Ralph Lee Woodward, Jr.

John J. Horton is Deputy Librarian of the University of Bradford and currently Chairman of its Academic Board of Studies in Social Sciences. He has maintained a longstanding interest in the discipline of area studies and its associated bibliographical problems, with special reference to European Studies. In particular he has published in the field of Icelandic and of Yugoslav studies, including the two relevant volumes in the World Bibliographical Series.

Robert A. Myers is Associate Professor of Anthropology in the Division of Social Sciences and Director of Study Abroad Programs at Alfred University, Alfred, New York. He has studied post-colonial island nations of the Caribbean and has spent two years in Nigeria on a Fulbright Lectureship. His interests include international public health, historical anthropology and developing societies. In addition to *Amerindians of the Lesser Antilles: a bibliography* (1981), *A Resource Guide to Dominica, 1493-1986* (1987) and numerous articles, he has compiled the World Bibliographical Series volumes on *Dominica* (1987), *Nigeria* (1989) and *Ghana* (1991).

Ian Wallace is Professor of German at the University of Bath. A graduate of Oxford in French and German, he also studied in Tübingen, Heidelberg and Lausanne before taking teaching posts at universities in the USA, Scotland and England. He specializes in contemporary German affairs, especially literature and culture, on which he has published numerous articles and books. In 1979 he founded the journal *GDR Monitor*, which he continues to edit under its new title *German Monitor*.

Hans H. Wellisch is Professor emeritus at the College of Library and Information Services, University of Maryland. He was President of the American Society of Indexers and was a member of the International Federation for Documentation. He is the author of numerous articles and several books on indexing and abstracting, and has published *The Conversion of Scripts* and *Indexing and Abstracting: an International Bibliography*. He also contributes frequently to *Journal of the American Society for Information Science, The Indexer* and other professional journals.

Ralph Lee Woodward, Jr. is Director of Graduate Studies at Tulane University, New Orleans, where he has been Professor of History since 1970. He is the author of *Central America, a Nation Divided*, 2nd ed. (1985), as well as several monographs and more than sixty scholarly articles on modern Latin America. He has also compiled volumes in the World Bibliographical Series on *Belize* (1980), *Nicaragua* (1983), and *El Salvador* (1988). Dr. Woodward edited the Central American section of the *Research Guide to Central America and the Caribbean* (1985) and is currently editor of the Central American history section of the *Handbook of Latin American Studies*.

VOLUME 149

Gabon

David E. Gardinier

Compiler

CLIO PRESS

OXFORD, ENGLAND · SANTA BARBARA, CALIFORNIA
DENVER, COLORADO

British Library Cataloguing in Publication Data

Gabon. – (World Bibliographical Series)
I Gardinier, David E.   II. Series
016.96721

ISBN 1–85109–174–2

Clio Press Ltd.,
55 St. Thomas' Street,
Oxford OX1 1JG, England.

ABC-CLIO,
130 Cremona Drive,
Santa Barbara,
CA 93116, USA.

Designed by Bernard Crossland.
Typeset by Columns Design and Production Services Ltd, Reading, England.
Printed and bound in Great Britain by
Bookcraft (Bath) Limited

THE WORLD BIBLIOGRAPHICAL SERIES

This series, which is principally designed for the English speaker, will eventually cover every country (and many of the world's principal regions), each in a separate volume comprising annotated entries on works dealing with its history, geography, economy and politics; and with its people, their culture, customs, religion and social organization. Attention will also be paid to current living conditions – housing, education, newspapers, clothing, etc.– that are all too often ignored in standard bibliographies; and to those particular aspects relevant to individual countries. Each volume seeks to achieve, by use of careful selectivity and critical assessment of the literature, an expression of the country and an appreciation of its nature and national aspirations, to guide the reader towards an understanding of its importance. The keynote of the series is to provide, in a uniform format, an interpretation of each country that will express its culture, its place in the world, and the qualities and background that make it unique. The views expressed in individual volumes, however, are not necessarily those of the publisher.

VOLUMES IN THE SERIES

To Josefina, Kenneth, Annemarie and Lourdes Marie,
with love

Contents

Contents

Contents

Introduction

Gabon, which is located in western equatorial Africa, has a population of only one million living in an area of 103,000 square miles (267,667 sq. km.), that is, half the size of France. The development of its extensive petroleum, manganese, uranium, and timber resources in recent decades has given its people one of the highest average per capita incomes on the continent, though these revenues have not been distributed equally or equitably. As a result of the recent economic development, close to 40 per cent of this population is now concentrated in two coastal cities, Libreville (the administrative capital and commercial centre) and Port-Gentil (an industrial centre). The majority still inhabit some four thousand villages scattered throughout the interior where they live mainly from subsistence agriculture. French colonial rule between the 1840s and 1960 has left a many-sided legacy: economic ties with the western world; continued use of the French language as the primary means of communication among the country's forty or more Bantu-speaking peoples; and French-derived educational, political and administrative institutions. This legacy is valued by most of the population, who remain more strongly attached to France, its language and culture than that of any other sub-Saharan African country except perhaps the Ivory Coast. At the same time the policies of the government, headed since 1967 by President Omar Bongo, have transformed Gabon's economy and society in ways that have brought material benefits, extensive urbanization, and unrest. The transformations helped to shape the popular dissatisfactions that led to the upheavals of 1990 and, in turn, to the restoration of a multi-party political system and freer exercise of civil liberties.

Location

Gabon lies astride the equator between 2°30' North latitude and 4° South latitude and between 9° and 14° West longitude. The average

Introduction

distance from north to south is 550 kilometres and from east to west 600 kilometres. On the western side the Atlantic Ocean stretches along 800 kilometres of frequently indented coast. To the north-west lies Equatorial Guinea; to the north, Cameroon; and to the east and south, the Congo (the capital of which is Brazzaville). The boundaries between Gabon and these three states separate the sources of several important rivers from their outlets along the Atlantic as well as dividing ethnic groups, for they were drawn by France, Germany and Spain in the late nineteenth century without much knowledge of the geography and peoples of the interior.

Climate

Gabon possesses an equatorial climate with uniformly high temperatures (averaging 26°C or 78°F), high relative humidities, and mean annual rainfalls from 150 to 300 centimetres. It has two rainy seasons (from mid-February to mid-May and from mid-September to mid-December) and two dry seasons (from mid-May to mid-September and from mid-December to mid-February).

Physical features

Like the other western and equatorial African countries that border the Atlantic, Gabon is watered by systems of rivers and streams that empty into the ocean. Supreme among them is the Ogooué River, which with its many tributaries drains close to four-fifths of the country (220,000 sq. km.). Its largest southern tributary is the N'Gounié River, which joins it 150 kilometres upstream, and its largest northern tributary is the Ivindo, which enters much farther east at a point 350 kilometres from the coast. The two other river systems of most significance are the Como or Gabon River to the north of the Ogooué, whose broad mouth has been known historically as 'the Estuary', and the Nyanga River to the south. The far north is drained by the Woleu and N'Tem Rivers, which rise within Gabon but reach the Atlantic through Equatorial Guinea and Cameroon respectively, and the streams such as the Noya and the Temboni, which form the Rio Muni or Muni Estuary between Gabon and Equatorial Guinea. South of the several mouths or estuary of the Ogooué lie several small rivers (the Rembo N'komi, Rembo N'gove and the N'dogo) which empty into the lagoons of Fernan Vaz, Iguéla, and N'dogo or Setté-Cama respectively. Only a very small portion of the south-east is drained by streams flowing into the northern tributaries of the Congo River system. Though Gabon has many waterways, most of them are cut at various points by falls and rapids, which make large portions of them unnavigable. For example, the Ogooué, though 1,200 kilometres in length, is navigable without interruption only one-third of this distance, that is, from its estuary to the island of N'Djolé.

These rivers flow through a terrain whose relief can be separated into three regions of unequal area: plains, plateaux and mountains. First of all, there is a low-lying coastal plain 30 to 200 kilometres in width that nowhere exceeds 300 metres in elevation. This plain is narrowest in the far south and broadest in the estuaries of the Como (Gabon) and Ogooué Rivers. Plains also extend towards the interior through the valleys of the Nyanga, N'Gounié and Ogooué, in the last case to within 100 kilometres of the frontier with the Congo Republic. Plateaux at altitudes from 300 to 800 metres cover most of the remainder of the country, in particular the north and east. Out of them rise two mountain chains, the Monts de Cristal in the north and the Massif du Chaillu in the south, separated by the Ogooué River valley. The highest point in Gabon is Mount Iboundji (1,575 metres) in the Massif du Chaillu and Mount Tembo near Oyem in the Monts de Cristal reaches 1,300 metres. In the extreme south-west parallel to the coast and flanking the Nyanga River is the less elevated Mayombe chain, the bulk of which extends into the Congo Republic. The mountains are covered with dense tropical rain forest as is nearly three-quarters of the country. Grasslands or savannas cover one-fifth, mainly in the upper Ogooué around Franceville, the upper N'Gounié above Mouila, and in the middle Nyanga River valley – especially beyond Tchibanga. Along the coast north of the Nyanga River stretches a narrow zone of marshes and mangrove trees.

Beneath the coastal plains and offshore lie cretaceous sedimentary rocks, which south of Port-Gentil have yielded petroleum and natural gas at shallow depth. Gabon's other important minerals (manganese, iron, uranium, gold) derive from the interior areas of Precambrian rocks. The heavy rains and high relative humidities have tended to leach the soil in most parts of the country, which has led to the practice of shifting cultivation.

Population

The population of Gabon has more than doubled since independence. Whereas the 1960-61 census showed 448,564 inhabitants, the best informed estimates three decades later average one million. A large part of the growth resulted from natural increase, the rate of which tripled as a result of improved medical care and diet, above all in urban areas. Among the one million people are 100,000 to 150,000 non-Gabonese Africans whose numbers fluctuate according to the economic situation, and approximately 30,000 Europeans, the bulk of whom are French. Whereas the Europeans play important roles in administration and the economy, the non-Gabonese Africans serve as labourers, clerical personnel, petty traders and transporters.

The rapid development of Gabon's mineral resources since the late 1950s has contributed to an even more rapid urbanization. Between 1960-61 and 1991 Libreville grew from 44,598 to an estimated 300,000 or more, of whom one-third are foreigners, including some 20,000 French. In those same decades Port-Gentil increased from 21,000 to an estimated 60,000, including approximately 2,500 Europeans, mostly French, and several thousand non-Gabonese Africans. Most of the country's Europeans and non-Gabonese Africans live in these two urban areas and to a lesser extent in the vicinity of other economic centres – Franceville, Moanda and Lambaréné. Approximately 40,000 persons are employed by the government, including the thousands in education. An estimated 80,000 wage-earners are involved in forestry, mining, industry, commerce and transport. Approximately one-half of the active population, including many women, are employed in agriculture, which is still mainly subsistence. They produce the staples of the traditional Gabonese diet – manioc, plantain bananas, other fruits and vegetables.

Peoples

Among the indigenous inhabitants there are a few thousand pygmies or Negrillos who are thought to be the descendants of the oldest known inhabitants. It is possible that the various pygmoid groups may have undergone some mixing with Negroid peoples in recent centuries. The remaining 99.5 per cent of the indigenous population has Negroid racial origins and has been differentiated through many centuries if not millennia into forty or more distinct peoples (a 'people' being a group linked by heredity, culture – including language – and historical experience). All of these peoples speak languages belonging to the Bantu group, the large group to which most of the inhabitants of central and southern Africa belong. These peoples vary in size from a few hundred to tens of thousands. Ethnologists have been able to distribute them among ten groups, mainly on the basis of linguistic similarities. But there is evidence of genetic, cultural and historical ties among certain groups as well so that in this sense the term 'Bantu' has a wider sense than just language. To complicate matters, in the course of the past century there is evidence of peoples who have abandoned their original language and adopted or adapted the languages of other peoples with whom they had contacts. Several of Gabon's smallest peoples are in the process of disappearing, with the remnants assimilating to neighbours, who are sometimes but not always of the same group.

Largest numerically of the ten groups (on the basis of the 1960-61 census) is the Fang with 31 per cent of the population, followed by the Mbédé with 25 per cent and the Eshira with 22 per cent. The remaining 22 per cent are distributed among the other seven groups, of which two (the Vili and the Téké) have the majority of their kin in the neighbouring Congo. Numerical size is not the same as historical importance, however, for the coastal Myènè group with only two-and-a-half per cent has played a larger role in the development of the country than several more numerous groups from the interior.

Main periods in the history of Gabon

The history of Gabon has been shaped by the interaction of both Africans and Europeans and by the interplay of both internal and external influences and events. On the basis of these factors, one can outline four general periods of unequal length, which can be designated by adjectives reflecting the dominant characteristics:

(1)   from ancient times to 1471 A.D. (Bantu Gabon)
(2)   from 1471 to 1843 A.D. (Atlantic Gabon)
(3)   from 1843 to 1960 A.D. (French Gabon)
(4)   since 1960 A.D. (Independent Gabon).

Bantu Gabon

Two thousand years before European peoples came along the Atlantic coasts, peoples of Negroid stock called the Bantu began their migrations into the forests which cover most of Gabon. It is believed that all of Gabon was once forest but portions were turned into grassland by human activities through the centuries. These Bantu peoples found small numbers of peoples of an older Pygmoid stock living at various points in the forest. The Bantu peoples came from the north, south and east, and though probably all of one stock and even of one proto-Bantu language, they became differentiated in the course of their travels. It was during these centuries, both before and after their arrival in Gabon, that they developed the foundations of their societies, in which roles were assigned on the basis of sex, generations within the sexes, and kinship, as well as the material culture for survival in the forest. They were peoples of the New Stone Age, who lived from hunting, fishing and subsistence agriculture, though the manioc and some of the varieties of bananas and plantains that would subsequently become the staples of the Gabonese diet had not yet been introduced from the New World. In this period we have called Bantu Gabon the extended family, the lineage and the clan formed the basic social units and governance seldom extended beyond them. Only on the Loango coast, centred in the Congo Republic but extending north into Gabon, were institutions developing on a larger scale.

Atlantic Gabon

The first Europeans who came along the coasts in the 1470s and 1480s were the Portuguese. They found the Mpongwe already living along the river or estuary to which they gave the name *gabāo*, meaning hood or sleeve. They also made contact with the Orungu at Cape Lopez and the Vili along the Loango coast. Indigenous trading networks that already extended from the interior down waterways to the ocean and along the coasts gradually acquired a new overseas dimension throughout the sixteenth and seventeenth centuries as Dutch and French traders joined the Portuguese. But the networks came to be focused upon the Atlantic coasts probably only in the late eighteenth and early nineteenth centuries as the slave-trade reached its height and British industrial manufactures gained a predominance. In the meantime movements of Bantu peoples continued throughout the interior. Frequently the stronger provoked the movement of the weaker and set off a veritable chain reaction of migrations. The largest in scope would be the southward and coastward movement of the Fang in the late eighteenth century and a large part of the nineteenth century whose impact would be felt throughout most of northern Gabon. Ultimately the Fang sought to make direct contact with European traders, a goal shared by other interior peoples who were moving towards the southern coasts in these same eras. The period of Atlantic Gabon also saw the sway of the Loango kingdom extend northward into Gabon at least as far as Setté-Cama and then decline in the nineteenth century.

French Gabon

France under King Louis Philippe founded a post in the Estuary in 1843 to promote commerce and to combat the slave-trade. Though the French made efforts to end the slave-trade, frequently as a result of British prodding, it continued clandestinely on a reduced scale until the 1860s. On the whole, the French exhibited much greater zeal in securing recognition of their sovereignty through treaties with the clan heads of the indigenous peoples as a first step in competing with the dominant British, American and German traders. French agents resorted to deception, threats and finally force in 1845 to gain the submission of the Mpongwe clan head at Glass who, unlike the other clan heads, refused to consent freely to the French establishment. During the next four decades the French made treaties with all of the coastal peoples from Loango to the Rio Muni (as well as with some farther north and offshore who would eventually be assigned to Spain). In the late 1860s they penetrated the lower Ogooué River valley. Their thrust into the middle and upper reaches of the river would take place between 1874 and 1885 under the leadership of Savorgnan de Brazza as part of France's competition with Leopold II, king of the Belgians, for control of the Congo. France in 1885 and 1894 partitioned the northern and north-eastern hinterlands with Germany. Then in 1900 it divided the disputed areas of the northern coasts with Spain. France would administer the Loango coast as part of Gabon until 1918, at which time most of it was transferred to the neighbouring French colony of the Middle Congo.

The boundaries drawn by the colonial powers in the north and north-west divided the Fang people among Gabon, Cameroon and Spanish Guinea as well as from the larger Pahouin group (Fang–Boulou–Beti) whose greatest numbers are located in Cameroon. The boundaries with the Middle Congo left small numbers of Vili and Téké within Gabon and split the Bakota, Bapounou and Mbédé groups (including the Nzabi). But the fact that France controlled the Middle Congo and, after 1916, the adjacent areas of Cameroon, helped to prevent irredentist or unification movements. The inland boundaries with Spanish Guinea (Rio Muni) posed few barriers to the movement of either peoples or goods during the colonial period.

Between 1843 and 1886 Gabon was always administered by French naval officers jointly with French West African territories. France instituted customs duties on foreign trade to help pay the expenses of its establishment. The French used force when necessary to protect European merchants seeking to bypass the coastal traders and to deal directly with the interior peoples as well as to punish Gabonese peoples who abused or attacked European traders. One of the ironies of this situation was that France was able to interest few of its own citizens to engage in commerce in Gabon. It therefore ended up providing protection for those very British, American and German traders with whom it had hoped the French merchants would compete. In one instance in the late 1840s in which a French entrepreneur, Le Cour, attempted to establish a commercial plantation in the Estuary, neither the Naval Ministry nor the local administration would give subsidies or aid in labour recruitment. Later on, in the 1860s, the administration aided a private company, Victor Régis of Marseilles, to recruit so-called 'free emigrants' for plantation labour in the French West Indies. The scheme deprived sparsely populated Gabon of several thousand workers who might have assisted in its own development. The French government helped Roman Catholic missionaries to establish in the Estuary in 1844 in the expectation that they would promote French cultural and political influence. Deaths and illnesses in the missionary ranks prevented them from evangelizing beyond the Mpongwe and Benga peoples or educating more than a few hundred persons at any time during their first thirty-five years. As far as the French government was concerned, however, the missionaries served the important purpose of providing competition to the American Protestant missionaries who had started work in the Estuary in 1842 and who entered the middle Ogooué in 1874.

In the 1880s French rule began to acquire a more typically colonialist character both in relation to the Gabonese and to other westerners. The French instituted a tax upon able-bodied persons of both sexes over ten years old and required unpaid labour for a certain number of days a year for projects deemed of public utility. In 1883 the administration closed the American Protestant schools, which had been teaching in English as well as local languages. It allowed them to reopen only after they had secured French-speaking teachers from Europe. After the Americans transferred their work to French Protestants and moved north into Cameroon, the administration showed much less zeal in enforcing the prohibition on the use of local languages for academic instruction but still vigorously encouraged the teaching of French. During the exploration and occupation of the interior, roughly from the mid-1870s through the First World War, the administration required various villages to provide foodstuffs to its posts and military units. The French paid for these provisions but generally at prices that were unattractive to both producers and transporters. The French instituted forced labour for portage and construction when free recruitment failed to yield the necessary manpower.

French colonialism saw its worst abuses and injustices as a result of the concessionary regime installed throughout the French Congo (of which Gabon formed part) in 1898-99 and not completely terminated everywhere until 1930. The regime effectively denied the land rights of the indigenous peoples. The companies systematically emptied the country of all its available resources, backed up in many cases by French-officered Senegalese militiamen. These exactions, taken together with the demands outlined above and a doubling of the head tax, caused the flight of tens of thousands of Africans in the Ogooué and N'Gounié valleys and the abandonment of food crops, with subsequent famines and epidemics. The companies and their supporters in the growing administrative machine nearly destroyed the existing commercial networks and sent the economy into a slump from which it did not begin to recover until the large-scale production of *okoumé* after the First World War. Concurrent with this devastation was the institution of the *indigénat* in 1910 at the time of the organization of the federation of French Equatorial Africa to which Gabon's interests would henceforth be subordinated, and the conscious abandonment of the cultural assimilation of the educated élite which had been official practice since the French arrival. From the institution of the federation, French educational policy aimed to create only subordinates and auxiliaries in a colonial situation where Frenchmen and French interests would be dominant for the forseeable future.

Is it therefore surprising in these circumstances to find an anti-colonialist reaction among the educated élite? Paradoxically, their numbers had increased significantly during the first two decades of the twentieth century as a result of the coming of the Brothers of Saint-Gabriel to Libreville and Lambaréné in 1900 and the establishment of public schools in the capital and other towns in 1907 and after. This agitation by educated elements from the Myènè and Fang peoples sought to curb the abuses of colonialism, which deprived them of the basic rights of liberty and property in the land of their birth, and to achieve legal and social equality with French citizens. The demands reflected élite interests almost entirely, for though the élite possessed close ties with the masses, the latter were too much in disarray and demographic decline, not to mention different in outlook, for meaningful political links to be established in this period. Members of the educated élite failed in their main objectives. But they were successful in securing appointments as chiefs among the Estuary peoples (including by this time the Fang) and as representatives in the consultative bodies established in the wake of the Popular Front regime in France (1936-37). Much of the post-war political leadership would come from these elements, plus a handful of educated Gabonese working at Brazzaville who rallied to Free France and gained advancement in the circle of Governor-General Félix Eboué between 1940 and 1944.

The Second World War generated decolonizing trends throughout the colonial empires that France tried to contain through a policy of assimilation, that is, by promoting the advancement of its Black African territories within a French Republic and Union dominated by Frenchmen. This policy, together with those of maintaining the federation of French Equatorial Africa and of treating all Black African territories alike, had the result of creating four different levels for Gabonese political activity (Gabon, FEA, all Black Africa, and the French Republic and Union). At the same time it projected some of the diverse interests and cleavages within French and Black African politics into Gabon. In addition to the opportunities for political participation, the Fourth French Republic (1946-58) saw the end of the worst abuses of colonialism and the granting of basic rights to the Gabonese. Public as well as private French investment improved and expanded the ports and roads with a view to promoting the expansion of wood production and later in the 1950s the exploitation of the mineral resources – manganese, uranium, iron and petroleum. Primary education in French was extended to the bulk of the school-age population. Much smaller numbers benefited from technical, secondary and higher education. Only in the mid-1950s were a few persons receiving secondary diplomas in Gabon itself and completing university programmes in France. With just a few exceptions, political life would be dominated by those educated within Gabon prior to 1945. Most influential among them were three men with similar education backgrounds and personal ties: Jean-Hilaire Aubame (1912-89), Gabon's deputy in the French National Assembly (1946-58); Léon Mba (1902-67), the first Gabonese mayor of Libreville in 1956 and the top African official in the first executive council in 1957; and Paul Gondjout (1912-90), member of the French Senate (1949-58) and the leading figure in the Territorial Assembly. Though both Aubame and Mba were Fang, they drew their support from different elements from within that people and had different Gabonese and European allies. Gondjout, who came from the Myènè peoples, used his considerable political talents to promote his own career, but from 1954 on allied with Mba against Aubame. On the whole, Gabonese politics were influenced by personal, regional and ethnic interests rather than by issues or ideologies. To complicate matters, independents held the balance of power between the two political parties that formed around Aubame, on the one hand, and Gondjout and Mba, on the other. In addition, the training of

Gabonese for the highest levels of territorial administration began only in 1956.

Independent Gabon

Gabon arrived at political independence on August 13, 1960, as a result of decolonizing forces elsewhere in the French Union that had contributed firstly to the collapse of the Fourth Republic in May 1958 and then to the demise of De Gaulle's French Community, which had limited the African territories to autonomy or self-government. At independence Gabon possessed neither the resources nor the personnel to operate its administration and economy, much less to develop them, without continued outside aid and assistance. Much of this support was forthcoming from France and was institutionalized in the fifteen *coopération* agreements signed a month before independence. At the same time private investors from France, other Common Market countries and the United States continued to develop the country's mineral resources. The early 1960s saw the first significant exports of manganese and uranium as well as the successful prospecting and construction of facilities that would lead to the exploitation of petroleum in the late 1960s and early 1970s.

In the meantime, within three years after independence, the political institutions modelled upon the Fifth French Republic had broken down, a victim of the rivalries of the politicians and parties. Central in the collapse was the determination of President Mba to provide a strongly authoritarian leadership, taken with the increasingly repressive measures necessary for him to do so. His actions provoked a military coup against his regime in February 1964. French military intervention, which restored Mba to office, allowed him to eliminate the restraints on his power represented by a multi-party National Assembly and to establish an authoritarian regime. It enabled him to transfer his power intact to his hand-picked successor, Albert-Bernard (later Omar) Bongo (b. 1935), whose selection involved agents from De Gaulle's office. Bongo would face the difficult task of maintaining political stability while trying to establish a less repressive and more broadly based regime.

For this task Bongo possessed a number of assets. As a member of the numerically small Téké people of the far interior, he stood outside the ethnic rivalries (Myènè vs. Fang, intra-Fang) that had plagued political life for two decades. Though young, he possessed a good education in business administration and a decade of governmental experience, including several years in the president's office. Yet he had not been personally involved in the rivalries or repression of the Mba presidency. Responding to the wishes expressed in the National Assembly, which by that time included only BDG deputies, Bongo between 1968 and 1972 released those involved in the coup and the members of the provisional government of 1964. Many of them re-entered government service while the remaining ones returned to private life in Gabon or abroad. Bongo took advantage of the BDG's control of the National Assembly to dissolve all existing parties and on March 12, 1968, announced the formation of a single party, the Parti Démocratique Gabonais (PDG). Bongo's main justification for such a course was his contention that the existing parties represented conflicting ethnic and regional interests which hindered effective government and national unity. Bongo recognized the strength of such interests in his appointments to the cabinet and civil service, where the desire to balance them often took precedence over professional qualifications. Bongo intended that the PDG would undertake a *rénovation* of national political life through greater participation and by means of *dialogue*. Henceforth all political discussion, debate and criticism could legitimately take place only within the framework of the PDG. During the early years of the Bongo presidency, a good deal of dialogue seems to have occurred within the regime with the chief executive ultimately making the important decisions himself.

The single-party system gave Gabon a new stability. But not surprisingly, it also provided the means to the president and ruling class for perpetuating themselves in power without regard to the wishes of the people. Those in power held the key positions in the party and influenced the selection of candidates for office, who ran unopposed. Revolt would have been futile because France was prepared to intervene militarily under the defence cooperation agreement to support Bongo. Jacques Foccart, De Gaulle's adviser on African affairs, aided Bongo to construct a security apparatus that relied on Frenchmen and other foreigners to protect those in power.

In April 1969 Bongo moved to curb the independence of the organized workers by requiring them to join a single labour federation, COSYGA, which in 1973 became a special organ of the PDG. Through these means the government sought to secure the workers' conformity with its policies and to control their relations with employers. Illegal strikes, work stoppages, and slow-downs periodically attested to the workers' dissatisfaction with arrangements that denied them effective representation but that they could not alter.

To a much greater extent than Mba, Bongo sought to secure Gabonese control of natural resources and greater benefits to the Gabonese from their exploitation. Thus came the requirements for greater Gabonese participation in the ownership and management of commercial and industrial enterprises. Given the paucity of private capital and its preference for investment in real estate and banks instead of industry or large-scale commerce, the state became the leading Gabonese participant. Gabonization advanced slowly as a result of the scarcity of Gabonese with advanced technical and managerial skills willing to work in industry instead of the civil service.

Bongo's accession to the presidency coincided with the beginning of a period of economic expansion based primarily on petroleum but also on manganese, uranium, and timber that multiplied the revenues hitherto available to the government. Between 1973 and 1985 revenues mainly from an increased petroleum production at higher prices multiplied eighteen-fold. On the assumption that the existing oil reserves would last only to the end of the 1980s (later additional reserves would be discovered), the government decided to use the bulk of the additional funds to promote the kind of development that would ultimately decrease dependence on petroleum and would create a much more diversified economy. To this end, it invested its own resources and sought foreign grants and loans to construct an infrastructure that would allow tapping of the minerals and timber of the interior. The cornerstone of this infrastructure was the Trans-Gabon Railway from the Estuary to the middle and upper Ogooué River valleys.

From the early 1970s the Bongo government pursued a more active foreign policy, primarily to get more aid for development and from greater numbers and kinds of sources. While establishing relations with additional western nations, it inaugurated relations with numerous Arab and Communist states. While becoming more independent of France in terms of policy formation, as reflected in the revised *coopération* agreements of February 1974, Gabon grew even more dependent in terms of personnel and capital investment. During the last half of the 1970s and the first half of the 1980s, several thousand additional European technicians and managers along with even larger numbers of non-Gabonese African labourers and employees entered Gabon to carry out the various development programmes. Additional Lebanese, Cameroonians, Senegalese and Malians arrived to participate in the growing commercial sector.

By the time a major part of the first section of the Trans-Gabon opened to Ndjolé in September 1978, heavy charges on foreign loans and less than anticipated petroleum revenues were forcing cutbacks and slow-downs in the development programmes. Also contributing to the financial woes were expenditures which *Africa Contemporary Record* estimated at as much as nine hundred million dollars for a lavish new presidential palace, beautification of the capital and luxury hotels for the 1977 OAU meeting. But by the early 1980s, with the aid of international institutions, the government was able to stabilize the country's finances and to reduce its debt. At the same time additional petroleum and uranium reserves were discovered.

The financial difficulties also contributed to a political malaise, which came into the open at the Second Extraordinary Congress of the PDG in January 1979. In unprecedented criticisms of the regime, the Congress called upon the government to tackle the related problems of inefficiency and multiple office-holding, which led to neglect of duties. One resolution lambasted the economic management of the country which it stated led to 'unbridled capitalism' instead of 'rational exploitation of our perennial resources' and called for agriculture to be made a top priority. The Congress failed to re-elect a number of top officials of the Central Committee and urged a democratization of the process for selecting party officials and National Assembly members. President Bongo responded by reshuffling his government and announcing several measures designed to satisfy the demands of the critics. In November 1979 an ordinary party congress renominated him and on December 30, 1979, he was popularly re-elected to another seven-year term. It thus appeared that he had received mandates both to continue in office and to institute reforms that might deal with the nation's ills. Following two-stage parliamentary elections in February 1980, Bongo reorganized the government as a step towards dealing with the current problems.

The previous month, the Paris semi-monthly *Afrique–Asie* had brought to public attention the underside of the Bongo regime. It alleged that misuse of public funds and corruption were a major source of Gabon's financial difficulties. It claimed that President Bongo, his wife Josephine, and her brother Jean-Boniface Assélé, director of the national police and Minister of Public Works, had acquired vast real estate holdings as well as majority interests in a score of companies involved in industry, construction, air transport, insurance and banking. The same magazine accused the regime of using violence to intimidate or to silence its critics.

The coming to power of a Socialist government in France in May 1981 made possible the publication of a work of investigative journalism that probably would not have survived the censor during the Gaullist and Giscardian eras. In the exposé *Affaires africaines* (1983), Pierre Péan, who had worked in the administration in Libreville for several years, made serious accusations concerning use of public funds for private purposes and of public office for private gain, political violence, and personal misconduct by the presidential couple. Péan alleged that Gabon was ruled by a *clan des Gabonais*, a coterie of Gabonese and Frenchmen who were enriching themselves while purportedly serving the interests of their respective countries. Though, as a result of the ensuing furore, the Socialist government ultimately had to conciliate Bongo in order to protect its economic and strategic interests in Gabon, his regime had acquired an unsavoury reputation in France. Even the conservative *Figaro Magazine* (Dec. 14, 1985) would thereafter comment: 'His country is a sort of equatorial emirate. It has for a long time been at the heart of numerous intrigues'.

In Gabon itself, the general prosperity of the late 1970s and early 1980s tended to mute popular criticism of the regime. When the Socialist–Communist victory in France encouraged the emergence of an opposition party, the Mouvement de Redressement National (MORENA), in Libreville in November 1981, it gained little popular support and was quickly crushed by the government. MORENA represented Fang and Bapounou elements who sought a more equitable distribution of wealth among provinces and individuals, a restoration of multi-party democracy, and a curb on abuses and corruption in government. After the leaders in Gabon were given harsh sentences, MORENA-in-exile continued in Paris among Gabonese intellectuals. They were led by a mild-mannered Spiritan priest, the Reverend Paul Mba-Abessolé, who emphasized that the group would work peacefully and through dialogue with those in power to achieve its goals.

The years of MORENA's challenge had seen unprecedented new levels of public income from petroleum because of higher prices and the appreciation of the dollar, the currency in which it was exchanged. Taxes derived from this source permitted the national budget to increase from close to forty billion francs CFA in 1973 to 328 billion in 1979 and over 669 billion in 1986. (The value of the franc CFA fluctuated from 200 to 250 per US dollar in these years.)

During the 1970s and 1980s the Bongo regime continued to neglect agriculture and the maintenance of the road network that brought both foodstuffs and export crops to market. Government inaction thus helped further to empty the countryside of its vital elements. The government had created a number of largely state-owned companies to provide food for the urban areas. Despite these efforts, Gabon was importing 85 per cent of its food. At the same time these agro-businesses tended to create a rural proletariat rather than to revitalize the peasantry. On the whole, government policies helped to transfer tens of thousands of rural populations into the urban areas, particularly into Libreville (the administrative and commercial centre) and Port-Gentil (the centre for mining, timber and industry). Into these centres also came the bulk of Europeans, non-Gabonese

Africans, and 60,000 Equatorial Guinean refugees from the two Nguema regimes. While some of the latter did agricultural work, including for the agro-businesses, the majority chose to settle in Libreville. Thus by the late 1980s an estimated forty-five per cent of Gabon's population, including the foreigners, were living in urban areas.

Within this urban population were great disparities in income. *Le Monde* (March 20, 1990) reported that during the 1970s and 1980s only two per cent of Gabon's population received 80 per cent of all personal income. Thus the ruling class enjoyed a standard of living comparable to the most privileged in western nations. At the same time the rest of the 40,000 government employees and 80,000 salaried workers in private enterprises shared to a lesser extent in the prosperity. Their families came to occupy decent housing with running water and electricity, and to have the convenience of a motor vehicle, an electric refrigerator and a television set. Many families obtained better health care and more of their children gained access to secondary, technical and higher education. Not so fortunate were the thousands of day labourers occupying makeshift housing without amenities and subsisting precariously from irregular employment and help from their extended families. Although the government devoted the bulk of its expenditures for social services to the urban areas, it could never keep up with the needs of this burgeoning population for housing, health care and education. While some of the non-Gabonese Africans held rather secure employment, most of them had uncertain incomes whose levels were linked to the health of the economy. A portion of them were small-scale independent retailers. Others, along with some of the Lebanese traders, risked the wrath of the government through their activities in the informal sector of the economy. The non-Gabonese Africans frequently lived in an unfriendly and sometimes insecure atmosphere. They were resented by many Gabonese, who saw them as necessary to the functioning of the economy in good times but as competitors to be sent away in bad times. Because the government required employers to compensate Gabonese workers nearly 25 per cent more than foreigners, employers preferred to hire the non-Gabonese Africans, and to lay off the Gabonese first in times of downturn.

Such conditions arrived in Gabon in the course of 1986 and persisted throughout the rest of the decade. Falling prices for oil in the world market and the weakness of the dollar drastically reduced the government's revenues. Whereas before 1985 oil had provided 65 per cent of the budget resources and 85 per cent of export receipts, in 1988 oil generated only 30 per cent and 18 per cent respectively. During the late 1980s income from manganese, timber, uranium, cocoa, coffee and palm oil barely remained stable or declined slightly. Thus in 1987 and 1988 the national budgets were only half those of 1984 to 1986. Development projects, in particular, were cut back severely. Whereas the investment budget had totalled 400 billion francs CFA in 1985 (8 billion FF), it fell to 60 billion francs CFA in 1988. At the same time higher interest rates increased the expenses of the government. In these circumstances unemployment grew to the point that domestic consumption dropped one-third. Schools lacked books and supplies, hospitals medicines and equipment, while the roads deteriorated further. In mid-1989 the secretary-general of Cosgya announced that 50,000 workers had lost their jobs since 1985, one-third of them in the private sector. Altogether, 200 companies had closed down. The public sector had been hard hit since completion of work on the Trans-Gabon in 1987.

A series of austerity measures which the government introduced between 1987 and 1989 in order to qualify for international loans reduced the income of employees in both the public and private sectors. During 1989 the ordinary people had reason to hope for the return of good times as the onshore oilfields at Rabi-Kounga began to produce, though the increased revenues would not become available to the government until 1990. As 1989 wore on, it became evident that the austerity measures were hitting hardest the portion of the population least capable of supporting them while allowing the ruling class to maintain its affluent lifestyle at only a slightly reduced scale. MORENA tracts circulated in Libreville identifying President Bongo as the 'Gabonese evil'. News of events in Europe, relayed into Gabon by international radio and television, also had an impact. The celebration of the 200th anniversary of the French Revolution throughout 1989 drew attention to a historic popular revolt against privilege. Focus on the rights of man and the citizen served to remind the Gabonese of the restraints on the exercise of such rights under the Bongo regime. The disintegration of the repressive communist regimes throughout Eastern Europe encouraged the dissatisfied to think of the possibility of replacing long-entrenched regimes and rather quickly. Bongo himself recognized these latter influences several months later as they began to affect several formerly French states in West Africa when he observed: 'The winds from the East are shaking the coconut trees'. To help defuse popular discontent, Bongo encouraged a week-long visit in May 1989 by Father Mba, whose proposals for change he promised to consider. Mba was treated more like a visiting dignitary than the leader of a suppressed political party, much to the consternation of some of the PDG's less flexible leaders.

In September and October 1989 the government announced that it had discovered and suppressed two related plots to assassinate the president and to overthrow the government. They were led by Bapounou elements that included civil servants and military men in league with foreign business interests and a religious sect led by a Malian trader. In mid-December, after new austerities provoked a strike by electricity and water workers that brought industry and commerce to a standstill, Bongo observed that the austerity measures had reached the limits of the supportable.

Then on January 16 began the wave of strikes and demonstrations that shook the foundations of the Bongo regime. On that date students at the Omar Bongo University who had been boycotting classes went on strike over the shortage of professors and library works, which diminished the quality of the education they were receiving. The students, most of whom were dependent upon the government for financial support, also showed concern about the impact of the austerities, which were eroding their purchasing power and limiting the expansion of educational facilities. The following day, the police forcibly evicted students from the economics and law faculty who were occupying the campus. On January 18 high school students took to the streets to demonstrate their solidarity. They were joined by adults who were not students and who the government claimed were mainly non-Gabonese Africans; these latter elements were blamed for the rioting that involved looting of Lebanese properties in the popular quarters and other criminal damage. Police firing at the feet of demonstrators killed five persons and injured at least seventy. Two hundred and fifty arrests took place. Bongo met with student representatives on January 22 to air their grievances and to defuse their discontent.

Following the riots of January 18, and despite government measures to curb protest, demonstrations intensified in Libreville and strikes spread to workers in both public and private sectors, bringing the capital almost to a standstill. Demands focused upon higher wages, fairer distribution of the country's wealth, and democratic reforms. Neither Bongo's concessions to particular groups between February 14 and 24 nor his banning of all strikes and demonstrations on February 22 failed immediately to halt the protests. The crisis peaked on February 26 when airport personnel, telecommunication workers and gas station attendants joined teachers and physicians striking for better pay and working conditions. Workers also demanded the creation of free trade unions not under government control and Gabonization of jobs. By the end of the month most strikers had returned to work after obtaining presidential promises to establish committees to consider their grievances and demands.

By that time, the events were pressuring the government to

undertake changes in the political system away from the one-party regime. From a commission on democracy created in January came the recommendation to dissolve the PDG in order to pave the way for a new political grouping, the Rassemblement Social et Démocratique Gabonais (RSDG), that would be open to various currents of opinion. The commission intended that the RSDG would provide an apprenticeship for political pluralism over a five-year period. For Bongo the RSDG was a means of permitting wider participation while maintaining his control over the nation's political forces. He summoned a national conference to begin on March 23 to discuss the new arrangements.

Then on February 26 Bongo announced a new provisional government replacing the one of August 1989. While he brought into office several younger and highly qualified ministers with well educated or experienced advisers, he retained most of the previous ministers who had held key posts. Among them as prime minister was Léon Mébiame, known to have little sympathy for democratic reform.

On March 21, amid continuing popular economic and social unrest, the government granted legal recognition to seventy-four political associations so that they might participate in the national conference which the president had summoned to discuss reforms. Although Bongo would have preferred to keep all parties under his control in the RSDG, the opposition rejected such incorporation. Though the opposition was splintered into many groups, there were broadly two tendencies among them. MORENA under Father Mba-Abessolé represented Christian democracy with a strong populist bent. MORENA had strong support from both Catholic and Protestant elements, including some troubled by the influences of masonry and Islam in the Bongo regime. It was most extensively implanted in the north and among the Fang people. The secular and socialist tendency was represented by the Parti Gabonais du Progrès (PGP), which had its strongest support among workers and in the coastal regions. Its leaders were respected professionals of aristocratic background, mainly Nkomi and Orungu from Port-Gentil, who included professors at the university who had been imprisoned during the 1970s for an alleged Marxist plot against the government. Among them were Joseph Rendjambe, professor of economics and a successful businessman, and his relative Pierre-Louis Agondjo-Okawe, former dean of the economics and law faculty at the university and currently head of the bar in Gabon. Because the PDG also included reformist elements, led, among others, by the president's son Ali Bongo, forces favouring reform had a majority in the national conference.

The national conference asked Omar Bongo to serve out the rest of his term as president (until December 1993) but to resign as head of the PDG and to put himself above parties. It also called for the return of a multi-party political system, which was re-established on May 22. A new government had been formed on April 27 under a respected technocrat, Casimir Oyé–Mba, in which minor posts were given to some opposition party members. Elections for a new National Assembly, which had been postponed pending the outcome of the national conference, were scheduled for September 1990.

In the meantime, also on May 22, the death of PGP leader Rendjambe in suspicious circumstances in a Libreville hotel owned by Bongo set off an explosion of violence in the main cities and towns the following day. The inability of the government to control the violence and destruction at Port-Gentil, which threatened French lives and property, led on May 24 to a French military intervention to restore order. Intervention had the effect of propping up the regime until it could regain control in Port-Gentil.

The circumstances of the assembly elections in September and October, which involved many irregularities, intimidation and fraud, allowed the PDG to retain a slight majority of the seats. It held 63 out of 120 with 27 going to the two factions of MORENA, 18 to the PGP, and 12 to other, mainly socialist, parties. Casimir Oyé-Mba gave minor cabinet posts to some opposition deputies in the new PDG-dominated government which he headed. On March 5, 1991, the National Assembly unanimously adopted a new constitution that restored multi-partyism and contained guarantees concerning civil liberties. The constitution provided for a strong president but strengthened the powers of the prime minister.

While the upheaval of 1990 restored multi-partyism and a freer exercise of speech, press and assembly, it left President Bongo and his associates of the PDG in control of all branches of government. Their actions are, however, now open to public scrutiny in the National Assembly and in the media. The regime has a strong political base only in the president's own Haut-Ogooué Province and among PDG office-holders in other provinces and the capital who have benefitted from arrangements that gave them both power and wealth. If the seats in the National Assembly had been distributed more strictly according to population, the PDG would not have retained its majority in that body or control of the government. At the same time the two markedly different broad tendencies within the opposition might make a coalition government among them difficult.

The increased revenues from the Rabi-Kounga oilfield during the early 1990s permitted the Bongo regime to secure the international loans to keep the government afloat. But its unwillingness or inability to institute a financial discipline that would lessen the privileges of the ruling class has delayed needed economic restructuring and the restoration of adequate levels of services in education and health care. As a result, chronic unrest has continued among the urban population, evidenced by periodic strikes, work stoppages and demonstrations by both public and private sector employees. Whether new leadership will emerge that can deal with these problems remains to be seen as the country awaits the presidential elections of 1993.

The bibliography

This bibliography is a selective one designed to serve the needs of both those whose only or primary language is English and those who read French. Because the bulk of the useful writing has been and continues to be in French, a majority of the entries describe or summarize publications in that language. At the same time a premium has been placed on including entries in English where they are available. In general, the bibliography aims to provide annotations on the most important writings for understanding Gabon present and past. It focuses on publications concerning history, external relations, politics, resources, the economy, society and culture while including some on other subjects and reference sources. Though many of the publications deal with just Gabon, quite a few treat the country as part of the larger ensembles to which it belongs, such as western equatorial Africa, French-speaking Black Africa and the franc zone. Hopefully the bibliography may contribute to a better understanding of Gabon and its place in the contemporary world as well as a desire among some for further study of this small but intriguing developing nation.

Acknowledgements

I should like to express my thanks to the staff of the Marquette University Memorial and Science Libraries, the Golda Meir Library of the University of Wisconsin–Milwaukee, the Memorial Library of the University of Wisconsin–Madison, the Herskovits Africana Library of Northwestern University, and the libraries of the Centre d'Etudes Africaines, Documentation Française and Académie des Sciences d'Outre-Mer in Paris who aided my search for materials. Particular appreciation goes to Maria Dittman, Susan Hopwood, David Henige, Mette Schayne, Daniel Britz and Zofia Yaranga. A grant from the Marquette University Graduate School for another project and an invitation to the De Gaulle Centenary made possible consultation of materials in Paris in 1990. A mini grant from the

Introduction

African Studies Program of the University of Wisconsin during the summer of 1991 facilitated use of Africanist periodicals.

The Scarecrow Press of Metuchen, New Jersey, has kindly given permission for me to draw upon materials in the introduction to the second, revised edition of the *Historical Dictionary of Gabon*, which will be published in 1993, for the introduction to this work.

I wish to dedicate this volume to my wife, Josefina Z. Sevilla, and our children, Kenneth, Annemarie and Lourdes Marie for their support during its research and writing. They assumed responsibility for many tasks that ordinarily would have been mine during my absence gathering materials and during my presence writing up and typing the results. My wife deserves special credit for explaining biological subjects in terms simple enough for one who never had the opportunity to study biology to understand.

Note on spelling

The absence of any universally accepted system of transliteration of African names into French or English and the development of variant spellings through the centuries that Europeans have been in equatorial Africa pose problems for any author who wishes to achieve accuracy and consistency.

Because French is the official language of Gabon, I have used the French transliteration for places and individuals. In the case of variant spellings, I have followed the usage in F. Meyo-Bibang and J.-M. Nzamba's *Notre pays, le Gabon* (1975). For the names of some of the Bantu peoples, one is faced with the additional problem of whether to use the basic stem or the plural, e.g. Kota or Bakota. In this case I have chosen the form most widely used in the sources I have consulted. Thus I have found Bakèlè, Bakota and Bapounou more frequently used than Kèlè, Kota and Pounou, on the one hand, and Loumbou, Téké and Vili more often than Baloumbou, Batéké and Bavili, on the other. To aid the reader, I have given both forms in some cases, e.g. Bakota or Kota, Loumbou or Baloumbou.

Note on personal names

During the French colonial period, most Gabonese adopted European first names and African last names. But many of them did not adopt African family names. Thus the brother of President Léon Mba was the Reverend Jean Obame. In recent decades last names have tended to become family names. For example, the older children of President Omar Bongo are Ali Bongo, Pascaline Bongo and Micheline Bongo. Around the time of independence, some Gabonese began to add the family name of their mother after that of their father. Thus Prime Minister Casimir Oyé-Mba is an Oyé on his father's side and an Mba on his mother's side. Confusion has arisen because some Gabonese do not hyphenate the two family names while others place the family name of their mother before that of their father and without hyphen. To complicate matters further, there is no uniform manner of indicating the family names of married women. Readers should be aware of these usages when they consult the indexes to this volume. In the indexes hyphenated names are listed under their first letter.

The Country and Its People

General

1 **Gabon: the development of a nation.**
Marc Aicardi de Saint-Paul. London: Routledge & Kegan Paul, 1989.
160p. 4 maps. bibliog.
This work is a translation of *Le Gabon du roi Denis à Omar Bongo* (Paris: Editions Albatross, 1987. 187p.) and contains chapters on the country and its peoples, history up to 1960, political and administrative institutions, economy, social policy and external relations (with France and its neighbours, in particular). Only the chapters on the evolution of the economy, particularly in the 1980s, rest on a database that is sufficient to ensure a reliable analysis. The sketchy chapter on history, in particular, creates false impressions by its amputations and omissions. The author's attitude towards the Bongo regime resembles that of a courtier rather than of a scholar. There are statistical tables and a bibliography that is strongest in articles on economic questions.

2 **Gabon: Beyond the colonial legacy.**
James F. Barnes. Boulder, Colorado: Westview, 1992. 135p. map.
bibliog. (Westview Profiles/Nations of Contemporary Africa).
This volumes provides a brief introduction to the country's political and economic evolution since 1960 in historical perspective. French military intervention in 1964 enabled President Léon Mba to establish a centralized one-party state that gave the country a kind of political stability for the next quarter century. At the same time France, and to a lesser extent other western nations, provided the investments necessary to develop its resources in manganese, uranium and petroleum, which brought unprecedented levels of wealth to the state and ruling class. This type of development perpetuated Gabon's dependence on France and subjected it to the fluctuations of world markets. Questionable government spending policies and the lack of financial discipline worsened the problems. The downturn that began in 1985 prompted an extended economic crisis that led to internal political disturbances at the

1

end of the decade. Though in 1990 Gabon re-established a multi-party political system, it was having difficulties coming to grips with its long-term economic problems and their social dimensions.

3   **Gabon.**

David E. Gardinier.   In: *Encyclopaedia Britannica, Vol. C.*   Chicago: Encyclopaedia Britannica, 1991, p. 652-55, 67. map. bibliog.

This up-to-date, brief introduction to Gabon, includes physical and human geography (land, people, religion, demographic trends, economy, administration and social conditions, cultural life), and history up to and including 1990. The article on Gabon is preceded by a larger one on Central Africa (p. 627-42), which provides a larger context for understanding developments in Gabon. Its section on history by David Birmingham gives a perceptive synthesis of the pre-colonial period in the region.

4   **Historical dictionary of Gabon.**

David E. Gardinier.   Metuchen, New Jersey. London: Scarecrow Press, 1981. 254p. 3 maps. bibliog.

Given the absence of a narrative history of Gabon in English, this reference work acquires unusual importance. It contains entries, detailed in many cases, that provide the elements for understanding the country's evolution from the 1470s to 1980. Various entries cover the forty indigenous peoples, the leading personalities (African, French and American, in particular), the economy, important events and institutions. The work gives particular attention to Christian missions and the development of western education. It devotes more space to the period of French colonial rule from 1843 to 1914 than to the era between the two World Wars, for which fewer primary sources were available. But it provides detailed data on the periods of decolonization and national independence. The volume contains a chronology, statistical tables and a selective bibliography of 741 works, mainly in French and English. The dictionary entries are linked to the bibliography through numbered references. A second revised and updated edition, including a bibliography of over 1,500 titles, is scheduled for publication in 1993.

5   **Le Gabon et son ombre.** (Gabon and its shadow.)

François Gaulme.   Paris: Editions Karthala, 1988. 211p. 3 maps. bibliog.

The title of this impressionistic yet authoritative and perceptive study refers to Gabon and what people think of it. The work gives careful attention to geographical influences, the population question, the indigenous peoples, the course of the country's contacts with Europeans on the coast from the 1470s until the 1830s, European exploration, and the establishment of French colonial rule and its development between the 1840s and the late 1950s. The most original and perhaps the most valuable sections are the chapters on the country's economic and political evolution, including its relations with France and the United States, since independence. The detailed account of the military coup and French military intervention of February 1964 provides new details on the role of Gaullist officials in Paris in the restoration of President Mba to power.

6 **Mission to civilize.**
Mort Rosenblum. New York: Doubleday, 1988. 480p.
This insightful work on the French presence in sub-Saharan Africa is written somewhat in the stye of *The New Yorker*. The chapter on Gabon in humorous fashion provides a devastating critique of the various myths concerning French activities over the past century and a half along with an amusing analysis of the contradictions and anomalies that they have produced in contemporary Gabonese society.

7 **The emerging states of French Equatorial Africa.**
Virginia Thompson, Richard Adloff. Stanford, California: Stanford University Press, 1960. 595p. 5 maps. bibliog.
This encyclopedic survey concentrates on the evolution of the federation and its four territories from the Second World War until the establishment of autonomous republics within the French Community in 1958. An individual chapter that utilizes the proceedings of the territorial assembly and the federal council, as well as other official documents, provides detailed information on Gabon's economic and political evolution.

Juvenile literature

8 **Gabon.**
Allan Carpenter. Chicago: Children's Press, 1976. 96p.
This juvenile literature presents the geography, peoples, history, government, resources and urban life of Gabon.

9 **Zaire, Gabon, and the Congo.**
Gerald Newman. New York: F. Walts, 1981. 66p.
This book for children includes a presentation on Gabon.

10 **Let's visit Gabon.**
Andrew Perriman. London: Macmillan, 1988. 96p. map.
This juvenile literature covers geography, peoples, history, developments since independence, villages and towns, religion and culture, and natural resources.

Geography

General

11 **Pour une géographie de l'habitat rural au Gabon.** (For a geography of rural habitat in Gabon.)
Claude Bouet. *Cahiers d'Outre-Mer*, vol. 33 (April–June 1980), p. 123-44.

The development of mining industries is having an impact on all aspects of traditional rural life in the forested regions of Gabon. It is essential that the modern housing that is being introduced should be adapted to the ecological and cultural settings of this environment. Most notably, it should be constructed from local, not imported materials.

12 **French Equatorial Africa and Cameroons.**
Great Britain. The Admiralty, Naval Intelligence Division, 1942. 524p. maps. bibliog.

This publication contains good descriptions of Gabon's physical and human geography and economy in the early 1940s.

13 **Libreville: la ville et sa région, Gabon, Afrique Equatoriale Francaise: étude de géographie humaine.** (Libreville: the city and its region, Gabon, French Equatorial Africa: study in human geography.
Guy Lasserre. Paris: Armand Colin, 1958. 347p. maps. bibliog.

This publication is also available in microfiche from Clearwater Publishers, New York. It represents the most important work on the evolution of Libreville, Gabon's administrative and commercial capital, from the 1840s up to and including the 1950s. It gives particular attention to demography and economic geography.

14   **Notre pays. Le Gabon. Géographie.** (Our country. Gabon. Geography.)
Frédéric Meyo-Bibang, Jean-Martin Nzamba.   Paris: Edicef, 1975. 80p.
maps.

This geography text for the secondary level contains clear and precise explanations as well as fine maps. It is particularly strong for economic geography.

15   **Le Gabon. Vol. 1, Espace–histoire–société; vol. 2, Etat et développement.**
(Gabon. Vol. 1, Space, history, society; vol. 2, State and development.)
Roland Pourtier.   Paris: Harmattan, 1989. 2 vols. 60 maps. bibliog.

This extraordinary work of scholarship deals with humankind's use of space through time to create an economy, society and state. It begins with the natural setting and the problem of underpopulation. It then turns to the formation of what is today Gabon as a result of the interaction of Africans with westerners and the institution of French rule. It reviews the delimitation of the frontiers and the major changes in international boundaries, including the transfer of Loango to the Congo Republic in 1918 and the recovery of the Haut-Ogooué Province in 1946. It deals with the economic utilization of the country's resources by the indigenous inhabitants before the French occupation and the transformations wrought by European activities, particularly the development of lumbering and the imposition of cash crops between the two World Wars. Among the most valuable sections are those dealing with economic development since independence that privileged mining at the expense of agriculture, and with the urbanization that has changed Gabon irrevocably. The study contains an excellent bibliography of works in economic geography and history. It includes travel accounts (p. 319-21), and maps and atlases (p. 314-16).

16   **Les climats au Gabon.** (Climates in Gabon.)
J. Saint-Vil.   *Annales de l'Université Nationale du Gabon, série Lettres et Sciences Sociales*, vol. 1 (Dec. 1977), p. 101-25. bibliog.

Gabon possesses an equatorial climate involving uniformly high temperatures averaging 26°C, high relative humidities, and mean annual rainfalls from 150 to 300 cm. The country has two rainy seasons, from mid-February to mid-May and from mid-September to mid-December, as well as two dry seasons, from mid-May to mid-September and from mid-December to mid-February.

17   **De l'Atlantique au fleuve Congo: une géographie du sous-peuplement**
(République du Congo. République gabonaise.). (From the Atlantic to the Congo River: a geography of under-population. Congo Republic, Gabonese Republic.)
Gilles Sautter.   Paris: Mouton, 1966. 2 vols. 1102p. maps. bibliog.

This is an important work for understanding the origins of underdevelopment, particularly its demographic dimensions. This massive study examines the problem of underdevelopment by looking first at the two countries as a whole, over half of which had population densities estimated at below one person per square kilometre and ninety-six per cent under six per square kilometre. The gross pattern of population distribution involved very low overall densities, great unevenness in distribution, frequently of linear patterns along the roads, dependence of several areas upon major internal waterways, and the general reduction of densities as one moves from south to north. Four-fifths of the work is devoted to more intensive analyses of six regions, including two in Gabon. Both of them are heavily forested; the lakes of the south inland from Port-Gentil, and the Woleu-N'Tem Province in the north, which forms a larger unit with adjacent areas in Cameroon. Sautter believes that the introduction of mining is well-suited to the characteristics of Gabon's population and that the cocomitant disadvantages of a dual economy are subject to correction.

Maps and atlases

18 **Africa, west coast approaches to Libreville and Owendo.**
Washington, DC: US Defense Mapping Agency. Hydrographic/ Topographic Center, 1989. 18th ed.
This map is both hydrographic and topographic.

19 **Géographie et cartographie du Gabon: atlas illustré.** (Geography and cartography of Gabon: illustrated atlas.)
Edited by Jacques Barret.   Paris: EDICEF, 1983. 135p.
This excellent atlas of Gabon contains clearly presented geographical information.

20 **Gabon.**
Washington, DC: Central Intelligence Agency, Government Printing Office, 1981.
This map of Gabon on the scale 1:1,690,000 is primarily a location and comparative area map, but also has maps of population, ethnic groups, economic activity and vegetation.

21 **Les sols du Gabon, pédogenèse répartition et aptitudes; cartes à 1:2,000,000.** (The soils of Gabon, pedogenesis, distribution and aptitudes; maps at 1:2,000,000.)
D. Martin, [et al.].   Paris: ORSTOM, 1981.
These maps chart the soils of Gabon.

22 **Afrique Centrale. Esquisse ethnique générale.** (Central Africa: general ethnic outline.)
Marcel Soret.   Brazzaville: Institut Géographique National, 1962.
This excellent map shows the locations of the various ethnic groups of Gabon as they were at the time of independence in 1960.

Le Gabon. Vol. 2, Etat et Développement. (Gabon. Vol. 2, State and development.)
See item no. 15.

Geology

23 **Brazil–Gabon geologic link supports continental drift: newly discovered tectonic province in Brazil matches province in Gabon.**
Giles O. Allard, Vernon J. Hurst.   *Science*, (Feb. 7, 1969), p. 528-32.
maps. bibliog.
This article discusses newly discovered geological links between Gabon and Brazil.

24 **Palynologie du crétace supérieur du Gabon.** (Palynology of the upper cretaceous in Gabon.)
Eugène Boltenhagen.   Paris: Bibliothèque Nationale, 1980. 191p.
bibliog.
In northern Gabon the coastal plain has an average width of 100 miles. Formed of sandstone and alluvium it has outcrops of chalk, limestone and cretaceous sandstone. This study treats the chalk formations.

25 **Bulletin de la Direction de Mines et de la Géologie.** (Bulletin of the Direction of Mines and Geology.)
Brazzaville: French Equatorial Africa, Direction of Mines and Geology, 1943-60. bi-annual.
This publication contains many announcements and articles about the study of the geology of Gabon during the Second World War and the Fourth Republic as well as the development of mineral resources.

26 **The Francevillian (lower Proterozoic) uranium ore deposits of Gabon.**
F. Gauthier-Lafaye, F. Weber. *Economic Geology*, vol. 84, no. 3
(1989), p. 2267-85. bibliog.

These deposits are the oldest high-grade uranium accumulations known. They are unique in that they contain evidence for natural nuclear fission reactors. Sedimentologic, tectonic, petrographic and geochemical studies have been performed in order to reconstruct the geologic conditions in which uranium mineralization took place. Uranium deposits are located in deltaic sediments overlying fluviatile deposits of coarse sandstone and conglomerates which are the source rocks for uranium. Deltaic sediments are overlaid by marine black shales (the FB formation). Petrographic observations, electron microscopic studies, and geochemical and carbon isotope data indicate that these FB black shales are source rocks for petroleum trapped in the uranium deposits. Tectonic studies show that all the uranium deposits are in tectonic structures that served as traps for both petroleum and uranium.

27 **Carte géologique de l'Afrique Equatoriale Française et du Cameroun.**
(Geological map of French Equatorial Africa and Cameroon.)
Designed by B. Leroy, edited by Maurice Nickles. Brazzaville: French
Equatorial Africa, Direction of Mines and Geology, 1952.

These three coloured maps on a scale of 1:2,000,000 depict the geology of French Equatorial Africa and the Cameroons.

Flora and Fauna

Plants

28 **Flore du Gabon.** (Flora of Gabon.)
Edited by A. Aubreville. Paris: Musée National d'Histoire Naturelle, 1961-73. 23 vols.
Most of Gabon lies within a zone of dense equatorial forest that includes some islands of grass woodland or savanna. There is also mangrove woodland on portions of the coast. This multi-volume series includes studies of trees, shrubs, plants, grasses, ferns, and flowers.

29 **Guide pour l'étude de quelques plantes tropicales.** (Guide for the study of some tropical plants.)
R. Paulian de Felice. Paris: Gauthier-Villars, 1967. 127p. bibliog.
Plants from Gabon are included in this volume.

30 **Les formations herbeuses au Gabon.** (The grassy formations of Gabon.)
J. Fontes. *Annales de l'Université Nationale du Gabon*, série Sciences et Techniques, no. 2 (Mar. 1978), p. 127-53. bibliog.
This study of the grasses of Gabon looks particularly at those in the savanna areas.

31 **Recherche sur quelques plantes médicinales du Gabon (deux ménispermacées): synclisin, scabrica, miers, jateorhiza macrantha.**
(Research on some medicinal plants of Gabon [two menispermaceae]: synclisin, scabrica, miers, jateorhiza macrantha.)
J. N. Gassita. Châteauroux, France: Imprimerie Badel, 1968. 138p. bibliog.
This study describes climbing shrubs of the menispermaceae family.

32 **Flore du Gabon: famille des sterculiacées.** (Flora of Gabon: families of
the sterculiaceae.)
N. Halle.   Paris: Musée National d'Histoire Naturelle, 1961. 150p.
bibliog.
Volume 2 of this work studies trees, shrubs and herbs of the sterculiaceae family.

33 **The tuberous plants of the Central Africa rainforest.**
Annette Hladik et al.   *Revue d'Ecologie* (*Terre et Vie*), vol. 39, no. 3
(1984), p. 249-96. bibliog.
Species of rainforest plants developing starchy tubers were studied around Makoukou
in north-eastern Gabon and in the Lobaye River district of the south-western Central
African Republic. A detailed description of the tuberous parts is given particularly in
wild yams (*dioscorea spp.*) to help to elucidate the taxonomic status of a number of
species.

34 **Les légumineuses du Gabon.** (The legumes of Gabon.)
F. Pellegrin.   Paris: Larose, 1948. 284p. bibliog.
This study describes 125 genuses and 450 species of leguminous plants.

35 **The forest vegetation of Gabon/Végétation forestière du Gabon.**
J. M. Reitsma.   Ede, Netherlands: Tropenbos, Technical Series 1,
1989. 142p. map. bibliog.
This study of rain-forest flora includes texts in both English and French. Reitsma made
intensive studies of the number of species to be found on one-hectare plots in four
different parts of the country. He found the greatest diversity (131 species) in the plot
at Oveng near the Monts de Cristal, which was nearly twice the number (69 species)
found in the Lopé Reserve in the middle Ogooué, with intermediate numbers located
in plots in the upper Ogooué and Ivindo river valleys. Only three percent of the
species identified were found in all four plots while seventy percent of them were
found in only one of the plots. Okoumé, the country's most important timber export,
was located in the forests of all regions of the country except the north-east. The
forests of Gabon are comparatively richer in the numbers of species of flora than most
of the forests of West Africa, having roughly three times as many species in relation to
area.

36 **Les plantes utiles au Gabon: essai d'inventaire et de concordance des noms vernaculaires et scientifiques des plantes spontanées et introduites; description des espèces, propriétes, utilisations économiques, ethnographiques et artistiques.** (The useful plants in Gabon: essay of inventory and concordance of the vernacular and scientific names of spontaneous and introduced plants: description of the species, properties, economic, ethnographic and artistic utilizations.)
André Raponda Walker, Roger Sillans.   Paris: P. Lechevalier, 1961. 614p. bibliog.

This handbook describes the useful plants of Gabon. Among them are such important food staples as the varieties of plantain bananas, manioc, sugar cane, and mushrooms, and the raphia used for making cloth and mats. Also discussed are the plants employed in decoration and traditional medicine.

Animals

37 **A la découverte des gorilles les plus secrets du monde.** (To the discovery of the most secret gorillas in the world.)
Madeleine Barbier-Decrozes.   *M'Bolo* no. 26 (1990), p. 40-49.

Since 1984 two researchers from the CIRMF, Caroline Tutin and Michel Fernandez, have been studying the life and habits of scarce gorilla species in the Lopé Reserve, a protected zone established by the government. An English summary is found in the appendix of the issue.

38 **Man determines the distribution of elephants in the rain forests of northeastern Gabon.**
R. F. W. Barnes, [et al.].   *African Journal of Ecology*, vol. 29, no. 1 (1991), p. 54-63. bibliog.

Loxodonta africana prefer secondary forest which grows on abandoned villages and plantations but avoid roads and villages. Thus elephant distribution is governed by the distribution of both past and present human settlement, even in the remotest and least disturbed forests of equatorial Africa.

39 **Ecology and behavior of nocturnal primates: prosimians of equatorial West Africa.**
Pierre Charles-Dominique.   New York: Columbia University Press, 1977. 277p. bibliog.

This work does not undertake a thoroughgoing review of our knowledge of all nocturnal primates in the region as the main title might suggest. Rather, the author concentrates on resolving the problems of behavioural ecology in the Gabonese prosimians. He demonstrates that no aspect or detail of structure or behaviour is without meaning in terms of the animals' survival.

Flora and Fauna. Animals

40 **Heureux éléphants au Gabon.** (Happy elephants in Gabon.)
Michel Fernandez-Puente. *M'Bolo*, no. 27 (1990), p. 38-50.

This article, illustrated with beautiful coloured photographs, describes the status of Gabon's 70,000 elephants and of the government's efforts to preserve them. An English summary appears in the appendix.

41 **Faune de l'Equateur Africain Français.** (Fauna of the French African
Equator.)
R. F. Malbrant, A. R. Maclatchy. Paris: Lechevalier, 1949. 2 vols.
bibliog.

The first volume discusses birds and the second mammifers. Among the latter are antelope, buffalo, monkeys, gorillas, chimpanzees, elephants, snakes, lizards, and various insects.

42 **Contribution à la Faune du Gabon. Mission A. Villiers 1969.**
(Contribution to the fauna of Gabon. A. Villiers Mission 1969.;
E. Pinhey. *Bulletin de l'IFAN, série A*, no. 4 (1971), p. 959-1044.
bibliog.

This special study on the animals of Gabon was undertaken in the late 1960s.

43 **Mammalian biomass in an African equatorial rainforest.**
H. H. T. Prins, J. M. Reitsma. *Journal of Animal Ecology*, vol. 58,
no. 3 (1989), p. 851-61. maps. bibliog.

Densities of mammals in a lowland rain forest in the Ogooué-Maritime were studied, including elephants, African buffalo, primates and pigs. The authors conclude that elephants play a key role in African rain-forest ecosystems in contrast to other rain forests where pigs are important.

44 **Gorilla diet in the Lopé Reserve, Gabon: a nutritional analysis.**
M. E. Rogers, [et al.]. *Oecologia*, vol. 84, no. 3 (1990), p. 326-29.
bibliog.

The diet is the most diverse so far analysed for gorillas. It consists of a balance between sugary fruit, proteinaceous leaves and relatively fibrous stems. Most fruits and herbaceous stems are succulent, but some drier, fibrous fruit and bark are also consumed. Seeds are another component of the diet, including unripe ones. Fruit, seeds, leaves and bark may all contain very high levels of total phenols and condensed tannins. But all herbaceous stems assayed contain low levels of these compounds. Alkaloids are not apparently a significant component of gorilla foods, and may be avoided. Gorilla g. gorilla tended to avoid fatty fruit and to select leaves that are high in protein and low in fibre compared to the general vegetation. When fruit and preferred young leaves are scarce, proteinaceous barks and mature leaves as well as sugary pith are important sources of nutrients.

45   A case study of a plant-animal relationship: 'cola-lizae' and lowland
      gorillas in the Lopé Reserve, Gabon.
      Caroline E. G. Tutin.   *Journal of Tropical Ecology*, vol. 7, pt. 2 (May
      1991), p. 181-99. bibliog.

The fruits of *cola-lizae*, an endemic tree with a limited geographic distribution, have
been a major food source for lowland gorillas in the Lopé Reserve during part of each
year over a six-year period. The open areas of forest which gorillas prefer as nest sites
are advantageous to the propagation of this species.

46   Nationwide census of gorilla (gorilla g. gorilla) and chimpanzee (pan t.
      troglodytes) populations in Gabon.
      Caroline E. G. Tutin, Michael Fernandez[-Puente].   *American Journal
      of Primatology*, vol. 6 (1984), p. 313-34. bibliog.

This article studies the natural distribution of these two primate species in Gabon.

Birds

47   **Birds from Gabon and Moyen Congo.**
      Austin L. Rand, Herbert Friedmann, Melvin Taylor.   *Fieldiana*, vol.
      41, no. 2 (1959), p. 221-411. map. bibliog.

An annotated list of 378 species contains 53 per cent of the possible avifauna in the two
countries. The forest element is an integral part of the Lower Guinea fauna and
racially its species are almost identical with those in Cameroon. Within the savanna
element, the relationship of those forms found both north and south of the forest is
slightly more with forms from Cameroon than with those from Angola. At the same
time there is a segment of savanna birds that reach their northernmost range in the two
countries and are not found north of the forest. The area of the two countries cannot
be considered a faunal subregion and its only endemic elements, nine subspecies and
one species, are confined to the coastal savannas.

Insects

48   **Les oiseaux des régions forestières du nord-est du Gabon.** (The birds of
      the forest regions of north-eastern Gabon.)
      A. Brossat, C. Erard.   Paris: Société nationale de protection de la
      nature, 1986. 200p., map, bibliog.

Over two decades French and Gabonese researchers have studied the distribution and
ecology of 410 species of sedentary or migratory birds found in the north-east of
Gabon. They represent roughly two-thirds of the 626 found in the whole country.

49 **Les lépidoptères de l'Afrique noire française.** (The lepidoptera of French
    Black Africa.)
    A. Villiers, H. Stempffer. 3 vols.   Dakar: IFAN, 1957. maps, bibliog.

The butterflies and moths of Gabon are included in this study. The first volume deals
with general matters, the second papillonids, and the third lycenids. Gabon abounds in
colourful species of lycenids, many of them common to other rain-forests of tropical
Africa. Among the lepidoptera found specifically in Gabon are the *graphium auriger*
(Butler), which has black wings, a white median band, and an orange and black body;
the *auslauga cura* (H. H. Druce), which has blue, black, and violet colouration; and
the *euliphyra mirifica* (Holland), which has reddish brown wings and a violet grey
body.

Shells

50 **Coquillages du Gabon/Shells of Gabon.**
    Pierre A. Bernard.   Libreville: The Author, 1984. 140p.

This work on the shells of Gabon has texts both in French and in English. It is
illustrated with many beautiful photographs.

Archaeology and Prehistory

51 **Bulletin de la Société Préhistorique et Prohistorique Gabonaise.** (Bulletin of the Gabonese Prehistoric and Protohistoric Society.)
Libreville: Société Préhistorique et Protohistorique Gabonaise, 1965-
irregular.
This periodical contains brief articles giving the results of recent research.

52 **Archaeology in review.**
Bernard Clist. *African Archaeological Review*, vol. 7 (1989), p. 59-95.
maps. bibliog.
This is a synthesis of the archaeological investigations undertaken in Gabon, particularly those of the 1980s that have caused revisions in the periodization of the various Stone and Iron Ages. Clist believes that the oldest tools found in Gabon were made by a hunting and collecting people in a savanna area of the Middle Ogooué more than 10,000 years ago. Late Stone Age tools dating from the Estuary around 6000 BC during a wetter phase seem to belong to forest dwellers, who possibly were pygmies. Evidence from the Late Stone Age suggests that the toolmaking industries in Gabon bear little resemblance to those in either southern Congo Republic and Zaire or in Cameroon in comparable periods. The earliest evidence for iron-smelting derives from sites in the Haut-Ogooué Province between 350 and 300 BC, and the Woleu-N'Tem Province between 280 and 200 BC. Iron-smelting reached the Gabon Estuary only around 100 AD. Iron-working skills most likely arrived in Gabon from the north, possibly introduced by speakers of Proto-Bantu languages. Recent research that produced evidence for village settlements in the Libreville area from around 2000 BC may lead to a redating of the early Bantu migrations into Gabon from the north.

53 **Métallurgie ancienne du fer au Gabon: premiers éléments de synthèse.**
(Ancient iron metallurgy in Gabon; first elements for a synthesis.)
Bernard Clist, Richard Oslisly, Bernard Peyrot. *Muntu*, no. 4-5
(1986), p. 47-55. map. bibliog.

Archaeological research carried on during the previous twelve months provides new
and precious information about the origins of iron-working in Gabon and Central
Africa. It has been learned that iron was known in all of the provinces studied since the
beginning of the Christian era. In addition, certain radiocarbon dates that predate this
period by several centuries enable the authors to hypothesize a very old beginning for
iron production in Gabon and to posit a north–south route along the Atlantic coast for
the diffusion of iron.

54 **Gabon: the earliest Iron Age of West Central Africa.**
Lazare Digombe. *Nyame Akuma*, no. 28 (1987), p. 9-11.

This discussion of the origins and spread of iron technology incorporates data from
recent excavations in the Haut-Ogooué and N'Gounié Provinces.

55 **The development of an Early Iron Age prehistory in Gabon.**
Lazare Digombe, [et al.]. *Current Anthropology*, vol. 29, no. 1 (Feb.
1988), p. 179-84.

Reports from ten more dates from Moanda in the Haut-Ogooué Province and three
more Early Iron Age dates from Lac Bleu near Mouila in the N'Gounié Province
provide the most coherent and earliest documentation for iron technology in the
equatorial forest zone of west Central Africa. In the N'Gounié there was found a
furnace of a shaft bowl type of structure. Slag was not tapped but collected in a bowl
surmounted by a one- to two-metre chimney shaft. The earliest phase of iron-smelting
in south-eastern Gabon began between the third and second centuries BC. At Moanda
manganese was used as a flux to lower the melting point of slag and more efficiently
separate bloom from the slag. Thus iron-smelting had a distinctively innovative
character in this area that is unique for the entirety of Gabon. Because Gabon lies
between the Bantu homeland on the Nigeria–Cameroon border and the interlacustrine
area of eastern Africa, its Iron Age archaeology promises to answer many questions
about the transition to iron technology upon Bantu-speaking peoples.

56 **Radiocarbon dates for the Iron Age in Gabon.**
Lazare Digombe, [et al.]. *Current Anthropology*, vol. 26, no. 4
(Aug.–Sept. 1985), p. 516. bibliog.

This is a report on the archaeological research programme undertaken by Omar Bongo
University since 1980. The two regions that have been surveyed to date are the Haut-
Ogooué and N'Gounié Provinces. The evidence obtained in the former region points
to a complete chronology. Eight C14 dates have been obtained through analysis of
charcoal samples from Iron Age sites.

57   **Esquisse archéologique des régions Teke.** (Archaeological outline of the
      Téké regions.)
      Raymond Lanfranchi.   *Muntu*, no. 7 (1987), p. 73-99. map. bibliog.

The Téké people of the Haut-Ogooué Province form part of a larger group living
mainly in the Congo Republic. The author believes that these regions have been
inhabited by *homo sapiens* for at least 70,000 years. The oldest industries belong to the
Middle Stone Age and particularly to the Sangoan in Central Africa. This Sangoan was
contemporaneous with a drying climatic phase. The Sangoan period was followed by
the Lupembian from 28,000 BC to 13,000-10,000 BC, which saw the maximum point of
aridity. The Tshitolian period which followed saw a rehumidification of the climate
involving a reconstitution of the forests. Limited evidence suggests that some of the
earliest agriculture using partially or completely polished stone hatchets and hoes
appeared at Franceville as well as at Kinshasa, Zaire. Iron tools first appeared in the
vicinity of Moanda during the second and first centuries BC. Copper use postdates iron
use.

58   **Aux origines de l'Afrique Centrale.** (To the origins of Central Africa.)
      Edited by Raymond Lanfranchi, Bernard Clist, under the direction of
      Théophile Obenga.   Libreville: Sépia for the Centre Cultural Français
      d'Afrique Centrale and CICIBA, 1991. 268p. map. bibliog.

This collection of essays represents latest scholarship on the prehistory and pre-colonial
history of Gabon and neighbouring areas.

59   **L'âge des métaux chez les Fang anciens: relations avec l'histoire générale
      et la chronologie absolue.** (The age of metals among the ancient Fang:
      relations with general history and absolute chronology.)
      Marc Ropivia.   *Mois en Afrique*, (Aug.–Sept. 1984), p. 152-63. map.
      bibliog.

This article continues the study of Fang origins begun in the following item (no. 60).
Ropivia tries to correlate general knowledge about copper and iron derived from
radiocarbon dates with references to the use of these metals in Fang oral tradition. He
concludes that the Fang lived in Nubia and the Great Lakes region of eastern Africa
from about 3000 BC. They began to move westward from these sites around 1500 AD.

60   **Les Fang dans les grands lacs et la vallée du Nil.** (The Fang in the Great
      Lakes and the valley of the Nile.)
      Marc Ropivia.   *Présence Africaine*, no. 4 (1981), p. 46-58. map.
      bibliog.

On the basis of a reading of the *mvet* in the edition by Tsira Ndong Ntoutoume (*see*
item no. 437) and the study of ancient documents on Egypt and the Nile Valley, the
young Gabonese scholar, Marc Ropivia, proposes a revised theory of Fang origins. He
concludes that the Fang in the distant past inhabited a huge area extending from Nubia
south to Lake Victoria from which they migrated west via the Ouellé and Oubangui
Rivers towards their later locations in northern Gabon.

61 **Migration Bantu et tradition orale des Fang.** (Bantu migration and oral tradition of the Fang.)
Marc Ropivia. *Le Mois en Afrique*, (Aug.–Sept. 1983), p. 121-32. maps. bibliog.

This continuation of item nos. 60 and 59 on Fang origins reviews the evidence for considering that people as of original Bantu stock and language.

62 **Newly dated Iron Age sites in Gabon.**
P. R. Schmidt, [et al.]. *Nyame Akuma*, no. 26 (1985), p. 16-18.

This article reports on findings from sites in the Haut-Ogooué and N'Gounié Provinces.

63 **Western Bantu expansion.**
Jan Vansina. *Journal of African History*, vol. 25, no. 2 (1984), p. 129-45. bibliog.

The author hypothesizes that Bantu-speaking people were already living in Gabon by at least 1000 BC. He concludes that linguistic evidence from Central Africa indicates that iron-working terms are derived from the eastern Bantu and not the western as once thought. This finding suggests the possibility of a reverse flow of iron-producing Bantu-speakers from the interlacustrine region of eastern Africa sometime during the first millenium BC. Whatever the origins of the technology, it is clear that iron production gained acceptance at a relatively early date in a heavily forested region of Africa. The Gabonese sites presently being studied hold great promise for understanding the development of technological traditions that display different adaptations and innovations suited to the specific resources in their regions. They provide enormous potential for explaining growth and variability of distinctive complex technological cultures in the African Iron Age.

Traditions orales et archives au Gabon. (Oral traditions and archives in Gabon.)
See item no. 106.

Inventaire et recensions de 130 récits migratoires originaux du Gabon. (Inventory and census of 130 original migratory accounts of Gabon.)
See item no. 115.

A natural fossil nuclear reactor.
See item no. 375.

The Oklo nuclear reactors: 1800 million years ago.
See item no. 376.

Le phénomène d'Oklo: comptes rendus d'un colloque sur le phénomène d'Oklo. The Oklo phenomenon: proceedings of a symposium on the Oklo phenomenon.
See item no. 377.

History

General

64 **Hommes et Destins. Dictionnaire biographique d'outre-mer.** (Men and
    Destinies. Overseas biographical dictionary.)
    Edited by Robert Cornevin.   Paris: Académie des Sciences d'Outre-
    Mer, 1975- . irregular.
A series of volumes containing biographical articles on important figures in the history
of France in Africa. In the volumes devoted to sub-Saharan Africa are found entries on
two dozen Gabonese, French and Americans from the nineteenth and twentieth
centuries.

65 **Colonial governors from the fifteenth century to the present: a
    comprehensive list.**
    Compiled by David P. Henige.   Madison, Wisconsin: University of
    Wisconsin Press, 1970. 401p. bibliog.
This work includes lists of colonial officials in France, French Congo/French Equatorial
Africa and Gabon for the period of the French presence in Gabon, 1843-1960.

66 **Paths in the rainforests: toward a history of political traditions in
    equatorial Africa.**
    Jan Vansina.   Madison, Wisconsin: University of Wisconsin Press,
    1990. 428p. 42 maps. bibliog.
This work reconstructs the history of the western Bantu peoples, including Gabon's
forty peoples, from the earliest times up to 1920, with particular attention to political,
economic and social dimensions and to concepts, values and ideologies. Among the
topics included are the original settlement of the forest by the western Bantu: the
periods of expansion and innovation in agriculture; the development of metallurgy; the
rise and fall of political forms and centres of power; the coming of the Atlantic trade

and colonial rule; and the conquest of the rain forest by European colonial powers and the destruction of a way of life.

67 **The peoples of the forest.**
Jan Vansina. In: *History of Central Africa, Vol. 1.* Edited by David Birmingham, Phyllis M. Martin. London: Longman, 1983, p. 75-117. 6 maps. bibliog.

This social history of the peoples of the equatorial rain forests focuses mainly on the late fifteenth to the late nineteenth centuries. The author sees a deep continuity in the social history of the forest peoples that extends from the days when they developed the house and village more than a millenium ago down to the European conquest. The colonial intrusion finally destroyed the nature and autonomy of these fundamental institutions between about 1870 and 1910. Prior to this destruction the Atlantic slave-trade had led to profound social change, including an increasingly rigorous social stratification throughout larger geographic areas leading to the widespread formation of social classes. This transformation proved deeper than any that had previously occurred and had greater effects than the emergence of kingdoms in the south-west, including in south-western Gabon, which formed part of the kingdom of Loango.

Historical dictionary of Gabon.
See item no. 4.

Regional

68 **Port-Gentil, centre économique du Gabon.** (Port-Gentil, economic centre of Gabon.)
Jacqueline Bouquerel. *Cahiers d'Outre-Mer*, vol. 20 (July–Sept. 1967), p. 247-74. maps. bibliog.

This article gives a detailed picture of the country's most important port and the centre of its timber and petroleum industries on the eve of the great expansion in oil production during the late 1960s and 1970s.

69 **Au Gabon: le district du 'bout du monde' [Mékambo].** (In Gabon: the district at 'the end of the world' [Mékambo].)
Louis Dermigny, Gérard Serre. *Cahiers d'Outre-Mer*, vol. 7 (July–Sept. 1954), p. 213-24. bibliog.

This account describes life in the Mékambo district of the Ogooué-Ivindo Province prior to the construction of road links with the rest of Gabon. It was in this region that extensive iron deposits were located but could not be developed for lack of means of evacuation.

70 **Franceville (Gabon). Activités et rôle dans l'organisation de son arrière pays.** (Franceville, Gabon. Activities and role in the organisation of its hinterland.)
Mamedi Kamara. *Cahiers d'Outre-Mer*, vol. 36 (July–Sept. 1983), p. 267-92.

The recent development of Franceville derives not only from economic factors but also from political ones. It is the capital of the Haut-Ogooué Province, which contains the manganese and uranium mines as well as state-sponsored agro-businesses. It is the terminus of the Trans-Gabon Railway (completed in 1986). As the home town of President Bongo it has become the site of a centre for medical research and a scientific and technological university. The transmitter of an international radio station, Africa No. 1, is located not far away at Moyabi. Between 1961 and 1976 the population of Franceville grew from 1,200 inhabitants to 16,000, a process which involved a good deal of social differentiation. The greatest degrees exist between the newly developed centre districts and undeveloped ones on the periphery of the city.

71 **Esquisse d'une étude urbaine des principales agglomérations de la province du Haut-Ogooué.** (Outline of an urban study of the principal agglomerations of the Haut-Ogooué Province.)
Emmanuel Ekarga Mba. *Muntu*, no. 7 (1987), p. 49-72. maps. bibliog.

Between 1925 and 1946, the Haut-Ogooué Province was attached to the Middle Congo Territory, today's Congo Republic. It was an economic backwater that was declining in population. After the Haut-Ogooué's reintegration into Gabon in 1946, the development of its considerable mineral resources, particularly manganese at Moanda and uranium at Mounana, gave it a new vitality and population growth. The coming to power of a native of the province, President Bongo, in 1967 led to the construction of the Trans-Gabon Railway connecting the province with the Gabon Estuary. Bongo was responsible for developing the provincial capital, Franceville, as an administrative centre. He transferred the faculties of physical sciences and engineering from Libreville to a new university at nearby Masuku in the late 1980s. Franceville is also the site of the Centre International de Recherches Médicales de Franceville (CIRMF), which undertakes research in the causes of infertility and morbidity that have until recently kept Gabon's rate of natural increase of population low.

72 **Millénaire de Mulundu, centenaire de Lastoursville.** (Millenary of Mulundu, centenary of Lastoursville.)
Bonjean Aba Nguoa, [et al.]. Libreville: Multipresse, 1986. 114p. map. bibliog.

A history of the Mulundu area of the Ogooé-Lolo Province from prehistoric times to recent days, and of Lastoursville, which was founded as a French post in 1883.

73 **Le peuple Teke en Afrique Centrale.** (The Téké people in Central Africa.)
Théophile Obenga. *Muntu*, no. 7 (1987), p. 11-31.

This article examines the geographic locations of the Téké people of Gabon, the Congo Republic and Zaire, and their various ethnic subdivisions.

74 **Les populations Batéké.** (The Batéké populations.)
Louis Papy. *Cahiers d'Outre-Mer*, vol. 2 (Apr.–June 1949), p. 112-34.
map. bibliog.

This article describes the Téké populations of the Congo Republic and Gabon shortly
after the Second World War, and includes their natural milieu, traditional economy
and society, and the influence of the French penetration.

75 **Chronique du pays Kota (Gabon).** (Chronicle of the Kota country,
Gabon.)
Louis Perrois. *Cahiers de l'ORSTOM. Série Sciences Humaines*, vol. 7,
no. 2 (1970), p. 15-110. map. bibliog.

The Kota people of eastern Gabon had a segmentary organization, patrilineal in the
north and matrilineal in the south. The oral traditions of the tribes (*ilongo*), the clans
(*ikaka*), and even of the villages, from which one may reconstruct the indigenous
version of their history, including the great migrations of the eighteenth and nineteenth
centuries, indicate that all Kota groups have the same origin, undoubtedly the middle
Sangha River valley. All of them have followed the same general north–south direction
under pressure from conquering neighbours and slave hunters. Because Kota migration
took place at the clan and village levels, the people spread in every direction within the
triangle formed by the Ivindo River in the north-west, and the Ogooué River and the
Sébé River in the south-east. They moved first from the Sangha to the Ivindo, then in a
more dispersed migration to the settlements of the early twentieth century. The
installation of French colonial rule between 1900 and 1930 ended the migrations and
also ruined the Kota tribes physically, socially and morally. The Kota are aware of
their great decline since the 1880s. By 1970 the earlier social and cultural features of
this people had barely survived.

76 **An ethno-historical study of the political economy of Ndjolé, Gabon.**
Michael Charles Reed. PhD thesis, University of Washington, Seattle,
Washington, 1988. 457p. bibliog. (Available from University Microfilms
International, Ann Arbor, Michigan, order no. 88-26,421.)

N'Djolé is a town of 4,000 situated at the upriver limit of year-round navigation on the
Ogooué River. It is a centre for administration, commerce and swidden subsistence
agriculture. N'Djolé has played these roles since its founding in 1883 by P. S. de
Brazza as a base for his explorations further into the interior. For the next two decades
the dominant local Fang exported ivory, rubber, wax and dyewood downriver to the
coast in return for Western manufactures. But between the establishment of a French
concessionary company in 1900, which wrecked Fang commerce, and the construction
of the Trans-Gabon Railway in the 1970s, the town's economy stagnated. The
dissertation aims to explain why the vigorous Fang entrepreneurial activity of the late
nineteenth century has been negligible ever since. Partial explanations are the lack of
indigenous market tradition, the restraints imposed by French colonialism, focus upon
capital intensive mineral exports, and the townspeople's reliance upon public sector
employment. The methodologies employed are those of radical political economy and
ethno-history.

77 **Port-Gentil: quelques aspects sociaux du développement industriel.** (Port
    Gentil: some social aspects of industrial development.)
    Micheline Roumegous. *Cahiers d'Outre-Mer*, vol. 19, no. 4 (Oct.–Dec.
    1966), p. 321-53. maps. bibliog.

This study was completed just before the large-scale expansion of Port-Gentil's oil
refinery and port. It seeks to clarify the originality of Port-Gentil's characteristics in
comparison with Libreville, and Gabon in general, by analysing its ecoomic and
demographic development, problems of salaried labour, and the socio-professional
achievements of a few enterprises. Before becoming a French town, Port-Gentil was a
Portuguese hunting and fishing station. Between 1880 and 1945 Port-Gentil became a
commercial and harbour centre, especially after the discovery of the *okoumé* and the
establishment of the timber yards in 1902. Between 1947 and 1955 the town developed
further with the introduction of timber industries followed by the exploitation of
petroleum deposits from 1956 on. As a result the population burgeoned from 4,500 in
1947 to 20,000 in 1962. The active percentage of the total population (42.5 per cent)
consisted mainly of single men drawn from all over Gabon and neighbouring countries,
the largest part having migrated from villages in the Ogooué basin without ever passing
by way of the timber yards. Most of the migrants were younger people who lacked
professional qualifications and who encountered severe problems in adjusting to work
with machines and assembly lines and to life away from their extended family. Some
women have also entered the work force. Few of the workers have joined trade unions
in an effort to protect their interests. The situation in Port-Gentil has spurred
government efforts to provide opportunities for basic education and professional
training to its workers.

78 **Les ports du Gabon et du Congo-Brazzaville.** (The ports of Gabon and
    Congo-Brazzaville.)
    Pierre Vennetier. *Cahiers d'Outre-Mer*, vol. 22, no. 4 (Oct.–Dec.
    1969), p. 337-55. bibliog.

The commercial activities of the French along the coasts of Gabon have a long history.
But from the 1500s to the early 1800s trade was carried on by barter and did without
fixed installations. The main stages in the establishment of French interests were
marked by the spread of trading factories, the setting up of the first military post in
1843 and the foundation of Libreville in 1849. The creation of Port-Gentil at the mouth
of the Ogooué River in the 1890s had significance for the exploitation of *okoumé* and
trade with the interior.

Exploration and travel

79 **One dry season: in the footsteps of Mary Kingsley.**
    Caroline Alexander. New York: Knopf, 1989. 290p. bibliog.

During 1981 the author retraced the travels of Mary Kingsley in 1895 throughout
regions of northern Gabon. Her account contains interesting descriptions of the
country and its people in our time.

80 **Ambiguous Africa.**
Georges Balandier. New York: Pantheon, 1966. 276p. translation of
Afrique ambiguë (Paris: Plon, 1957. 294p.)

This includes a brief description of Gabonese art and a chapter on the author's travels
throughout Gabon during the 1950s while doing research.

81 **A new and accurate description of the coast of Guinea: divided into the
gold, slave, and ivory coasts.**
William [Willem] Bosman. London: Frank Cass, 1967. 577p.

This translation of the Dutch edition of 1704 represents the most important European
source on Gabon in the early eighteenth century by a Dutch visitor.

82 **Mission from Cape Coast Castle to Ashantee.**
Thomas Edward Bowdich. London: J. Murray, 1819. 3rd ed.
Reprinted, London: Frank Cass, 1966. 512p.

Included in this volume is the account of an English visitor in Gabon during the early
nineteenth century.

83 **Canonization by repetition: Paul du Chaillu in historiography.**
Henry H. Bucher. *Revue Française d'Histoire d'Outre-Mer*, vol. 66,
no. 242-43 (1979), p. 15-32. bibliog.

A review of the evidence about the life and career of the explorer Paul du Chaillu
challenges many of the beliefs that by repetition over time became 'facts'. Born in
Réunion in 1831, du Chaillu followed his French merchant father to Gabon in 1848.
He sailed from there in 1852 to teach French at a private girls' school in New York. He
applied for American citizenship but there is no proof that he ever received it. His
return trip to Gabon in 1856 began a series of controversies about what he actually did
there. The Academy of Natural Sciences in Philadelphia disclaimed support of du
Chaillu's expedition. His antagonists were leading scientists and men knowledgeable
about Africa in general, and Gabon in particular, while his supporters were high
society friends with money, prestige and influence in the publishing world. Clear
evidence exists of prevarication and plagiarism by du Chaillu concerning his
explorations and discoveries. He was an insecure young man of unrecorded parentage
who was determined to make a name for himself by providing what the western world
wanted from Africa – intrigue, drama and erotica. Du Chaillu certainly made some
contributions to ornithology and ethnography but the deeds for which he is most
famous need re-examination in the light of new evidence.

84 **Brazza et la prise de possession du Congo. La mission de l'ouest africain,
1883-1885.** (Brazza and the taking possession of the Congo. The West
African Mission, 1883-1885.)
Catherine Coquery-Vidrovitch. Paris: Mouton, 1969. 502p. maps.
bibliog.

The third expedition of Brazza established French control on the upper Ogooué River
as well as on the Loango coast, which formed part of the colony of Gabon until 1918.
This work deals with the organization and activities of the expedition. There are
detailed accounts of the peoples of Gabon during the late nineteenth century as well as

of the French penetration and installation. Half of the volume reproduces a selection of documents relevant to the subject.

85 **The life and works of Alfred Aloysius Horn. An old visiter. Vol. 1 The Ivory Coast in the earlies.**
Alfred Aloysius Horn.   London: Jonathan Cape, 1927. 320p.
'Trader' Horn, as he was known, called the coast of Gabon adjacent to the mouths of the Ogooué River the 'Ivory Coast'. That term is usually reserved for the West African country that is known in French as the Côte d'Ivoire. Horn was a colourful figure who provides interesting perspectives on travel, trade and peoples along the Ogooué during the late nineteenth century.

86 **Travels in West Africa – Congo français, Corisco & Cameroons.**
Mary H. Kingsley.   New York: Macmillan, 1897. 743p. Reprinted, London: Frank Cass, 1965.
Mary Kingsley was an English traveller who visited Gabon in 1895. After a period in the Gabon Estuary, she went up the Ogooué as far as Talagouga, the site of a French Protestant mission. Then she returned overland to the Estuary via its southern tributary, the Remboué River. Her keen observations of nature and society are a valuable source for understanding Gabon during the late nineteenth century. Kingsley questioned whether the Christian missionaries were serving the interests of Africans by introducing the moral values of western civilization. But she was hardly critical at all of the economic penetration of western traders, which often injured African interests and well-being.

87 **A Victorian lady in Africa: the story of Mary Kingsley.**
Victoria Grosvenor Meyer.   Southampton, England: Ashford Press, 1989. 221p. bibliog.
This popular biography of the famous English traveller includes her visit to Gabon during 1895.

88 **Early knowledge of the Ogowe River and the American exploration of 1854.**
K. David Patterson.   *International Journal of African Historical Studies*, vol. 5, no. 1 (1972), p. 75-90.
The first European exploration of the Ogooué River is usually credited to two French naval officers, Lt. Paul Serval and Dr. Marie-Théophile Griffon du Bellay in 1862. But they were not the first to collect reliable information about the Ogooué nor the first to sail its waters. The Englishman, T. E. Bowdich, in 1818 described the river and its commercial importance. In 1861 the Franco-American adventurer, Paul du Chaillu, published his data on the Ogooué, which, though second-hand, had much value. Earlier, in 1854, two American missionaries based on the northern shore of the Gabon Estuary, the Reverends William Walker and Ira Preston, had made a pioneering exploration up the Nazareth mouth of the Ogooué half way to the site of Lambaréné Island. The text of Walker's report to the American Board of Commissioners for Foreign Missions in Boston is included.

89 **Paul B. du Chaillu and the exploration of Gabon, 1855-1865.**
K. David Patterson. *International Journal of African Historical Studies*, vol. 7, no. 4 (1974), p. 648-67. bibliog.
This article describes and analyses the travels of du Chaillu (1831-1903), the first European to visit any portion of the Gabon hinterland outside the Estuary since the seventeenth century. His books, despite their shortcomings, are essential sources for the study of pre-colonial Gabon.

90 **Paul du Chaillu: gorilla hunter.**
Michel Vaucaire. New York: Harper, 1930. 322p.
This popular biography is based in part on interviews with those who knew the nineteenth-century adventurer and explorer.

91 **Brazza of the Congo: European exploration and exploitation in French Equatorial Africa.**
Richard West. London: Cape, 1972. 304p. map. bibliog.
The Italian-born aristocrat, Pierre Savorgnan de Brazza (1852-1905) undertook explorations between 1875 and 1883 that laid the foundations for the extension of French colonial rule throughout the Ogooué River basin and along the southern coasts of what is today Gabon. The enlarged Gabon formed a colony of the French Congo, which was called French Equatorial Africa after 1910. His activities had the effect of linking the evolution of Gabon to that of the other territories – Middle Congo, Oubangui-Chari, and Chad – and drawing off many of its revenues for their benefit and the neglect of its own development. Brazza served as commissioner-general of the French Congo from 1886 to 1897 during which time French administration was established in the interior of Gabon. In 1905 Brazza was summoned from retirement to head an inquiry into the abuses of the concessionary regime which the French government had installed in 1899 to promote economic development by private companies. He was overwhelmed by the injustices and brutalities of the system, to which his exaggerations about the riches of equatorial Africa had inadvertently helped to give support. His report resulted in the mitigation of some of the worst abuses and scaling down of many of the concessions. Moreover, Brazza retained his reputation among the peoples of the Ogooué as a peaceful explorer and friend.

Slave-trade

92 **The Atlantic slave trade and the Gabon Estuary: the Mpongwe to 1860.**
Henry H. Bucher. In *Africans in bondage: studies in slavery and the slave trade*. Edited by Paul E. Lovejoy. Madison, Wisconsin: African Studies Program, University of Wisconsin–Madison, University of Wisconsin Press, 1986, p. 137-54. 2 maps. bibliog.
The volume of slave exports from the Gabon Estuary was always relatively small. Yet the slave-trade had an important impact on the local society and economy. Mpongwe society experienced structural changes related to the efforts to control trade, including but not exclusively the trade in slaves. Among these changes were the development of

commercial institutions that derived from slave-trading, social contracts based on the use of women as collateral for trade and as the link in establishing trading alliances, and a regional stratification based partly on wealth from trade and partly on ethnicity, particularly clan loyalty.

93 **The Atlantic slave trade: a census.**
Philip D. Curtin.   Madison, Wisconsin: University of Wisconsin Press, 1969. 338p. 25 maps. bibliog.
This work synthesizes a vast amount of data in order to measure the forced movement of peoples in the Atlantic region. It contains a useful chapter on the French slave-trade of the eighteenth century, which included Gabon.

94 **The tropical Atlantic in the age of the slave trade.**
Philip D. Curtin.   Washington, DC: American Historical Association, 1991. 47p. 3 maps. bibliog.
This introduction aimed at college students represents a synthesis of the latest scholarship on the Atlantic slave-trade during the eighteenth century. Although it does not deal specifically with Gabon, it is most useful for establishing the framework within which developments there took place.

95 **Répertoire des expeditions françaises à la traite illégale (1814-1850).** (List of French expeditions in the illegal slave-trade, 1814-1850).
Edited by Serge Daget.   Nantes, France: Centre de Recherche sur l'Histoire du Monde Atlantique. Comité Nantais en Sciences Humaines, 1988. 603p. bibliog.
Although France agreed in 1815, under British pressure, to end the slave trade north of the Equator, and subsequently south as well, illegal slaving expeditions continued until at least 1850 on the Atlantic coasts of Africa. The founding of the French post on the northern shore of the Gabon Estuary in 1843 led to the drastic curtailment of these expeditions there and on the Ogooué. Although Gabon was never a major focus of the slave trade, as were the Congo and Niger basins it was the scene of a number of illegal expeditions. The available details about these are provided in this list.

96 **The Dutch in the Atlantic slave trade, 1600-1815.**
Johannes Menne Postma.   London: Cambridge University Press, 1990. 428p. maps. bibliog.
The work provides an understanding of the international dimensions of the Dutch slave-trade on the Atlantic coasts of Africa during the seventeenth and eighteenth centuries. It contains specifics on the trade centred at Loango which drew upon the southern portions of Gabon.

97 **Libération d'esclaves et nouvelles servitudes.** (Liberation of slaves and new servitudes.)
François Renault. Dakar: Nouvelles Editions Africaines, 1976. 236p. bibliog.

Detailed information is included on the recruitment of labourers from Gabon between 1857 and 1862 for French plantations in the Caribbean. Their departure worsened the labour shortage in a colony that already had a serious lack. Though the labourers were indentured servants, the conditions of their recruitment, waiting on shore and transport closely resembled those of the discredited slave-trade. Growing British criticism led to French agreement to abolish the scheme.

98 **Traite des noirs et navires négriers au xviiie siècle.** (Slave-trade and slaving ships in the eighteenth century.)
Patrick Villiers. Grenoble, France: Editions des Quatre Seigneurs, 1982. 162p. bibliog.

This study is useful for understanding French involvement in the slave-trade in Gabon during the eighteenth century.

Liberty and labor: the origins of Libreville considered.
See item no. 123.

Freed slave colonies in West Africa.
See item no. 127.

Les villages de liberté en Afrique noire française, 1887-1910. (Freedom villages in French Black Africa, 1887-1910.)
See item no. 226.

Pre-colonial (1471-1843)

99 **Esquisse d'histoire ethnique du Gabon.** (Sketch of the ethnic history of Gabon.)
Aganga Akélaguélo. *Présence Africaine*, no. 4 (1984), p. 3-32. bibliog.

A review of the publications available on the history of the ethnic groups of Gabon from the time of the first contacts with Europeans indicates that the Mpongwe, Orungu, Nkomi, Ngowé, Baloumbou, Vili and Batéké peoples were already in their present locations in the late 1400s.

100 **Structures communautaires traditionnels et perspectives coopératives dans la société altogovéenne (Gabon).** (Traditional community structures and cooperative perspectives in the altogovean society, Gabon.)
Martin Alihanga. PhD thesis, St. Thomas Aquinas University of Pontifical Studies, Rome, 1976. 625p. bibliog.

Alihanga derived the adjective *altogovean* from Latin to describe the pre-colonial civilization of the upper Ogooué River valley. He advocated a social philosophy called 'communitarianism', which is rooted in the traditional structures and values of the Altogovean peoples and updated in the light of Christianity and contemporary needs, as the best way to promote a development that is morally and materially sound.

101 **Un peuple gabonais à l'aube de la colonisation: le bas Ogooué au xixe siècle.** (A Gabonese people at the dawn of colonization: the lower Ogooué in the nineteenth century.)
Joseph Ambouroué-Avaro. Paris: Karthala, 1981. 285p. map. bibliog.

This is a doctoral dissertation that was completed at the University of Paris in 1969 and was posthumously published in 1981 without revision. Yves Person has provided an introduction with references to subsequent works by other scholars, including K. David Patterson (1975). Ambouroué seeks to reconstruct the societies of the lower Ogooué River before the arrival of the Europeans. Unfortunately there are no written sources of consequence for Cape Lopez and the lower Ogooué prior to 1826. Thereafter, the author employs the French ones but not the British, American and Portuguese, along with some oral traditions. He is thus able to provide sketchy accounts after 1850 about individual rulers of the Orungu state, treaties, the slave-trade and European exploration. But these data are not tied together sufficiently to give a strong sense of sequential change and chronological development, much less the processes of change on the lower Ogooué. The work is thus useful primarily for the factual material it contains and the viewpoint of the author, who wished to revitalize his own society through the restoration of traditional Orungu moral and social values.

102 **Northern Central Africa.**
David Birmingham. In: *The Cambridge History of Africa, vol. 5, From c.1790 to c.1870.* Edited by J. D. Fage, Roland Oliver. Cambridge, England: Cambridge University Press, 1976, p. 254-67. bibliog.

This is a brief discussion of the patterns of external trade, movements of peoples, and beginnings of European penetration of Gabon seen as part of the forested areas of western equatorial Africa from 1790 to 1870.

103 **Mpongwe origins: historical perspectives.**
Henry H. Bucher. *History in Africa*, vol. 2 (1975), p. 59-90. maps. bibliog.

The majority of the people known as the Mpongwe began arriving in the Gabon Estuary or coalescing there after the sixteenth century. This process may have continued into the late seventeenth century and even into the early eighteenth. Not all of the people called 'Pongo' by the Dutch and later by other Europeans may have been Mpongwe but the fact that they were called 'Pongo' led to the adoption of 'Pongwe' by the people controlling the Estuary from at least 1600 up to and including the nineteenth century. Who the Mpongwe were originally remains unanswerable in the sense that present-day Mpongwe culture and language are the results of a long process of assimilation involving most of the societies that preceded them in the Estuary and possibly by others nearby. In trying to understand the history of the peoples of the Estuary, scholars have often failed to give sufficient attention to oral traditions, which generally complement and supplement the written records.

104   **The settlement of the Mpongwe clans in the Gabon Estuary: an historical synthesis.**
       Henry H. Bucher.   *Revue Française d'Histoire d'Outre-Mer*, vol. 64, no. 1 (1977), p. 148-75. maps. bibliog.
The last half of the eighteenth century witnessed intense competition for western trade among the Mpongwe clans and caused them to migrate to the mouth of the Gabon Estuary. Traced in considerable detail are the most probable routes taken by some of the two dozen clans in a journey which gradually brought them to what was to become modern Libreville.

105   **The migrations of the Fang into central Gabon during the nineteenth century: a new interpretation.**
       Christopher Chamberlain.   *International Journal of African Historical Studies*, vol. 11, no. 3 (1979), p. 429-56. map. bibliog.
On the basis of a wide range of American and French sources, Chamberlain argues that the Fang migrations into Gabon were not continuous but took place in stages. By 1800 a first stage had brought the Fang into northern Gabon, particularly into the areas of the headwaters of the Woleu, N'Tem and Ivindo Rivers. Then around 1840 there began a second stage which brought the Fang into central Gabon, that is, the areas of the rivers leading to the Estuary and to the north side of the Ogooué River. The Betsi branch of the Fang began moving from their homes in the escarpment east of the Monts de Cristal down the streams leading to the Estuary in order to bypass the Bakèlè and Séké intermediaries and to trade directly with the Mpongwe and the whites. They saw the whites as the ghosts of their ancestors who would bring them wealth and prosperity. Then around 1860 the Maké branch of the Fang left the headwaters of the Ivindo, where it appears that they were being besieged by the Mvele, and descended the Ivindo into the middle Ogooué River valley. Thus the second stage of migrations had two sub-stages which together would place the Fang throughout the northern half of Gabon where they live today. Fang hopes of trading alliances with the Mpongwe and whites did not materialize; instead their contacts led to conflict and periodic violence.

106   **Traditions orales et archives au Gabon.** (Oral traditions and archives in Gabon.)
       Hubert Deschamps.   Paris: Berger-Levrault, 1962. 172p. maps. bibliog.
These oral traditions, which were collected in the late 1950s and early 1960s, contain material on genealogies and migrations, among other things. At independence some records of the colonial administration were transferred to the depository of the French National Archives at Aix-en-Provence while others were left in the newly created National Archives of Gabon at Libreville and in provincial and local sites.

107 **Le commerce entre sociétés lignagères: les Nzabis dans la traite à la fin du xixᵉ siècle (Gabon–Congo).** (Commerce between lineage societies: the Nzabi in trade at the end of the nineteenth century, Gabon–Congo.)
Georges Dupré. *Cahiers d'Études Africaines*, vol. 12, no. 4 (1972), p. 616-58. bibliog.

This article examines the view of trade held by merchants, the position and production of the Nzabi, their methods of trade, and the influence of trade on the Nzabi social hierarchy. There is also a discussion of the effects of Nzabi ironworkers, slavery and tribal movements during the late nineteenth century.

108 **A history of São Tomé Island, 1470-1655.**
Robert Garfield. PhD thesis, Northwestern University, Evanston, Illinois, 1971. 337p. bibliog. (Available from University Microfilms, Ann Arbor, Michigan, order no. 8722382.)

On São Tomé Island off the coast of Gabon, the Portuguese established sugar plantations using slaves obtained from the mainland. Portuguese merchants used São Tomé as their base for trade with Gabon after 1598 in competition with the Dutch.

109 **Bibliographie critique pour servir à l'anthropologie historique du littoral gabonaise (époque pré-coloniale xviᵉ–xixᵉ siècles).** (Critical bibliography serving the historical anthropology of the Gabonese coast, pre-colonial period, 16th to 19th centuries.)
François Gaulme. *Journal des Africanistes*, vol. 47, no. 1 (1977), p. 157-75.

This bibliographical essay focuses on the published sources for the study of the pre-colonial period on the southern coasts of Gabon.

110 **Le pays de Cama: un ancien état côtier du Gabon et ses origines.** (Cama country: an ancient coastal state of Gabon and its origins.)
François Gaulme. Paris: Karthala, 1981. 269p. maps. bibliog.

This work is based on the meticulous examination of a limited range of sources in Europe and the USA. The author studies the evolution of the institutions of the peoples inhabiting Cama country, that is, the portions of coastal Gabon between Cape Lopez and Pointe Sainte-Catherine, including the shores of the Lagoon of Fernan Vaz from the arrival of the Portuguese until the establishment of the French post in 1894. He concludes that the centralized state involving a pyramidal structure which developed among the Nkomi resembled closely that of Loango and other states to the south rather than the Mpongwe segmentary states of the Gabon Estuary. The Portuguese and the Dutch did not disorient the Nkomi structures because the monarchy retained control of trade. But the slave-trade later weakened the monarchy, which could no longer control it. Only the small volume of that trade lessened the disaggregation. The monarchy retained importance and much power until undermined by the French in the late 1800s because the ruler was considered to have supernatural powers and because of his capacity to administer justice fairly.

111 **Etude historique sur les Mpongoués et tribus avoisinantes.** (Historical study on the Mpongwe and neighbouring tribes.)
Jean M. Gautier. Montpellier, France: Imprimerie Lafitte-Lauriol for the Institut d'Etudes Centrafricaines, 1950. 69p. maps. bibliog.

This is a brief study of the history of the Mpongwe and such neighbouring peoples as the Séké (Shékiani) and Bakèlè based upon Catholic missionary records since the 1840s and oral traditions.

112 **Le 'Mauritius', la mémoire engloutie.** (The *Mauritius*, memory engulfed.)
Michel L'Hour, [et al.]. Paris: Castermann, 1989. 271p. maps.

This work contains studies from historical and archaeological perspectives concerning a Dutch ship that was wrecked off Cape Lopez in 1609 and recovered in part in 1985.

113 **The external trade of the Loango coast, 1576-1870: the effects of changing commercial relations on the Vili kingdom of Loango.**
Phyllis M. Martin. Oxford: Clarendon, 1972. 193p. map. bibliog.

The Loango kingdom, which was at one time loosely linked with the Congo kingdom, extended its influence throughout large areas of south-western Gabon between the fifteenth and nineteenth centuries. Martin's study deals with the various changes in the political and social structures of the Loango kingdom resulting from three centuries of overseas trade during which the Dutch and the French were the leading merchants on the coast. During much of this period Vili traders controlled the trade between the coast and the N'Gounié River valley. The study includes the development of the slave-trade during the last half of the 1600s, its organization and supply. Until the nineteenth entury Loango was able to maintain trade largely on its own terms. But the increase in the number of trading points and the establishment of Europeans in trade factories during the last decades of the slave-trade diffused economic and social power and thereby weakened centralized state structures. In 1883 Loango came under French control and until 1918 was administered as part of Gabon.

114 **Power, cloth, and currency on the Loango coast.**
Phyllis M. Martin. *Muntu*, no. 7 (1987), p. 135-47. bibliog.

The term Loango coast refers to the coastal regions between southern Gabon and the Congo or Zaire River. Cloth was a basic resource for the peoples of the Loango coast throughout their pre-colonial history. It was used in daily life for furnishings and clothing. It was essential in such key events as initiation and burial ceremonies. It formed part of key transactions that cemented lineage and state alliances. It also served as currency. The importation of European and East Indian cloth from the mid-seventeenth century began a transition from raffia cloth produced by African men to a reliance on foreign cloth. But the significance of cloth as a key resource at all levels of society continued. Access to sources of cloth and control of its distribution were closely associated with the wielding of power, whether by royal administrators, lineage elders, religious specialists or merchant-brokers. This was the case in the late eighteenth century when the central government of Loango weakened through the challenge of a class of merchant-brokers who had gained access to imported goods independently of the royal administration of the capital.

115 **Inventaire et recensions de 130 récits migratoires originaux du Gabon.**
(Inventory and census of 130 original migratory accounts of Gabon.)
Raymond Mayer. *Pholia*, vol. 4 (1989), p. 171-216.
This is an annotated bio-bibliography on Gabonese oral historical traditions relating to ethnic migrations and settlement narratives. The main sources are materials in indigenous languages collected by students from the Omar Bongo University and privately held unpublished manuscripts.

116 **Le Gabon pre-coloniale: étude sociale et économique.** (Pre-colonial Gabon: social and economic study.)
Elikia M'Bokolo. *Cahiers d'Études Africaines*, vol. 17, no. 2-3 (1977), p. 331-44. bibliog.
This discussion of the situation of the various coastal peoples in Gabon at the time of the end of the slave-trade, around 1850, is based on written French and British records in the absence of recoverable oral traditions. The economy, politics and social organization had developed as a function of the slave-trade. Thus the Mpongwe had evolved a decentralized society as a result of their favoured position along the shores of the Gabon Estuary while the Orungu and Nkomi farther south had retained a more centralized organization in response to a somewhat different trading context.

117 **Autour du Loango, XIVe–XIXe siècle: histoire des peuples du sud-ouest du Gabon au temps de Loango et du Congo français.** (Around Loango, sixteenth to nineteenth centuries: history of the peoples of the south-west of Gabon in the time of Loango and the French Congo.)
Edited by Annie Merlet. Libreville: Sépia for the Centre Culturel Français Saint-Exupéry, 1991. 550p. maps. bibliog.
This work represents the latest scholarship on the peoples of south-western Gabon who were part of the Loango state or were influenced by its economic activities between the 1500s and the 1800s prior to the French occupation.

118 **Notes sur l'économie des côtes du Gabon au début du xviiie siècle.** (Notes on the economy of the Gabon coasts at the start of the eighteenth century.)
Robert Reynard. *Bulletin de l'Institut d'Etudes Centrafricaines*, vol. 13-14, no. 49-54 (1957), p. 49-54. bibliog.
In the sixteenth and early seventeenth centuries, the Portuguese abandoned plantations on São Tomé but kept that island as a base for trading with the Gabon coasts for the next three centuries. The Portuguese were somewhat supplanted by the Dutch, who rapidly came to control the ivory trade.

119 **Nouvelles recherches sur l'influence portugaise au Gabon.** (New research on the Portuguese influence in Gabon.)
Robert Reynard. *Bulletin de l'Institut d'Etudes Centrafricaines*, no. 9 (1955), p. 36-50, and new series, no. 11 (1956), p. 5-20. bibliog.
This discussion of the Portuguese impact on Gabon includes names of places and words transmitted into the local Bantu languages.

120 **Notes d'histoire du Gabon.** (History notes on Gabon.)
André Raponda Walker. Montpellier, France: Imprimerie Charité for the Institut d'Etudes Centrafricaines, 1960. 158p. bibliog.

André Walker (1871-1968), son of a British trader and an Mpongwe princess, was the first Catholic priest to be ordained in Gabon. During his pastoral work in different parts of Gabon, he collected the oral histories of many of its peoples. His work is most substantial for the Myènè group, among which his own Mpongwe people is the most extensively presented.

121 **Anglais, espagnols et nord-américains du Gabon au xixe siècle.** (English, Spanish and North Americans in Gabon in the nineteenth century.)
André Raponda Walker, Robert Reynard. *Bulletin de l'Institut d'Etudes Centrafricaines*, new series, no. 12 (1956), p. 253-79.

This brief review of the activities of English, Spanish and American traders in Gabon during the nineteenth century is based upon Catholic missionary records and oral histories.

The Mpongwe of the Gabon Estuary, a history to 1860.
See item no. 124.

Noirs et blancs en Afrique Equatoriale Française: les sociétés cotières et la pénétration française (vers 1820-1874). (Blacks and whites in Equatorial Africa: the coastal societies and the French penetration [towards 1820–1874].)
See item no. 129.

The northern Gabon coast to 1875.
See item no. 132.

Early colonial (1843-86)

122 **John Leighton Wilson and the Mpongwe: the 'Spirit of 1776' in mid-nineteenth-century Africa.**
Henry H. Bucher. *Journal of Presbyterian History*, vol. 54 (fall 1976), p. 291-316. bibliog.

John Leighton Wilson (1809-86) of South Carolina founded the American Protestant mission in the Gabon Estuary in 1842 and directed its work until his definitive departure in 1853. The article discusses the issue of Wilson's role in the initial resistance by the Mpongwe to the establishment of French colonial rule. Wilson's defence of the Africans' attempts to retain their independence led to serious difficulties with the French naval authorities who were administering the region.

123 **Liberty and labor: the origins of Libreville reconsidered.**
Henry H. Bucher. *Bulletin de l'IFAN*, series B, vol. 41, no. 3
(1979), p. 478-96. 3 maps. bibliog.
The tourist-guide version of Libreville's myth of origin is challenged on the basis of
Mpongwe oral traditions and French archival data. What emerges is not the story of a
modern African capital whose first inhabitants were a group of mainly Vili slaves freed
by France to seek their fortunes in the new 'village of liberty'. Instead, Libreville was a
forced settlement created to provide labour for French colonial ambitions at a time of
crisis. Furthermore, the colony of fifty-two slaves in 1849 was located on the ancestral
lands of the Mpongwe people who then numbered several thousands. The settlement
was supposed to be both French and Catholic, a shining model for the Mpongwe to
emulate, but by 1854 the Librevilleois had become absorbed and soon assimilated by
the Mpongwe. All that remains of the tourist-book version is the name Libreville itself.

124 **The Mpongwe of the Gabon Estuary, a history to 1860.**
Henry H. Bucher.   PhD thesis, University of Wisconsin–Madison,
1977. 455p. bibliog.   (Available from University Microfilms, Ann
Arbor, Michigan, order no. 77-19,088).
After 1500 the Gabon Estuary was a regional centre of economic and political
movement. By the late 1700s the area was controlled by numerous clans, collectively
called the Mpongwe, who were middlemen traders between westerners and the inland
peoples. The greatest impact of the West on the institutions of Mpongwe society may
have occurred between 1500 and 1840, a period for which there is meagre
documentation. The decline in Mpongwe control of their estuary and the weakening of
their social structure greatly accelerated between 1840 and 1860. During the 1840s the
French made treaties with clan heads and established a fort. American Protestant and
French Catholic missionaries arrived, and western traders opened trading houses on
the shore. Thus began the process by which the powerful clan heads and their chief
traders lost their trade monopoly as younger men with little capital or experience, but
western backing entered the competition and widened social stratification. During the
1840s and 1850s the two Agekaza clans, particularly the Agekaza-Glass, had
dominated local trade and politics. But by 1860 a breakdown in the old order,
symbolized by a shift from a local economy under Mpongwe to a market economy
under external controls, had taken place.

125 **The village of Glass and western intrusion: an Mpongwe response to the
American and French presence in the Gabon Estuary.**
Henry H. Bucher. *International Journal of African Historical Studies*,
vol. 6, no. 3 (1973), p. 363-400. 2 maps. bibliog.
This valuable account, the first to be based on American and British sources as well as
French, reviews in much detail Mpongwe settlement and society in the early 1800s, the
inner dynamics of the main villages, the arrival of westerners in the Gabon Estuary in
the early 1840s, and the responses of the Mpongwe to the establishment of French
rule. The Mpongwe of the Estuary were organized around four trading polities that
profited as intermediaries between western merchants and the peoples of the interior.
The absence of a centralized government facilitated the French penetration. While
three of the polities accepted French sovereignty willingly, the village of Glass, which
was the centre for British and American traders and Protestant missionaries from
Boston, sought to retain its independence. In March 1844 French agents obtained a
treaty from the ruler of Glass by deception. In 1845 the French crushed popular

protests, with which the American missionaries sympathized, by bombarding the village of Glass. The French footholds in the Estuary would form the basis for their later expansion along the coasts and into the interior.

126 **Quinze ans de Gabon: les débuts de l'établissement français, 1839-1853.**
(Fifteen years of Gabon: the beginnings of the French establishment, 1839-1853.)
Hubert Deschamps. Paris: Société Française d'Histoire d'Outre-Mer, 1965. 98p. map.

This very detailed account of the beginnings of the French colony in the Gabon Estuary is nevertheless incomplete and partisan because it is based solely on official French records at Dakar and Paris. In particular, the author did not use important missionary records in France and the USA that would have contributed to a better rounded and more accurate picture of French relations with indigenous peoples.

127 **Freed slave colonies in West Africa.**
Christopher Fyfe. In: *Cambridge history of Africa. Vol. 5, c.1790–c.1870.* Edited by John Flint. London: Cambridge University Press, 1976, p. 170-99. bibliog.

A brief summary is included concerning the founding of Libreville in August 1849 by the French navy as a home for freed Vili slaves.

128 **L'historicité des paroles attributées au premier évêque du Gabon à propos du maintien du comptoir entre 1871 et 1873.** (The historicity of the words attributed to the first bishop of Gabon concerning the maintenance of the post between 1871 and 1873.)
Otto Gollnhofer, Bernard Noël, Roger Sillans. *Revue Française d'Histoire d'Outre-Mer*, vol. 59, no. 4 (1972), p. 611-44. bibliog.

Because of various political and religious events which occurred in Gabon between 1858 and 1873, a legend developed linking the territory's political destiny to an imaginary decision of Monsignor Jean-Rémy Bessieux to remain in the face of a possible official withdrawal. The proposal to exchange Gabon for the Gambia, a British colony, during the early 1870s, proved abortive, but not because of the imagined action of the first Catholic bishop.

129 **Noirs et blancs en Afrique Equatoriale: les sociétés côtières et la pénétration française (vers 1820-1874).** (Blacks and whites in Equatorial Africa: the coastal societies and the French penetration [towards 1820-1874].)
Elikia M'Bokolo. Paris: Mouton, 1981. 302p. maps. bibliog.

In this work the peoples of the Gabon Estuary and adjacent coasts are seen almost exclusively through the eyes of French naval officers. The failure to use important American missionary and trading archives leads to an incomplete and unbalanced picture of Mpongwe responses to French imperialism. Ignorance about the motives and activities of the ABCFM missionaries and Yankee traders in turn contributes to the repetition of the same kinds of inaccuracies and biases found in Hubert Deshamps's *Quinze ans de Gabon* (q.v.). M'Bokolo also fails to address the findings of Schnapper,

Patterson and Bucher. His contribution to the understanding of the Estuary in the nineteenth century lies in its more extensive and exhaustive analysis of certain aspects of the French penetration of coastal societies and their responses. He provides a clear and perceptive narrative of French elimination of the coastal middlemen traders and the slave-trade, and of their establishment of direct contact with the interior peoples. The most original sections deal with periods that Deschamps did not cover, 1820-41, and 1857-70; they deal respectively with the two decades before the French takeover and the expansion into the Ogooué River basin and along the coasts. There are also fresh details on the free emigrants' scheme of the late 1850s.

130 **La résistance des Mpongwe du Gabon à la creation du comptoir français
(1843-1845).** (The resistance of the Mpongwe of Gabon to the creation
of the French post, 1843-1845.)
Elikia M'Bokolo. *Afrika Zamani*, no. 8-9 (Dec. 1978), p. 5-32.
bibliog.

This is an account, based on official French archives, of the different forms of resistance of the Mpongwe clans to the establishment of French sovereignty in the Gabon Estuary. The open resistance of the village of Glass in March 1845 is given particular attention. By August of that year the French had been able to establish their authority on both shores of the Estuary. The Mpongwe had made their submission but did not give their adherence. Their attitude was not one of collaboration but of resignation. Thereafter they would resort to methods other than resistance to show the persistence of their hostility, or at least the depth of their distrust and the vigour of their resentment.

131 **Le roi Denis, la première tentative de modernisation du Gabon.** (King
Denis, the first attempt at modernization of Gabon.)
Elikia M'Bokolo. Paris: ABC; Dakar: Nouvelles Editions Africaines,
1976. 94p. bibliog.

King Denis or Antchouwe Kowe Rapontchombo (c.1780-1876), the most eminent of the Mpongwe clan heads in the Estuary, was the first to accept French sovereignty and to promote French influence in Gabon. His Asiga clan occupied the peninsula at the extreme western tip of the southern shore of the Estuary and along the Atlantic. There in the last third of the 1700s and the first half of the 1800s its members actively engaged as middlemen in a slave-trade with the interior and Cape Lopez to the south. Denis personally profited from the trade. He possessed 300 to 400 domestic slaves and forty to fifty wives. Despite this involvement, he impressed European visitors by his intelligence and cultivation. He acquired a reputation for wisdom and honesty and enjoyed great respect. Denis maintained good relations with the Catholic mission on the northern shore of the Estuary and sent some of his children to its boarding schools, including his heir, Félix Adandé. But he refused to allow the priests to establish a mission at his capital. Ultimately the association with France helped to undermine the slave-trade on which his people's prosperity was built.

132 **The northern Gabon coast to 1875.**
K. David Patterson. Oxford: Clarendon Press, 1975. 167p. 2 maps.
bibliog.

The greatest originality of this pioneering study is the detailed account of political and economic developments on the northern coast between 1815 and 1875, for which the author is the first to use the full range of sources – Portuguese, French, British and American. During the nineteenth century the Mpongwe of the Gabon Estuary and the Orungu of Cape Lopez were middlemen specializing in long-distance trade. The Mpongwe sold slaves but also ivory, dyewood and wax drawn from interior peoples to Europeans on the coast. The Orungu concentrated upon slaves drawn from the Ogooué River basin. The Orungu became organized into a single state under a despotic monarch while the Mpongwe were divided among four political units under weak rulers. The establishment of French sovereignty in the Estuary during the early 1840s, which was achieved through bribery, threats and deception, led by the 1860s to economic disaster for the Mpongwe. Protected by the French regime, British and other western traders established posts from which they dealt directly with the peoples of the interior. Long before the French in 1862 forced the Orungu to cede the mouth of the Ogooué, French and British naval patrols had shut off most slave exports. The closure of the Brazilian markets in 1850 was a disaster only slightly alleviated by the clandestine trade to São Tomé and Príncipe, which continued into the 1870s. The power of the Orungu monarch disintegrated by 1870 and the clans emerged as the only effective political units. Bypassed by the European officials and merchants who ascended the Ogooué, the Orungu maintained an impoverished independence until the 1860s.

133 **La politique et le commerce français dans la Golfe de Guinée.** (Politics and French commerce in the Gulf of Guinea.)
Bernard Schnapper. Paris: Mouton, 1961. 286p. bibliog.

This work is essential for understanding the international diplomatic and economic contexts that led to French involvement in the territories along the Gulf of Guinea, including Gabon, in the late 1830s and early 1840s.

134 **Western Africa: its history, condition, and prospects.**
John Leighton Wilson. New York: Harper, 1856. 527p. bibliog.
Reprinted, New York: Negro University Press, 1970.

This account, concerning the Gabon Estuary in the 1840s and early 1850s, was written by the founder of the American Protestant mission and is useful for understanding the life of the peoples, their response to Christian evangelization and French rule, and anti-slaving activities.

Colonial (1886-1940)

135 Equatorial Africa under colonial rule.
Ralph A. Austen, Rita Headrick. In: *History of Central Africa, Vol. 2.*
Edited by David Birmingham, Phyllis M. Martin. London: Longman,
1983, p. 27-94. 6 maps. bibliog.

This is a detailed and perceptive account of the impact of French colonial rule in the
four states of ex-French Equatorial Africa and Cameroon from the nineteenth century
up to and including independence in 1960. Only after the Second World War and
independence did France finally achieve its long-term economic hopes for markets and
raw materials as well as its political hopes for prestige. The hardship which colonial
rule imposed prior to 1945 was replaced thereafter by a general increase in material
well-being and social opportunity. An obvious colonial legacy has been the continued
dependence on France for aid and assistance as well as occasional armed intervention
to prop up unpopular regimes favourable to western interests.

136 The sociology of Black Africa: social dynamics in Central Africa.
Georges Balandier. London: André Deutsch) New York: Praeger,
1970. 540p. maps. bibliog.

It is the subtitle of this work that best indicates its contents. The study deals with social
change among two peoples, the Fang of northern Gabon, and the Bakongo of the
Congo Republic, under the impact of French colonial rule. Balandier coined the term
'colonial situation' to describe the context that colonial rule created for the evolution
of these peoples from the latter part of the nineteenth century until 1960. The impact
of the European presence on traditional Fang institutions is discussed as well as their
efforts to reconstruct new frameworks for meaningful life. The work is translated from
Sociologie actuelle de l'Afrique Noire. (Paris: Presses Universitaire de France, 2nd ed.
1963. 532p. bibliog.).

137 Expéditions punitives au Gabon (1875-1877). (Punitive expeditions in
Gabon, 1875-1877.)
Henri Brunschwig. *Cahiers d'Études Africaines*, vol. 2, no. 3
(1962), p. 347-61. bibliog.

In the course of penetrating the interior of Gabon, the French came into conflict with
African middlemen traders, who resisted their attempts to deal directly with the
producers or primary sellers of goods. This article describes punitive expeditions
against the Fang in the Gabon Estuary and the Bakèlè on the Ogooué who blocked
French advances.

**138 Competition and conflict: the development of the bulk export trade in
central Gabon during the nineteenth century.**
Christopher Chamberlain. PhD thesis, University of California, Los
Angeles, 1977. 351p. bibliog. (Available from University Microfilms,
Ann Arbor, Michigan, order no. 77-12,927).

During the 1840s and 1850s several developments combined to alter significantly the
commercial patterns of central Gabon. In 1843 the French navy established a post on
the Gabon Estuary at almost the same time that the Fang settled the river's upper
reaches. Soon after 1850 the first exports of wild rubber left the Estuary while slave

exports declined rapidly. European trading companies built permanent factories along the Estuary and by 1860 the companies, aided by French gunboats, had established substations on the upper Estuary in order to obtain the rubber, ivory, ebony and dyewood that the increasingly more numerous Fang were harvesting or collecting. Conflicts soon arose over the terms of trade. During the late 1860s this same bulk export trade and endemic episodes of conflict were extended into the middle Ogooué, the country's main artery, where they continued until 1900. Much multiplied numbers of Fang searching for the items that could be traded and company agents seeking to purchase them contributed to conditions under which Africans received very low profits while western companies, backed by the French administration, managed to prosper as before.

139 **The concessions policy in the French Congo and the British reaction, 1898-1906.**
S. J. S. Cookey. *Journal of African History*, vol. 7, no. 2 (1966), p. 263-78. bibliog.

In 1899 the French Colonial Ministry parcelled out the greater part of the French Congo, of which Gabon formed part, among forty concessionary companies in imitation of a similar policy adopted earlier by the Congo Free State. British companies which had pioneered in the trade found themselves being treated as squatters and interlopers subject to legal prosecution. Among them were Hatton & Cookson and John Holt, which had traded in Gabon since 1857 and 1869 respectively and together had over half of the principal posts of the entire French Congo. British agents trading in rubber came into conflict with the Société du Haut-Ogooué in the upper Ogooué River valley and with other French companies in the N'Gounié River valley and on the southern coasts at Nyanga and Mayumba. The British companies claimed that the French government had infringed the provisions of the Berlin Act and called for the diplomatic support of the Foreign Office. Their call was backed by the British chambers of commerce. Already British humanitarians had been decrying the treatment of Africans in the Congo basin whose lands were being expropriated. They had repeatedly appealed to the British government to ensure that the provisions of the Berlin Act were enforced. In the face of joint agitation by merchants and humanitarians, the Foreign Office had to act. Protracted Anglo–French negotiations ended only in 1906 when Paris, while maintaining the principle of concessions, agreed to compensate the British firms for their losses.

140 **Le Congo au temps des grandes compagnies concessionnaires, 1898-1930.** (The Congo in the time of the big concessionary companies, 1898-1930.)
Catherine Coquery-Vidrovitch. Paris, The Hague: Mouton, 1972. 598p. maps. bibliog.

The concessionary regime which France installed in Gabon and its other colonies in equatorial Africa in order to develop them by private means with little public expense is the subject of this important study based on archival materials. The concessionary regime paralysed the economy of these countries. By constraint the companies extracted the existing wealth without regard for the future. They invested almost exclusively to secure short-term gains and put very little into infrastructure. Many of the companies were stillborn or miscarried. Most of the survivors were transformed after the First World War into commercial and/or industrial enterprises of a non-monopolistic nature. They operated concurrently with new trading and industrial firms along patterns developed in French West Africa. During the 1920s the production of woods such as *okoumé* and of peasant exports such as cocoa appeared as harbingers of a new era. But then came the world depression of 1930. As for the peoples of Gabon and other countries, the concessionary regime severely disrupted their traditional economy and society. Its aftermath gave rise to the modern sector of the economy which exists today. Among the most disastrous consequences of the concessionary regime was a demographic decline from which Gabon began to recover only after independence. The work as a whole contributes much to an understanding of underdevelopment in Gabon, especially to those dimensions of African and not European origin.

141 **French Congo and Gabon, 1886-1905.**
Catherine Coquery-Vidrovitch. In: *The Cambridge history of Africa*: *Vol. 5: From 1870 to 1905*. Edited by Roland Oliver, G. N. Sanderson. Cambridge, England: Cambridge University Press, 1985, p. 298-315. map. bibliog.
This is a discussion of French expansion into the interior of Gabon, the establishment of the colonial administration, and the installation of the regime of the concessionary companies, 1898-1905, which had such devastating effects on the well-being of the inhabitants.

142 **Investissements privés, investissements publics en AEF, 1900-1940.**
(Private investments, public investments in FEA [French Equatorial Africa], 1900-1940.)
Catherine Coquery-Vidrovitch. *African Economic History*, no. 12 (1983), p. 13-32. 5 maps. bibliog.
Between 1910 and 1960 Gabon was administered as a territory within French Equatorial Africa. The author has projected that name back into the period when the federation was actually called the French Congo. Most of the concessionary companies to whom France entrusted the economic development of FEA between 1900 and 1920 turned out to be commercial enterprises that lacked the necessary capital and were concerned mainly with short-term gains. They became involved in an economy of pillage that emptied the countryside of its resources. Among the handful that was sufficiently capitalized and earned a good level of profits was the Société du Haut-Ogooué. After 1920 the federation itself invested directly in infrastructure and development projects using aid from the French budget as well as local funds. The major aprt of the investments in this era came from public rather than private sources.

143 **Wongo ou la révolte d'un chef gabonais contre l'impôt et le travail forcé.**
(Wongo or the revolt of a Gabonese chief against taxes and forced labour.)
Catherine Coquery-Vidrovitch. In: *Les Africains, Vol. 11*. Paris: Editions Jeune Afrique, 1978, p. 267-86. maps. bibliog.
The Awandji people live south of Lastoursville in the upper Ogooué River valley. They had already been victimized for three decades by the commercial monopoly of the Société Commerciale, Industrielle et Agricole du Haut-Ogooué when the colonial administration began to increase its demands upon them in the early 1920s. The French instituted a head tax in 1923 and a prestation or unpaid required labour in 1926. In December 1927 they demanded that the Awandji bring provisions regularly to the

market in Lastoursville for the benefit of the French post. Not only were the prices paid unattractive but appearance at market made the Awandji more liable for enforcement of the head and labour taxes, not to mention recruitment for construction of the Congo–Ocean Railway (1921-34). Starting in January 1928 Chief Wongo led twelve other chiefs and about 1,500 villagers in resisting French demands for bringing foodstuffs to Lastoursville. French attempts at repression encountered a guerrilla warfare, which was not suppressed until May 1929. At the Awandji surrender, the Senegalese militia executed scores of resisters and took 150 prisoners. Chief Wongo and another leader, Chief Lessibi, died three months later aboard a steamer in transit to Bangui for trial.

144 **Extracting people from precapitalist production: French Equatorial Africa from the 1890s to the 1930s.**
Dennis D. Cordell. In: *African population and capitalism: historical perspectives.* Edited by D. E. Cordell, J. W. Gregory. Boulder, Colorado: Westview, 1987, p. 137-52. map. bibliog.
This includes data on labour recruitment and utilization in Gabon during the era of the concessionary companies before the First World War and the introduction of peasant-produced cocoa and coffee in the north between the two World Wars.

145 **La colonisation française et une minorité ethnique de l'Afrique centrale: les pygmées.** (French colonization and an ethnic minority of Central Africa: the pygmies.)
Jean-Michel Delobeau. In: *Histoires d'outre-mer: mélanges en l'honneur de Jean-Louis Miège.* Aix-en-Provence, France: Publications de l'Université de Provence, 1992, p. 373-88. bibliog.
This is a discussion of the impact of French rule on the various pygmies of western equatorial Africa, including Gabon.

146 **Un problème d'histoire du Gabon: la sacre du Père Bichet par les Nkomi en 1897.** (A problem in the history of Gabon: the consecration of Father Bichet by the Nkomi in 1897.)
François Gaulme. *Revue Française d'Histoire d'Outre-Mer*, vol. 61, no. 3 (1974), p. 395-416. bibliog.
Father Marie-Georges Bichet, a missionary of the French Holy Ghost Fathers, was granted royal honours by the Nkomi in 1897. He was given the title *renima* or 'chief of the whole country'. He nevertheless remained subordinate to the *regondo* or paramount chief. The presence of missionaries had the effect of stimulating factionalism among the Nkomi and making centralized control more difficult.

147 **Spain and the scramble for Africa: the 'Africanistas' and the Gulf of Guinea.**
Billy Gene Hahs, Jr. PhD thesis, University of New Mexico, Albuquerque, New Mexico, 1980. 319p. bibliog. (Available from University Microfilms, Ann Arbor, Michigan, order no. 8123.)

By a treaty of 1778, Spain acquired Portugal's claims to the coastal lands between the Niger and Ogooué Rivers. But Spain moved to make good on these claims only in the nineteenth century when nationals of other western states began to establish posts on offshore islands and river mouths. Spain's claims to Equatorial Guinea (formerly called both Spanish Guinea and Rio Muni) and to adjacent areas subsequently assigned to Gabon under France were defended by Madrid's Society of Africanists (the *Africanistas*). Into the upper reaches of the Noya and N'Tem rivers in 1884-85 the Society sent explorers and agents whose activities limited French expansion into the area. The efforts of the Africanistas to secure a sub-Saharan realm for Spain were only partially successful. While they re-established Spanish claims to some coastal areas which France also claimed, they saw their country relinquish its claims to the interior of Africa in favour of a clear title to the enclave of Spanish Guinea or Rio Muni in 1900. Earlier the Spanish government had established control over the island of Corisco, where American Presbyterians had established a mission in 1850, the two Elobeys and smaller islands. Ownership of some of the last named would become a matter of dispute between Gabon and Equatorial Guinea during the 1970s, in part because of their possible oil resources.

148 **The impact of colonialism on health in French Equatorial Africa, 1880-1934.**
Rita Headrick. PhD thesis, University of Chicago, Chicago, Illinois, 1987. [n.p.] bibliog. (Available for purchase from the Regensburg Library, University of Chicago.)

Compared to other regions of the continent, French Equatorial Africa had a sparse population and relatively little long-distance trade. Beginning in the 1880s the French occupation of additional areas of Gabon and the three states that are today the Congo Republic, the Central African Republic, and Chad as well as increasing relations with the outside world led to a series of health crises that lasted for half a century. Movements of soldiers, porters, administrators, and traders into the new areas brought diseases from the outside or spread indigenous ones. An epidemic of sleeping sickness, starting in 1900, led to formation of a health service and a Pasteur Institute. But mass diagnosis and treatment took place only after 1918 and eradication was not achieved until the 1930s. The few doctors in the colony before 1914 succeeded only in controlling the spread of smallpox. Construction of the Congo-Ocean Railway (1918-24) led to massive labour recruitment in Gabon, disrupting the economy of large areas and forcing labourers into dangerously unsanitary camps. Among the results were local famines, including among the Fang, and an upsurge of mortality from respiratory diseases, beriberi, and dysentery. During the period from the 1880s to the 1930s sterility, low birth rates, and high infant mortality persisted, and in areas of Gabon even worsened. Despite the shortage of doctors, mainly military officers, the French regime discouraged missionaries, Albert Schweitzer being the only successful physician outside the official establishment. By the 1930s better organization of public health services, increased budgets and the dedication of medical personnel (including African male nurses who handled great responsibilities) began to overcome the previous negative impact of colonialism on the health of the population.

149 **La délimitation des frontières du Gabon (1885-1911).** (The delimitation of the frontiers of Gabon 1885-1911.)
André Mangongo-Nzambi. *Cahiers d'Études Africaines*, vol. 9, no. 1 (1969), p. 5-53.

The convention concluded between France and Britain in 1885 left the boundaries between the German Cameroons and French settlements in the Congo vague, particularly in the regions situated east of the meridian 7°40′ east of Paris. Exploration of this region was undertaken by the missions of the German Crampel and the Frenchman Fourneau. In 1894 the first boundary was fixed, the eventual revision of which was foreseen. From 1900 to 1903 the Cureau mission explored these boundary regions for France. Then from 1905 to 1907 a Franco–German commission headed by Captain Cottes on the French side led to the signature of a new convention in 1908. Subsequently the Franco–German agreement of 1911 giving France a free hand in Morocco ceded important territories to the Germans. Rio Muni had its boundaries fixed in 1901 by the Franco–Spanish commission which was led for the French by Bonnel de Mézières. Unfortunately the boundary fixed then gave rise to quarrelling and the differences were not resolved until 1924.

150 **L'implantation coloniale. Vol. 1. Résistance d'un peuple.** (Colonial implantation. Vol. 1. Resistance of a people.)
Nicholas Métégué N'nah. Paris: Harmattan, 1979. 79p. bibliog.

This brief work dispels the myth that all of the Gabonese peacefully submitted to the establishment of French rule and thereafter cooperated docilely with their colonial masters. It shows that elements of the Fang and Awandji resisted French efforts to tax them and to interfere with their trading advantages.

151 **Brazza, commissaire-général: le Congo français, 1886-1897.** (Brazza, commissioner-general: the French Congo, 1886-1897.)
Elisabeth Rabut. Paris: Ecole des Hautes Etudes en Sciences Sociales, 1989. 490p. maps. bibliog.

This is a detailed study based on archival materials of Pierre Savorgnan de Brazza's tenure as head of the French Congo, which comprised the countries of Gabon and the Congo (capital Brazzaville). Brazza laid the foundations for French administration in the interior of Gabon.

152 **Les résistances gabonaises à l'impérialisme de 1870 à 1914.** (Gabonese resistance to imperialism from 1870 to 1914.)
Ange Ratanga-Atoz. PhD thesis, University of Paris, 1973. 266p. bibliog. (Microfiche edition available from Clearwater Publishers, New York.)

This thesis shows that various Gabonese peoples and leaders resisted the imposition of French rule in the late nineteenth century as well as French attempts to monopolize trade and to tax.

153 **Histoire du Congo. Capitale Brazzaville.** (History of the Congo. Capital
Brazzaville.)
Marcel Soret. Paris: Berger-Levrault, 1978. 237p. maps. bibliog.
Prior to the establishment of French rule in the late nineteenth century, the kingdom
of Loango, which was loosely attached to the Kongo kingdom farther south, held sway
over portions of southern Gabon. Much of the trade of south-western Gabon was
focused on the capital and port of Loango. Between 1883 and 1918 France ruled
Loango as a part of the colony of Gabon. After the First World War the French
detached these regions and added them to the colony of the Middle Congo so that the
route of the Congo–Ocean Railway from the coast to the Pool, on whose northern
banks Brazzaville was located, could be completed within a single colony. The new
inter-colonial boundary divided such peoples as the Vili, Nzabi, Babuissi and
Bapounou. Thus Soret's detailed account of these peoples' history has much value for
the understanding of developments in southern Gabon.

**The vanishing Mpongwe: European contact and demographic change in the
Gabon River.**
See item no. 190.

**My Ogowe: being a narrative of daily incidents during sixteen years in
equatorial Africa.**
See item no. 241.

Histoire militaire de l'Afrique Equatoriale Française. (Military history of
French Equatorial Africa.)
See item no. 304.

**Colonial conscripts. The 'tirailleurs sénégalais' in French West Africa,
1857-1960.**
See item no. 305.

French colonial rule in Africa [1914-62]: a bibliographical essay.
See item no. 542.

First World War (1914-18)

154 **La double défi de l'AEF en guerre (1914-1918).** (The double challenge
of FEA [French Equatorial Africa] in war, 1914-1918.)
Colette Dubois. *Africa* (Rome), vol. 44, no. 1 (1989), p. 25-49. map.
bibliog.
During the First World War France used the resources of its colonies in equatorial
Africa, in cooperation with Britain, to defeat the Germans in the Cameroons, and then
to aid its war effort in Europe. Volunteer troops from Gabon were used to reoccupy
the portions of the country ceded to Germany in 1911 and to defeat the German forces
in the Cameroons in January 1916. Forced recruitment of thousands of porters led to
huge tensions involving uprisings, desertions from villages, flights during transfer and

self-inflicted injuries to secure medical excuses. Drastic reductions in the subventions France had been providing to the territorial budget led to huge increases in the rate of the head tax. The average Gabonese had to spend four to five times as many hours as before the war working to pay this tax, with the resulting neglect of food crops. In January 1918 France drafted 1,500 Gabonese for military service on the western front in Europe. In Gabon itself shortages of transport for the increased palm production led to spoilage. At war's end Gabon was on the verge of famine, a situation made worse by requisitions to feed troops and porters. These demands proved particularly disastrous for the Fang areas, where a real crisis in food production between 1918 and 1920 contributed during the following years to famines in which thousands died. Other thousands, weakened by malnutrition, succumbed to the epidemics of Spanish influenza during 1918 and after.

155 **Le prix d'une guerre: deux colonies pendant la Première guerre mondiale (Gabon-Oubangui-Chari, 1911-1923).** (The price of a war: two colonies during the First World War, Gabon and Oubangui-Chari, 1911-1923.)
Colette Dubois. Aix-en-Provence, France: University of Provence, Institut d'Histoire des Pays d'Outre-Mer, 1985. 792p. maps. bibliog.

This detailed account of the impact of the First World War on Gabon and Oubangui-Chari is based on archival sources. It discusses the course of events from the time of the transfer of portions of the two colonies to Germany in 1911 up to and including the first five years of the war's aftermath. It shows how largely forced participation in the French war effort had disastrous consequences for the African populations, including demographic dislocation and decline.

156 **La bataille de Cocobeach.** (The battle of Cocobeach.)
Jean-Pierre Fourés. *M'Bolo*, no. 28 (1991), p. 16-23.

On September 20, 1914, French-led Gabonese troops took Cocobeach, on the northern coast next to Equatorial Guinea, from superior German forces. There is an English summary in the appendix of the issue.

157 **Les Gabonais et la première guerre mondiale (1914-1918).** (The Gabonese and the First World War, 1914-1918.)
Théophile Loungou, Alike Tshinyoka. In: *Les réactions africaines à la colonisation en Afrique Centrale.* Kigali: Université Nationale du Rwanda, 1985, p. 243-72. bibliog.

This study of the impact of the First World War on Gabon covers much the same ground as the works by Colette Dubois (q.v.). It does not present as much detailed information and statistics but comes to the same conclusion that Gabon suffered much and with long-term consequences as a result of its contributions to the French war effort.

Second World War (1940-45)

158 Quand Libreville était en guerre – il y a 50 ans. (When Libreville was at war – fifty years ago.)
Jean-Pierre Fourés. *M'Bolo*, no. 26 (1990), p. 31-37. map.

This article contains an eye-witness account of the Gaullist take-over in Libreville between November 6 and 9, 1940.

159 Le Gabon devant le gaullisme. (Gabon in the presence of Gaullism.)
René Labat. Bordeaux, France: Delmas, 1941. 79p.

On August 30, 1940, Governor Pierre Masson, after consultation with influential settlers, rallied Gabon to the Free French movement under General Charles de Gaulle. But on September 1, he reversed his decision. Apparently he was influenced by the criticism of the Catholic bishop of Libreville, Monsignor Louis Tardy, and the prominent businessman, René Labat, as well as by the arrival of two Vichy gunboats on the coast and high Vichy colonial appointees by air. Thereafter Gabon became the scene of a struggle between the Free French, based in the Cameroons and the Middle Congo, and their French supporters in Gabon, on the one side, and the Vichy forces and their local French supporters, on the other. Free French forces led by Colonel Parant in the south and by Colonel Leclerc in the north succeeded in wresting the territory from the Vichyites by November 11. Labat provides an account of these events from the perspective of the Vichyites.

160 L'A.E.F. et le Cameroun pendant et depuis la guerre. (FEA and the Cameroons since the [Second World] War.)
Charles Robequain. *Annales de Géographie*, vol. 55 (July–Sept. 1946), p. 188-95. bibliog.

The shortage of transportation reduced the export of timber from Gabon drastically from 300,000 tons in 1938 to 50,000 tons in 1944. Oil prospecting was pursued during the war with very promising possibilities.

161 Eboué.
Brian Weinstein. New York: Oxford University Press, 1971. 350p. bibliog.

This is the most authoritative and complete biography of Félix Eboué (1884-1944), a French colonial administrator from French Guyana who served for many years in Oubangui-Chari. As governor-general of French Equatorial Africa from 1940 to 1944 under the Free French he took many actions that had an impact upon Gabon. He improved the status of African civil servants in the colonial service and encouraged discussion groups among them. He took a personal interest in the careers of such future leaders as Jean-Hilaire Aubame, Jean-Rémy Ayouné and René-Paul Sousatte. He solicited their views about the reform of the colonial system at the time of the Brazzaville Conference of January–February 1944, which General de Gaulle summoned to refashion France's postwar relationship with sub-Saharan Africa. Despite the problems of wartime, Eboué tripled expenditures for education, including important subsidies to the schools of the Catholic and Protestant missions, so that they could play a larger role in expanding educational opportunities. In 1942 he opened the first *école supérieure* (US grades seven to ten) in Libreville, which facilitated the preparation of larger numbers of Gabonese for middle-level positions in the administration and upper-primary teaching.

Le capitaine Charles N'Tchoréré. (Captain Charles N'Tchorére.)
See item no. 300.

Colonial conscripts. The 'tirailleurs sénégalais' in French West Africa, 1857-1960.
See item no. 305.

Decolonization (1945-60)

162 **The development of political parties in French Equatorial Africa.**
John A. Ballard.   PhD thesis, Fletcher School, Tufts University, Medford, Massachusetts, 1964. 495p. bibliog.   (Available through interlibrary loan.)

This thesis includes a study of the development of political groups in Gabon from the end of the First World War up to the end of the Fourth French Republic. The period between the two World Wars saw the French-educated élite organize groups that sought to end the abuses of colonialism and to achieve equality of rights with French citizens. The Popular Front of the late 1930s in Paris and the Free French government in French Equatorial Africa during the Second World War provided new but limited opportunities for élite participation in administration and local government. The aftermath of the war and the organization of the Fourth Republic brought new opportunities for political participation by the Gabonese at several levels: the territory, the federation, the French Republic and Union. Gabonese political parties were organized to compete for office at these various levels. They generally affiliated with metropolitan parties directed by Europeans. Thus the Union Démocratique et Sociale Gabonaise, led by Jean-Hilaire Aubame, and the Bloc Démocratique Gabonais, under Léon Mba and Paul Gondjout, reflected not only the regional, ethnic and religious divisions within Gabon but the ideological, economic and social orientations of the metropolitan parties with which they were affiliated. European participation in the Gabonese and federation assemblies further reinforced these characteristics.

163 **Four equatorial states.**
John A. Ballard.   In: *National unity and regionalism in African states.*   Edited by Gwendolyn Carter.   Ithaca, New York: Cornell University Press, 1966, p. 231-336. bibliog.

This includes an examination of the internal politics and external ties of Gabon, particularly from the Second World War until the military coup of February 1964.

164   **Le rôle des milieux coloniaux dans la décolonisation du Gabon et du Congo-Brazzaville (1945-1964).** (The role of the colonial circles in the decolonization of Gabon and Congo-Brazzaville, 1945-1964.) Florence Bernault-Boswell.   In: *Les décolonisations et les indépendances en Afrique noire.*   Edited by Robert Ageron and Marc Michel.   Paris: Editions du CNRS, 1992. [n.p.] bibliog.

Several thousand Frenchmen lived in Gabon during the age of decolonization. They staffed the administration, education and social services, and ran private businesses in commerce and lumbering. During the Fourth French Republic (1946-58) French citizens elected a deputy to the French National Assembly and a third of the representatives in the Territorial Assembly in Libreville. In these capacities settlers played an influential role in territorial politics, which reflected metropolitan political divisions as well as local interests. The support of the territorial administration and the Christian missions helped to elect Jean-Hiliare Aubame as the Gabonese voters' deputy to Paris. The shift of important lumbering men's support from Aubame to Léon Mba in 1957 enabled Mba to supplant Aubame at the territorial level. Mba thus became the country's highest African executive officer under the *loi-cadre* (enabling act) reforms of 1956-57 and later its first prime minister and president of the republic. Mba was able to install an authoritarian regime that survived the military coup of February 1964 because of French intervention.

165   **L'évolution politique et juridique de l'union française depuis 1946.** (The political and juridical evolution of the French Union since 1946.) François Borella.   Paris: R. Pichon & R. Durand-Auzias, 1958. 499p. bibliog.

Between 1946 and 1958 Gabon was an overseas territory of the Fourth French Republic while the Republic itself formed part of the French Union. The Gabonese were citizens of both the republic and union. As a result, they had token representation in the French National Assembly, Council of the Republic and Assembly of the French Union. They possessed a territorial assembly and sent representatives to the federal council of French Equatorial Africa in Brazzaville. This work provides a detailed analysis of the constitutional and institutional framework of the overseas territories and its evolution. As a result of the reforms of April 1957 the assemblies of the overseas territories acquired greater powers concerning local matters and embryonic executives were formed under the chairmanship of the territorial governors. This work was completed prior to the collapse of the Fourth Republic in May 1958.

166   **Chroniques d'Outre-Mer.** (Overseas Chronicles.) Paris: Ministry of Overseas France, 1951-58. 10 times per year.

This periodical provides a valuable source for studying French development projects (e.g. economy, education, health care) and policies in the overseas territories during the Fourth Republic.

167 **Barthélémy Boganda ou du projet d'état unitaire central africaine à celui d'Etats-Unis d'Afrique Centrale.** (Barthelemy Boganda or from the project for a unitary Central African state to that for a United States of Central Africa.)
Philippe Decraene. *Relations Internationales*, (summer 1983), p. 215-26. bibliog.

Between 1886 and 1958 Gabon was always administered as part of a larger entity, at first the French Congo, and then after 1910, the federation of French Equatorial Africa. Its revenues were used for the benefit of the other colonies, including for the construction of a railway in the Congo while it lacked a railway to promote its own development. The development of Gabon's considerable resources in manganese, uranium and petroleum in the late 1950s encouraged its tendencies to separate from the federation and to seek direct ties with France, the major source of investment capital and trading partner. While Gabon later agreed to customs and monetary cooperation with the other three equatorial African states and Cameroon, it rejected the proposal of Barthelemy Boganda, prime minister of the Central African Republic, for a unitary state or a new federation.

168 **Affirmation of things past: Alar Ayong and Bwiti as movements of protest.**
James W. Fernandez. In: *Protest and power in Black Africa.* Edited by Robert Rotberg, Ali Mazrui. New York: Oxford University Press, 1970, p. 427-57. bibliog.

Alar ayong means 'to unite the clans' in Fang. It was a movement during the late 1940s and early 1950s to revitalize their traditional structures and values by the regrouping of their 150 or so clans. While the French administration favoured a regrouping of the Fang populations for convenience in providing services and securing revenues, it was suspicious of the movement because of its links with the Cameroons and its American Presbyterian missions. It also feared that the Alar Ayong leaders might try to displace the chiefs installed by the French. In these circumstances the movement did more to restore Fang self-esteem by affirming the relevance of the ancestors and the clans than it did to modernize society along western lines. Bwiti is a syncretic religion adopted by thousands of Fang in the course of the twentieth century as a means of dealing with the impact of French political control as well as European economic and cultural penetration. Though it borrowed from Roman Catholicism, its followers benefited psychically from its incorporation of African values under solely Gabonese leadership. The organizational fragmentation of the movement after 1950 weakened its potential for protest against the colonial situation.

169 **Bibliographical essay: decolonization in French, Belgian, and Portuguese Africa.**
David E. Gardinier. In: *Transfer of power in Africa*: *decolonization, 1940-1960.* Edited by Prosser Gifford, Wm. Roger Louis. New Haven, Connecticut: Yale University Press, 1982, p. 516-66.

This is a historiography of works dealing with decolonization in French Africa, including Gabon, particularly for the period 1945-60. Lists of colonial officials in France and in Africa are included.

170 **Decolonization in French, Belgian, Portuguese, and Italian Africa: Bibliography.**
Compiled by David E. Gardinier. In: *Decolonization and African independence: the transfers of power, 1960-1980.* Edited by Prosser Gifford, Wm. Roger Louis. New Haven, Connecticut: Yale University Press, 1988, p. 573-635.

This bibliography encompasses mainly those works published in the preceding decade dealing with decolonization, including after formal independence. Material on Gabon is found in many of the references dealing with France in Africa or the Francophone states.

171 **French Equatorial Africa.**
David E. Gardinier. *Current History*, vol. 34 (Feb. 1958), p. 105-10. bibliog.

This article provides an introduction to the political and economic evolution of the four equatorial African states during the Fourth French Republic.

172 **Hommage à Léon Mba.** (Homage to Léon Mba).
Libreville: Ministry of Information, 1971. 100p. bibliog.

Information is provided on the life and accomplishments of Gabon's first prime minister and president.

173 **Forces sociales et idéologies dans la décolonisation de l'Afrique Equatoriale Française.** (Social forces and ideologies in the decolonization of French Equatorial Africa.)
Elikia M'Bokolo. *Journal of African History*, vol. 22, no. 3 (1981), p. 393-407. bibliog.

The initiatives for decolonization in French Equatorial Africa came less from the Africans than from the colonial power, both at the metropolitan and territorial levels. From start to finish French officials controlled the movements for political emancipation. It is not that the African submitted passively to this evolution. Rather, such groups as traditional chiefs and workers that might have given other directions to the movements were too weak to perform such roles. The main role in emancipation fell to the lower middle class (*petite bourgeoisie*), who were anti-colonialist but not anti-imperialist. They thus wanted to replace the French in power in order to have all the benefits of a ruling class. But they did not wish to reorganize economic relations with the western world, which might have been a step towards a re-ordering of their societies towards greater equality of opportunity.

174 **French colonial policy in equatorial Africa in the 1940s and 1950s.**
Elikia M'Bokolo. In: *The transfer of power in Africa: decolonization, 1940-1960.* Edited by Prosser Gifford, Wm. Roger Louis. New Haven, Connecticut: Yale University Press, 1982, p. 173-210. map. bibliog.

Between 1940 and 1944 changes initiated by Governor-General Félix Eboué aimed chiefly at correcting the backwardness of French policy with respect to conditions in French Equatorial Africa were only partially achieved. Between 1944 and 1952 the policy of change continued but initiative passed into the hands of the authorities in Paris. Basically pursuing the policy worked out by Eboué, they also mapped out a policy of political participation and socio-economic development for all of French Black Africa. This new policy aggravated the tensions peculiar to FEA. From 1952 to 1957 the government-general in Brazzaville, faced with an accelerated course of events, particularly following reforms decided upon the government in Paris, redoubled its efforts to meet the most urgent situations while at the same time endeavouring to make up for past delays and to appease opposition. The last phase consisted in the march to independence between 1957 and 1960, during which the initiatives reverted once more to Paris. Throughout all these periods French policy consisted in granting more power to the Africans without jeopardizing fundamental European interests. This approach succeeded the more easily in FEA because the élites, surprised by the swift pace of events, cut off from the masses and won over by the idea of collaboration, conceived of independence as merely obtaining powerful positions without changes in the structure of society or in the nature of their relations with France. That is why in FEA colonialism was replaced by neocolonialism.

175   **Le colonisateur colonisé.** (The colonizer colonized.)
Louis Sanmarco.   Paris: ABC, 1983. 229p.

The memoirs of Sanmarco, French colonial governor at the time of the creation of the French Community, provide colourful details on France's refusal to allow Gabon the option of becoming an overseas department of the Fifth Republic. He also gives interesting vignettes of some of the leading Gabonese personalities of the era.

176   **Gabon: nation-building on the Ogooué.**
Brian Weinstein.   Cambridge, Massachusetts; London: MIT Press, 1966. 287p. 2 maps. bibliog.

This valuable introduction to the political evolution of Gabon under French colonial rule and in the early years after independence is presented in terms of 'nation-building', a concept popular among Africanist political scientists in the 1960s. There is a useful annotated bibliography.

177   **Black Africa and De Gaulle: from the French empire to independence.**
Dorothy Shipley White.   University Park, Pennsylvania: Penn State University Press, 1979. 314p. bibliog.

This authoritative account of the decolonization of French Black Africa emphasizes the role of General Charles de Gaulle in the periods 1940-46 and 1958-61. In 1958 Gabon would have preferred to have become an overseas department of the Fifth French Republic rather than an autonomous republic of the French Community. But the Gaullist regime was unwilling to offer it such a status, thus detaching it from the French Republic and heading it along the same path as the other French territories towards independence in 1960 and membership in the stillborn French Community.

National (1960-)

178 **Echec aux militaires au Gabon en 1964.** (Failure for the military in
Gabon in 1964.)
Moise N'Sole Biteghé. Paris: Editions Chaka, 1990. 159p. bibliog.
In February 1964 military elements staged a coup to prevent President Léon Mba from
establishing a single-party regime. They summoned Jean-Hilaire Aubame, deputy in
Paris from 1946 to 1958, to head a civilian provisional government. But French military
intervention, authorized by General Charles de Gaulle, restored Mba to power,
thereby permitting him to create a dictatorship that persisted under his handpicked
successor Omar Bongo. N'Sole Biteghé found no evidence, as some have charged, that
Aubame was involved in planning the coup or that he was conniving with Americans.
The author carries his account through the elections of April 1964, which showed how
limited Gabonese support for Mba really was, and the trials at Lambaréné that
punished the surviving coup leaders and members of the provisional government.
Annexes contain documents issued by that government and various political groups.

179 **La République gabonaise: treize années d'histoire.** (The Gabonese
Republic: thirteen years of history.)
Gilbert Comte. *Revue Française d'Etudes Politiques Africaines*: *le
Mois en Afrique*, (June 1973), p. 39-57.
This article describes Gabon's internal political and economic evolution in the first
thirteen years after independence as well as its relations with France.

180 **African betrayal.**
Charles F. Darlington, Alice B. Darlington. New York: David
McKay, 1968. 359p. 2 maps. bibliog.
Charles Darlington served as the first American ambassador to Gabon from 1961 to
1964. The Darlingtons witnessed the military coup of February 1964 against President
Mba and the French military intervention to restore him to power. They contend that
French President Charles de Gaulle betrayed the people of Gabon by a restoration that
permitted Mba to establish a dictatorial regime that destroyed democracy while serving
foreign interests. The work contains firsthand observations about the leading
personalities of Gabon and the country's relations with the United States and France.

181 **Hommage à Léon Mba.** (Homage to Léon Mba.)
Europe–France–Outre-Mer, no. 454 (1967), p. 9-12.
This article briefly surveys the career and accomplishments of Gabon's first prime
minister and president.

182 **French-speaking Africa since independence.**
Guy de Lusignan. New York: Praeger, 1969. 416p. bibliog. This work
is a translation of *L'Afrique noire depuis l'indépendance. L'évolution
des états francophones* (Paris: Fayard, 1970. 410p.).
It includes a section on politics in Gabon during the presidency of Léon Mba and
relations with France.

183 **Gabon.**
In: *The new Africans.* Edited by S. Taylor. New York: Putnam, 1967, p. 128-45.
Detailed biographies are supplied of the first generation of post-independence leaders, including Léon Mba and Jean-Hilaire Aubame.

184 **Léon Mba: the ideology of dependence.**
Brian Weinstein. *Genève–Afrique*, vol. 6, no. 1 (1967), p. 49-62. bibliog.
This article provides a detailed discussion of the ideas of Gabon's first prime minister and president about the country's society and polity, and its relations with France. Léon Mba drew his notions concerning a dependence on France which would ultimately lead to independence not only from his experience under colonial rule and decolonization but also from Fang culture. The article makes a real contribution to understanding the political behaviour of Mba that led to a military coup against him in 1964 and to the policies he adopted in relation to France, the role of Frenchmen within Gabon, and the French language and culture.

185 **The northern republics, 1960-1980.**
Crawford Young. In: *History of Central Africa, Vol. 2.* Edited by David Birmingham, Phyllis M. Martin. London: Longman, 1983, p. 291-335. map. bibliog.
This includes a brief account of Gabon's internal political evolution and external relations in the first two decades after independence.

Gabon. Beyond the colonial legacy.
See item no. 2.

Le Gabon et son ombre. (Gabon and its shadow.)
See item no. 5.

Hommage à Léon Mba. (Homage to Léon Mba.)
See item no. 172.

Gabon: nation-building on the Ogooué.
See item no. 176.

Gabon: a neocolonial enclave of enduring French interest.
See item no. 333.

Population

186 **African historical demography: a multi-disciplinary bibliography.**
Compiled by Joel W. Gregory, Dennis D. Cordell, Raymond
Gervais.   Los Angeles: Crossroads, 1984. 248p.
This bibliography includes citations on Gabon and French Equatorial Africa, and all of
French Africa.

187 **Studying the population of French Equatorial Africa.**
Rita Headrick. In: *Demography from scanty evidence: Central Africa in
the colonial era.*   Edited by Bruce Fetter.   Boulder, Colorado;
London: Lynn Rienner, 1990, p. 273-98. 2 maps. bibliog.
Data from Gabon from the 1920s through 1960 indicate rising infertility. Gonorrhoea,
malaria and the poverty of rain-forest diets contributed to sterility as well as to
secondary sterility, the inability of mothers to bear additional children. Economic
conditions, linked to the absence of thousands of men from their villages to work in
lumber camps, contributed to prostitution and to the diffusion of venereal diseases.
Auxiliaries of the administration did more to spread such diseases than the health
measures of the administration achieved in trying to eradicate them. Infant mortality,
which was roughly two hundred per thousand during the first two years of life, did not
diminish until after the Second World War. Gabon's population remained remarkably
stable between 1920 and 1960 with a slow growth from 1930 as result of improved
medical care. But the percentage of children was low in comparison with the rest of
French Equatorial Africa and did not increase after 1929. Between 1920 and 1960 there
were always more women than men.

188 **Gabon.**
François D. Michel. In: *Evaluation des effectifs de la population des pays africains, Vol. 2. (Evaluating the population figures of the African countries.)* Paris: Groupe de Démographie Africaine–IDP–INED–INSEE–MINCOOP–ORSTOM, 1984, p. 135-48. bibliog.

Because the government of Gabon inflated the results of the 1970 and 1980 censuses and concealed portions of the data upon which the population figures were based, accurate counts have to be made from other sources, which the author proceeds to do.

189 **Gabon.**
François D. Michel. In: *Population growth and socio-economic change in West Africa.* Edited by John C. Caldwell. New York: Columbia University Press, 1975, p. 630-56. map. bibliog.

This item reviews demographic trends through the early 1970s. Colonial censuses indicate that Gabon's population remained basically stagnant during the four decades between the First World War and independence. The census of 1921 showed 389,000 and that of 1959 416,000. The censuses and other administrative inquiries provided evidence of rising infertility under colonial rule. Malaria may have contributed to infertility by causing miscarriages that led to sterilizing infections. Almost all ethnic groups suffered from high sterility rates during these decades. The direct medical cause of sterility among women who were examined by French physicians was blockages in the fallopian tubes due to scarring and lesion from infection usually suspected to be gonorrhoea. The poverty of rain-forest diets may also have contributed to sterility. The absence of reliable census data after 1960-61 hinders the analysis of population trends since independence. But administrative surveys and studies by international organizations indicated that the rate of population growth increased. Between 1960 and 1970 the birth rate remained constant, thirty-five per thousand, while the death rate fell from thirty to twenty per thousand. Thus the rate of natural increase tripled from 0.5 per cent to 1.5 per cent. Explanations for the growth are linked to the improved standard of living, particularly in diet and access to medical care, and above all for the increasing percentage that lived in urban areas.

190 **The vanishing Mpongwe: European contact and demographic change in the Gabon River.**
K. David Patterson. *Journal of African History,* vol. 16, no. 2 (1975), p. 217-38. bibliog.

European commercial and imperial expansion sometimes contributed to a drastic decline in the aboriginal populations in coastal regions of sub-Saharan Africa through social disruption and the spread of diseases. Because of the presence of European and American observers in Gabon from 1842 onward, it is possible to have a fairly accurate picture of the decline of the Mpongwe population of the Estuary from 1840 to 1880. Whereas in 1842 there were 6,000 Mpongwe freemen and 6,000 slaves (some part Mpongwe), by 1874 there were only 3,000 to 4,000 Mpongwe and slaves all told. Among the chief causes for a decline in the birth rate were prostitution involving Mpongwe women and westerners, which spread syphilis and gonorrhoea; the practice of abortion because pregnancy interfered with prostitution and field-work; the marriage of younger women to polygynous older men; and alcoholism. Among the main causes of mortality were smallpox epidemics, particularly the one of 1864-65, which killed nearly half the population. In the same period the Mpongwe continued to absorb a considerable number of non-Mpongwe through adoption and enslavement, which often led to marriage between Mpongwe men and non-Mpongwe women.

Libreville: la ville et sa région, Gabon, Afrique Equatoriale Française: étude de géographie humaine. (Libreville: the city and its region, Gabon, French Equatorial Africa: study in human geography.)
See item no. 13.

Le Gabon: Vol. 1, Espace-histoire-société. (Gabon: Vol. 1, Space, history, society.)
See item no. 15.

Extracting people from precapitalist production: French Equatorial Africa from the 1890s to the 1930s.
See item no. 144.

Languages

Bantu

191 **Présentation du Yi-Lumbu dans ses rapports avec le Yi-Punu et la Ci-Vili à travers un conte traditionnel.** (Presentation of Yi-Loumbou in its relationships with Yi-Pounou and Ci-Vili as seen in a traditional tale.) Jean A. Blanchon. *Pholia*, vol. 1 (1984), p. 7-35. bibliog.

Examination of a traditional story of the Loumbou revealed that 65 per cent of the vocabulary was common to the language of the Pounou and that their phonological and tonological systems were very close. The author concludes, therefore, that Yi-Loumbou is a variety of the same language as Yi-Pounou. It was also discovered that 65 per cent of the vocabulary of the Loumbou tale was common with Ci-Vili but that the phonology and tonology of Ci-Vili were very different. The author concludes that through contact with Ci-Vili Yi-Loumbou speakers have borrowed 25 per cent of Ci-Vili's vocabulary.

192 **Notes towards a description of Teke (Gabon).** V. L. Fontaney. *Pholia*, vol. 1 (1984),p. 47-70. bibliog.

This articles describes the phonology and morphology of the Téké language spoken in the Haut-Ogooué Province of Gabon.

193 **Notes on the Nzebi (Gabon).** Malcolm Guthrie. *Journal of African Languages*, vol. 7, no. 2 (1986), p. 10-29. bibliog.

This presents a sketch of the grammar of Nzabi, including the verbal system, the nominal system (classes, tone patterns), the sounds, and word lists divided according to grammatical criteria.

194 **The western Bantu languages.**
Malcolm Guthrie. In: *Linguistics in sub-Saharan Africa*. Edited by
Thomas A. Sebok. Paris: Mouton, 1971, p. 357-66. bibliog.
This provides a brief introduction to the western Bantu family of languages of which
Gabon's forty-odd languages form a part.

195 **Bibliographie des langues du Gabon.** (Bibliography of the languages of
Gabon.)
Jean-Marie Hombert, A. M. Mortier. *Pholia*, vol. 1 (1984), p. 165-
84.
This bibliography lists 200 citations of works dealing with the languages of Gabon.

196 **Les Fang sont-ils Bantu?** (Are the Fang Bantu?)
Jean-Marie Hombert, Pither Medio, Raymond Nguéma. *Pholia*, vol.
4 (1989), p. 133-47. bibliog.
Various Bantu-speaking neighbours of the Fang have questioned whether the Fang are
a Bantu people. While the Fang may not have been originally of Bantu stock, the Fang
of today (using the Fang of Bitam as an example) speak a language that has grown
from Proto-Bantu according to the rules of regular phonetic evolution. Data on vowels
and consonants for regular sound correspondences between Proto-Bantu and Fang
support this conclusion.

197 **Etude de phonologie et morphologie myène.** (Study of Myènè phonology
and morphology.)
André Jacquot. In: *Etudes bantoues II (myène et laadi)*. Edited by
André Jacquot, [et al.]. Paris: SELAF, 1976, p. 13-78. bibliog.
Under Malcolm Guthrie's system of classifying Bantu languages, the Myènè group or
cluster is labelled B.10. It includes Adjumba, Enenga, Galwa, Orungu, Nkomi and
Mpongwe. In 1976 only 100 persons were speaking Enenga.

198 **A grammar of the Bakele language with vocabularies.**
Ira M. Preston, Jacob Best. New York: Prall, 1854. 117p.
American Protestant missionaries prepared this grammar with vocabularies at a time
when the Bakèlè were still a hunting and trading people of major importance in the
Gabon Estuary. The work has value for the historical dimensions of language
development.

199 **Orthographic systems and conventions in sub-Saharan Africa.**
A. N. Tucker. In: *Linguistics in sub-Saharan Africa*. Edited by
Thomas A. Sebok. Paris: Mouton, 1971, p. 618-53. bibliog.
This is a useful introduction to the systems for transcribing the western Bantu
languages through the Latin alphabet.

200 **A grammar of the Mpongwe language with vocabularies.**
John Leighton Wilson. New York: Snowden & Prall, 1847. 94p.
Wilson, founder of the American Protestant mission in the Gabon Estuary in 1842, was the first to transcribe Mpongwe using the Latin alphabet. His work has considerable value for understanding the historical evolution of that language.

Pygmy

201 **Langues des groupes pygmées au Gabon: un état des lieux.** (Languages of the pygmy groups in Gabon: a status of the places.)
Raymond Mayer. *Pholia*, vol. 2 (1987), p. 111-23. bibliog.
The pygmies of Gabon are distributed at various places throughout the nine provinces. The pygmies do not have a single language, nor are all of their languages mutually intelligible. A language spoken by pygmies in the Ogooué-Ivindo Province (north-east) is neither an original pygmy language nor a Bantu language absorbed through contact with later African arrivals. Rather it exhibits an exceptional heterogeneity involving elements from both pygmy and Bantu sources perhaps over many centuries. A language spoken by pygmies at M'Bigou in the N'Gounié Province (south-central) is apparently Bantu in origin but is not the same as the other Bantu languages spoken in the vicinity. This basically Bantu language, however, reflects the original pygmy tendency to create plurals through suffixes. Elsewhere pygmies have retained their own language while learning the Bantu languages of their neighbours as well. The article contains a list of pygmy locations as well as a bibliography of published literature and theses, phonography and discography, and filmography and videography.

French

202 **Langue française en République gabonaise.** (The French language in the Gabonese Republic.)
Claude Couvert. Paris: Haut Comité de la Langue Française, 1982. 200p. bibliog.
This study includes the linguistic context in the pre-colonial and colonial periods as well as the place of the French language in Gabonese society and the educational system today.

203 **French in Gabon.**
John Ogden. *Contemporary French Civilization*, vol. 8 (spring 1984), p. 339-48. bibliog.
This article discusses the place of the French language in Gabon during the early 1980s. French has continued to be the national language of Gabon and is the sole medium of instruction in secular subjects. (Religion is often taught in the vernacular.) Reasons for

the primacy of French include: the absence of an African vehicular language; preference for a long-established foreign language in the face of ethnic rivalries that make it impossible to select a Gabonese language as the national language; the access to modern learning and international communication; and the presence of greater numbers of Frenchmen in the country since independence than before, including hundreds of *coopérants*, who staff the secondary, technical and higher institutions. The competence of a Gabonese speaker of French is influenced by the length of schooling, the amount and quality of the French spoken at home and the degree to which the language is used in daily activities. During the 1970s Gabon modified the content of its school curriculum to include more African and Gabonese subject matter (e.g. stories and legends) but French was still used to teach this material. In 1981-82 there were experiments in three elementary schools of Libreville whereby French was taught as a second language rather than as a primary one as had previously been the case everywhere.

Language question

204 **Langue nationale et langues nationales. Commentaire sur un projet de langue commune au Gabon.** (National language and national languages. Commentary on a project for a common language in Gabon.)
André Jacquot. *Cahiers de l'ORSTOM, série Sciences Humaines*, vol. 24, no. 3 (1988),p. 403-16. bibliog.
This article discusses the issues involved in using a Bantu language of Gabon as a common language.

205 **Quelques réflexions à propos de l'enseignement en langue vernaculaire.** (Some reflections concerning teaching in a vernacular language.)
André Jacquot. *Cahiers de l'ORSTOM, série Sciences Humaines*, vol. 21, no. 2-3 (1985), p. 355-60. bibliog.
Because Gabon has over forty Bantu languages many of which do not possess a vocabulary for expressing western philosophical and scientific ideas, French has continued to be used as the sole medium of instruction. At the same time it is recognized that young children learn best in their own language and that the sole use of French leads to much repeating and dropping out. This article discusses the issues involved in attempting instruction in vernacular languages in a situation of great fragmentation.

Religions and Missions

Traditional and syncretic

206 **Cosmologie bantu: origine de la vie, du monde et de Dieu chez les Fang.**
(Bantu cosmology: origin of life, the world, and God among the Fang.)
Blandine Engonga Bikoro. *Muntu*, no. 6 (1987),p. 105-19. bibliog.
This article discusses traditional Fang conceptions about life, the world and the
Supreme Being, as they existed before the coming of the Europeans, as derived from
the Fang epic, the *mvet*.

207 **Drugs and mysticism: the Bwiti cult of the Fang.**
Jacques Binet. *Diogenes*, vol. 86 (summer 1974), p. 31-54. bibliog.
This article discusses the use of the hallucinogenic drug *iboga* or *eboga* within the Bwiti
cult of the Fang people.

208 **Quelques aspects métaphysiques du bouiti mitshogo.** (Some
metaphysical aspects of the Mitsogo Bwiti.)
Paul-Louis Esparre. *Genève-Afrique*, vol. 7, no. 1 (1968), p. 53-57.
The Mitsogo people inhabit the lands east of Mouila in the N'Gounié Province. A
matrilineal people, they originated the Bwiti cult which they have transmitted to other
peoples. Unlike the Fang Bwiti, which mixes the sexes, the Mitsogo Bwiti is only for
men, the women's cult being the *nyemba*. Mitsogo Bwiti comprises three levels of
initiation that lead the initiate towards the 'unknowable', which is represented by the
nine spheres of the universe corresponding to the nine bodies of man. The syncretist
Bwiti cult of the Fang appears as the sublimation of the autism of a group threatened
by change. It is the product of collective anxiety produced by acculturation.

tars (TCI-Selbsteinschätzung). Verhaltensther Verhaltensmed 1997; 18:95–110.

Roman T, Bau CHD, Almeida S, Hutz HM. Lack of association of the dopamine D4 receptor gene with alcoholism in a Brazilian population. Addict Biol 1999;4:203–7.

Ronai Z, Szekely A, Nemoda Z, Lakatos K, Gervai J, Staub M, Sasvari-Szekely M. Association between Novelty-seeking and the -521 C/T polymorphism in the promoter region of the DRD4 gene. Mol Psychiatry 2001;6:35–8.

209 **Bwiti: an ethnography of the religious imagination in Africa.**
James W. Fernandez.   Princeton, New Jersey: Princeton University
Press, 1982. 731p. bibliog.

Bwiti is a syncretist religion derived from a variety of autochthonous and Christian traditions in response to the impact of the West on the Fang people of northern Gabon. It received the adherence of as many as 8 to 10 per cent of the Fang. Bwiti's members claim that their imaginative elaborations of liturgy and belief come to them in dream communications with the ancestors or under the influence of *eboga*, a hallucinogenic drug to which they are deeply attached. Bwiti is one of the few African religions to argue its potency from the constant use of a psychoreactive drug rather than possession by supernatural beings or the impersonation of such beings by means of masks. Bwiti is at the same time a highly polymorphous religion that exhibits substantial variations in doctrine, worship and symbolism from one branch to another, depending among other things upon the degree to which affinity with Christianity is emphasized or de-emphasized. Fernandez's study is limited to the branch known as the *asumeje ening*, up to and including 1960, which he treats more as a reinterpretation of old Fang cults than as a variation of Christianity, despite its adoption of such biblical figures as Jesus and Mary.

210 **Christian acculturation and Fang witchcraft.**
James W. Fernandez.   *Cahiers d'Études Africaines*, vol. 2, no. 2
(1961), p. 244-70.

Traditional Fang society involved belief in witchcraft. The Fang believed that peoples are divided into *mimia* (simple humans without magical power), *engolengola* (those who possess for themselves *evus* or magical power) and *nnem* (those who possess an aggressive *evus* that leads them to power and cannibalism). The *evus* is distinct from the spirit and soul of the individual in whom it is incarnated and thus has a separate existence. Because the Fang considered the goods of this world to be in constant number, the one who increases his possessions by magic causes prejudice to others. That is why the ancestors as guarantors of the social order are opposed to sorcery. Like the ancestors, the Christian missions have tried without much success to combat sorcery. Within Fang society movements are manifest to draw the divinity more closely to humanity and to introduce into spiritual life other principles of responsibility. Attached to Fernandez's account of these situations is an essay by a Christian-educated Fang, P. Bakalé, entitled 'Concerning evil or sorcery renovated'; he calls upon such figures as St. Michael to aid the people in their struggle against sorcery.

211 **Fang representations under acculturation.**
James W. Fernandez.   In: *Africa and the West*.   Edited by Philip D.
Curtin.   Madison, Wisconsin: University of Wisconsin Press, 1972,
p. 3-48. bibliog.

An examination is presented of the Fang response to pressure put upon their thinking about the world as a consequence of both French colonial administrative organization and Christian missionary evangelization. It concerns primarily the reactions of the forest villagers as they experienced the direct intervention of administrator and missionary in village affairs and not the reactions of the intellectual élite in the trading centres and coastal cities. The process of acculturation emanating from this intervention has led to a greater self-consciousness and a greater awareness of their patterns of behaviour. They have become anxious to explain their way of life to themselves. Various kinds of mythology appeared, which explained the differences

Religions and Missions. Traditional and syncretic

between whites and blacks. In contrast, the Bwiti cult was a conscious attempt to syncretize and harmonize the cultures in contact, to find a satisfactory explanatory network for the anomalies produced by that contact. Less frequent reactions included self-isolation so as to suppress the claims of the acculturated consciousness. But in general, increasing self-consciousness is the lot of the acculturated. This should be seen as an intellectual reaction, for at least in western experience knowledge of self has been one of the hallmarks of the intellectual tradition. The new models of cosmology, religion and family structures that the Fang have elaborated under acculturation have manifestly less complexity than their traditional systems.

212   **Symbolic consensus in a Fang reformative cult.**
      James W. Fernandez. *American Anthropologist*, vol. 67, no. 4
      (August 1965), p. 902-29. bibliog.

The concepts 'consensus' and 'symbol' and their relationship are discussed here with reference to the Bwiti cult, which was found among up to 10 per cent of the Fang of northern Gabon and Equatorial Guinea. When Bwiti first appeared at the turn of the century, it represented a reworking of the Fang ancestral cult, *bieri*. The history of the cult is briefly considered but primary concern focuses upon the cult as it appeared during fieldwork in 1958-60. There is a variety of sub-cults in Bwiti but in this essay only the main one, *Dissoumba* or *Asunge Ening* (literally 'beginning of life'), which is found primarily in Gabon, is discussed. Variable interpretations of the symbols involved in ritual interaction were found simultaneously with unanimous recognition of the effectiveness of the ritual that was resulting in the kind of cohesiveness and solidarity the Fang call *nlem mvore* (one-heartedness). Thus a social consensus exists in the sense of an agreement with respect to the interaction requirements of signals and signs. But a cultural consensus is lacking given the absence of agreement over the meaning of the symbols. Attempts to achieve a cultural consensus might threaten the cohesiveness already achieved among Bwiti followers.

213   **Le Bwiti chez les Nkomi: association cultuelle et évolution historique sur
      le littoral gabonais.** (Bwiti among the Nkomi: cultic association and
      historical evolution on the Gabon coast.)
      François Gaulme. *Journal des Africanistes*, vol. 49, no. 2 (1979),
      p. 37-87. bibliog.

Although Bwiti is the most prominent of cultic associations for males in Gabon, it never had widespread appeal among the Myènè peoples of the Gabon coast. Among the Nkomi, Bwiti had to compete with a more popular therapeutic cult called Elombo. Until the nineteenth century Nkomi men had an association called Okuyi, which assured the transition from childhood to manhood for tribesman. It paralleled Ndjembe, the female association that is still flourishing today. The term *ombwiri*, which is now reserved for some of the Myènè therapeutic cults, probably had a wider meaning in the past; it then included a classic aspect of the cult of the ancestors, which is fairly comparable to the supposedly primary form of Bwiti that arose among the Mitsogo. In the late nineteenth century some Nkomi were attracted to Bwiti as a means of gaining personal power in a society that was being disrupted by European colonial penetration. But Bwiti has always had a bad reputation because of its association with sorcery.

214 **Le Ngo, société secrète du Haut-Ogowe (Gabon).** (The Ngo, secret
society of the Haut-Ogooué, Gabon.)
A. Hée. *Africa* (London), vol. 10, no. 4 (1937), p. 472-80.
The Ngo or panther society among the peoples of the Haut-Ogooué Province had the
function of preserving the bones of the ancestors where, it was believed, their souls
came to live. The Ngo also preserved the traditions and customs of their peoples and
exerted pressures on those who deviated from traditional norms and values.

215 **L'alternative de la vision et de la possession dans les sociétés religieuses
et therapeutiques du Gabon.** (The alternative of vision and possession in
the religious and therapeutical societies of Gabon.)
André Mary. *Cahiers d'Études Africaines*, vol. 23, no. 3 (1983),
p. 281-310. bibliog.
The Fang Bwiti cult has retained vision as an initiatory experience involving absorption
of a hallucinogenic drug (*eboga*) and a privileged medium of surrealist communication.
Vision displays a number of traits that differentiate it from possession as practised in
other Gabonese therapeutic cults. Complementary relations between vision and
possession in the religious and therapeutic field demarcate the male-dominated Bwiti
societies from the women-controlled Ombwiri communities. The regulations pertaining
to these two kind of initiatory experiences govern the logic of ceremonial activities, the
conception of worship, and the calling forth of spirits of genii through trance-inducing
dances or mask parades. Since independence in 1960 there has been a weakening of
the significant oppositions between vision and possession along with a shifting of
functions. The stressing of the divinatory use of vision arising from the constraints of a
neocolonial situation, and the struggle to dominate the ritual scene bear witness to a
new distribution of power favouring women with political and social meaning as yet
ambiguous.

216 **La naissance à l'envers: essai sur le rituel du Bwiti Fang au Gabon.**
(Birth on the inverse: essay on the ritual of the Fang Bwiti in Gabon.)
André Mary. Paris: Harmattan, 1983. 386p. bibliog.
This work centres on the ethnography of the Bwiti rituals, of which it gives minute
descriptions. It insists on their symbolic and syncretic dimensions.

217 **Fetishism in West Africa: forty years' observations of natives customs
and superstitions.**
Robert Hamill Nassau. New York: Scribners, 1904. 389p. bibliog.
Reprinted, New York: Negro Universities Press, 1969.
The American Presbyterian missionary Nassau observed African use of fetishes during
his years on the Ogooué River between 1874 and 1890.

218 **Ekang Ngoua, réformateur religieux au Gabon.** (Ekang Ngoua,
religious reformer in Gabon.)
Stanislaw Świderski. *Anthropos*, vol. 79, no. 4-6 (1984), p. 627-35.
In Gabon today the encounter of western civilization and the local civilization and
culture has provoked a profound regrouping in the socio-economic and religious
domain. At the start of this century the Fang started to inaugurate a new religion in

order to consolidate their tribal and cultural conscience. Bwiti has been developed out of an ancestor cult of the Apindji, to which the Fang have added their religious tradition and Roman Catholic liturgy. So the present Fang Bwiti is a syncretic religion. It was organized to correspond to the atavistic taste of the people but also to the present sociocultural and religious demands. It proves its identity by numerous spiritual guides, reformers and founders of sects and communities. One such spiritual guide, who, inspired at the same time by the manner of philosophical thinking of the Bwiti and by the practical spirit of the Ombwiri, a feminine initiating healing society, has given a new aspect to the spiritual life of Gabon. In his testimony one can recognize a great need of reflection on all the manifestations of life in the capacity of a reflection on the presence of God. He established a programme of cultural and spiritual action to respiritualize man. Ekang Ngoua can be distinguished from other guides by the prophetic conscience he preserved until his death. By the originality of the cultic ceremonies, this prophet differs in his thoughts from both authentic Bwiti and missionized Christianity.

219 **La harpe sacrée dans les cultes syncrétiques au Gabon.** (The sacred harp in the syncretic cults of Gabon.)
Stanislaw Świderski. *Anthropos*, vol. 65, no. 5-6 (1970), p. 833-57. map. bibliog.

In the Fang syncretic cults Bwiti and Ombwiri, the sacred harp (*ngoma* or *ngombi*), through the accompaniment of lyrics reactualizes and dramatizes, in the course of nocturnal ceremonies, the mythic account of the death of a woman who has been sacrificed. The harp symbolizes the Holy Virgin, around whom the Fang have composed numerous hymns. She is venerated as the saviour of the Black race to whom the cultists each week consecrate prayers and dances. Formerly the harp was a sacred object of music and symbol of the mythical past. As a result of the acculturation that has occurred under the impact of the West, it has become the means of a new socio-religious cohesion and source of inspiration for the formation and development of a people's consciousness of itself.

220 **Meyo Mé Nguéma Minko. Réformateur oecuméniste de la religion Bwiti.** (Meyo Mé Nguéma Minko. Ecumenical reformer of the Bwiti religion.)
Stanislaw Świderski. *Journal of Religion in Africa*, vol. 17, no. 1 (1987), p. 32-43. bibliog.

The syncretic religion, Bwiti, reflects well the tendency to reactualize the ancestral religious tradition. At the same time it shows the tendency to restructure its educational, social and religious role to serve multiple functions in new socio-political and cultural dimensions. Bwiti among the Fang has gone through several periods. There was first a period of adaptation and acculturation of the Bwiti borrowed from the Apindji to the Fang milieu towards 1920. Then, after an intense and rapid syncretization between 1930 and 1955, there was a strong separatist tendency within Bwiti from 1950 to 1968. Today one observes a spontaneous return to liturgical authenticity. In adapting, Bwiti not only split into numerous sects; because of individualism it lost its spiritual purity, leaning either towards esoteric mysticism or materialism. Meyo Mé Nguéma Minko opened a new period in the Bwiti, marked by the tendency towards unification, which during the course of years had been weakened in its role as a cultural and religious institution. Minko seeks internal reform and government recognition of Bwiti along with Christianity and Islam. He wishes all Bwiti congregations to share the same philosophical, theological and structural characteristics. Another ecumenical reformer, Mba Amvéné Victor, had sought liturgical reform through a *rapprochement* with Roman Catholic practices as well as administrative reform. Both reformers use Catholic models in their structure and external organization. They wish to revive the spiritual and cultural past in a new setting to prove the validity of Bwiti's experience of the sacred.

221 **Le mouvement oecuménique dans la religion Bouiti au Gabon.** (The ecumenical movement in the Bwiti religion in Gabon.)
Stanislaw Świderski. *Journal of Religion in Africa*, vol. 18, no. 2 (1988), p. 125-40. bibliog.

Bwiti is a syncretic religion created by the Fang at the start of the twentieth century by adapting to their milieu an ancestral cult found in its original form among the Apindji, Mitsogho and other peoples of central Gabon. Bwiti includes elements from those cults, as well as from Christianity, particularly Roman Catholic liturgy. But it also incorporates elements from Fang culture that reflect their beliefs, religious practices and psychosociological aspirations. In Bwiti the Fang abandoned their traditional liturgical language in favour of the vernacular. Bwiti acquired many different forms under diverse leaders, which led to social and political disaggregation among the Fang. To counter this situation, in 1948 there came into being a popular movement for unification of all Bwiti groups and seeking government recognition of a single Bwiti sect. Whereas traditional Bwiti discriminated functionally between the sexes so that women were excluded from the liturgy and hierarchy, contemporary leaders desire to end this discrimination. They also wish to seek total cultural emancipation and the reconquest of their identity.

222 **Nguema Mba Evariste, fondateur de la communauté Eglise Romaine de Saint-Pierre de Jerusalem.** (Nguema Mba Evariste, founder of the Roman church community of St. Peter of Jerusalem.)
Stanislaw Świderski. *Journal of Religion in Africa*, vol. 14, no. 1 (1983), p. 74-83.

This article reports on the life, personality and teachings of Nguema Mba Evariste (1929-79), who in 1966 founded a small sect to which adhered mainly his family and friends. According to his autobiographical writings, Evariste in a vision was commanded by St. Peter to reform spiritually the indigenous religious beliefs and to purify the Roman Catholic missions. He introduced Christian mysticism into the local religion and envisioned a society free of witchcraft and based on mutual respect and justice.

223 **L'Ombuiri, société d'initiation et de guérison.** (Ombwiri, initiation and healing society.)
Stanislaw Świderski. *Studi e Materiali di Storia delle Religioni*, vol. 41 (1970-71), p. 125-204. bibliog.

This is a study of the Fang syncretic cult for women, Ombwiri, which is in some ways the counterpart of Bwiti.

224 **Synkretyzm religijny.** (Syncretic religions.)
  Stanisław Świderski. *Socjiologiczny*, vol. 26 (1975), p. 133-74. bibliog.
This analysis of the origin and development of syncretic sects in Gabon, which were formed as Christianity encountered African religions, shows that they are both a reaction to the new French culture and religion and a spontaneous popular movement.

225 **Rites et croyances des peuples du Gabon: essai sur les pratiques
  religieuses d'autrefois et d'aujourd'hui.** (Rites and beliefs of the peoples
  of Gabon: essay on the religious practices of yesterday and today.)
  André Raponda Walker, Roger Sillans.   Paris: Présence Africaine,
  1962. 377p. bibliog.
This study describes the traditional religious beliefs and practices of Gabon's peoples, and their evolution in recent decades. The work takes up the agents and accessories for the religious rites, the ritual practices and ceremonies, and initiatory rites. Included among the latter are those of the Bwiti of the Mitsogo, the Mwiri of the Duma, and the Ngambe (women's society) of various peoples.

Affirmation of things past: Alar Ayong and Bwiti as movements of protest.
See item no. 168.

L'art sacré du Bwiti. (The sacred art of the Bwiti.)
See item no. 456.

Catholicism

226 **Les villages de liberté en Afrique noire française, 1887-1910.** (Freedom
  villages in French Black Africa, 1887-1910.)
  Denise Bouche.   Paris: Mouton, 1968. 280p. maps. bibliog.
At the beginning of the twentieth century the French Anti-Slavery Society, founded by Cardinal Lavigerie with papal support, sponsored the organization of three villages in the Gabon interior for slaves whose freedom it had helped to purchase. These communities were located adjacent to the mission posts of the Holy Ghost Fathers (Spiritans) on the lower N'Gounié River in 1899, at Franceville on the upper Ogooué River in 1902, and at Lambaréné on the lower Ogooué in 1903. The inhabitants were mostly adults whereas earlier the Spiritans had concentrated on the liberation of ill-treated orphan children whom they subsequently raised, educated and prepared for Christian marriage. The Spiritans also formed two other villages, among the Eshira of the southern coast in 1887 and at Fernan-Vaz in 1901, without external support. Though the freedom villages did not promote evangelization to the extent that the missionaries had hoped, they nevertheless secured permanent freedom for several hundred persons in an era when the French colonial administration was not yet in a position to terminate the worst forms of domestic slavery.

227 **Missions catholiques et administration française sur la côte d'Afrique de 1815 à 1870.** (Catholic missions and French administration on the coast of Africa from 1815 to 1870.)
Paule Brasseur. *Revue Française d'Histoire d'Outre-Mer*, vol. 62, no. 3 (1975), p. 415-66. bibliog.
The French government gave material aid to French Catholic missionaries (the Holy Ghost Fathers and Immaculate Conception Sisters in the case of Gabon) to establish and maintain churches and schools in Senegal, Gabon and other points on the Atlantic coast of Africa. The colonial administration's pursuit of the goal of spreading French cultural and political influence through these missions sometimes conflicted with the Catholic congregations' goal of spreading the gospel and establishing the Church through the creation of native agents. Anticlerical and antichristian officials sought at times to undermine the work of the missionaries or set a bad example for the Africans.

228 **Libermann 1802-1852: une pensée et une mystique missionnaire.** (Libermann, 1802-1852: a missionary thought and mystique.)
Edited by Paul Coulon, Paule Brasseur. Paris: Cerf, 1988. 938p. bibliog.
This collection of essays on the work of the Holy Ghost Fathers (Spiritans) in west and equatorial Africa from the 1840s on treats their efforts from historical, theological or missiological, and sociological perspectives. Several essays deal in part with Gabon.

229 **The beginnings of French Catholic evangelization in Gabon and African responses, 1844-1883.**
David E. Gardinier. *French Colonial Studies*, no. 2 (1978), p. 49-74. bibliog.
The Holy Ghost Fathers (Spiritans) and the Immaculate Conception Sisters of Castres laid the foundations of Roman Catholicism in northern Gabon between 1844 and 1883. In that period, with French government financial aid, they established missions among the Mpongwe, Benga and Fang peoples of the Gabon Estuary and nearby coasts. Schools for boys and girls proved to be the main agency for evangelization among the Mpongwe. Through them the missionaries sought to form Christians among whom they could select and prepare teachers, catechists, religious and clergy. It proved more difficult to attract and retain adults in a Christian life because of the competing values and customs of Mpongwe trading society. But by the time of the second wave of expansion into the interior of Gabon in the 1880s, a small Christian community had taken shape and was beginning to multiply.

230 **Les Frères de Saint-Gabriel au Gabon, 1900-1918: la naissance d'une nouvelle élite africaine.** (The Brothers of St. Gabriel in Gabon, 1900-1918: the birth of a new African élite.)
David E. Gardinier. *Mondes et Cultures*, vol. 46, no. 3 (1986), p. 593-606. bibliog.

The French Holy Ghost Fathers (Spiritans) had run schools for boys in Gabon since 1844 to educate teachers, catechists and hopefully an indigenous clergy. Their considerable efforts had produced only one priest, in part, they thought, because they were not professionally trained teachers. In 1900 the Holy Ghost Fathers obtained the assistance of such personnel from the Brothers of Saint-Gabriel, who took charge of schools in Libreville and Lambaréné. While the Spiritans had usually viewed education as a means of evangelization, the brothers saw it as developing the whole person and thus opposed the subordination of instruction to the limited aim of spreading the gospel. From this difference arose not only conflicts but also more success in achieving the religious goals toward which the Spiritans had been striving. The schools soon produced several additional Gabonese priests. But they also turned out dozens of better educated employees for the colonial administration and European commerce. From the ranks of this new élite would emerge pro-French but anti-colonialist critics of French rule during the period between the two World Wars. Graduates of the brothers' schools would form the bulk of the representatives in the territorial assembly and middle-level employees of the administration during the era of decolonization under the Fourth French Republic.

231 **To the ends of the earth: a general history of the Congregation of the Holy Ghost.**
Henry J. Koren. Pittsburgh, Pennsylvania: Duquesne University Press, 1983. 548p. bibliog. This work also appears in translation as *Les Spiritains, trois siècles d'histoire religieuse et missionnaire* (Paris: Beauchêne, 1982. 633p. bibliog.).

This includes a discussion of Roman Catholic evangelization in Gabon within the context of the work of the Holy Ghost Fathers (Spiritans) in west and equatorial Africa from 1844 to 1983. In Gabon progress in terms of numbers was slow until the First World War and then accelerated during the 1930s and after. The Church in Gabon still relies heavily on missionary priests. In 1980 seventy mainly French and Dutch Spiritans worked among 330,000 Catholics in four dioceses under Gabonese bishops.

232 **Mission de Frère Macaire, 1905-1980.** (Mission of Brother Macaire, 1905-1980.)
Paris: Editions Saint-Paul, 1983. 63p. bibliog.

Brother Macaire Clémenceau was the moving spirit within the congregation of the Brothers of St. Gabriel, who conducted several schools for boys in Gabon, from the 1930s up to and including the 1960s. He wrote a series of successful textbooks and served as a representative in the Territorial Assembly during the age of decolonization, where he was a sympathetic spokesman for African advancement.

233 **Le pionnier du Gabon, Jean-Rémy Bessieux.** (The pioneer of Gabon,
     Jean-Rémy Bessieux.)
     L. Roques. Paris: Alsatia, 1971. 176p. bibliog.

Monsignor Bessieux (1803-76) founded the French Roman Catholic mission in the
Gabon Estuary in September 1844 and presided over its destinies until his death in
April 1876. He was a missionary of the Holy Ghost Fathers and the first bishop of
Libreville. He prepared a grammar in Mpongwe which facilitated evangelization
among the Estuary peoples. He opened a boys' school from which he sought to recruit
young men for service to the Church. He secured the assistance of the Immaculate
Conception Sisters of Castres, France, in 1849 for work among girls and women.
Bessieux's experiences in Gabon influenced the missionary doctrine of his congregation, which in its comparative lack of ethnocentrism was far ahead of its time.
Bessieux's determination to remain in Gabon, even without official support if
necessary, on several occasions when the government was thinking of withdrawing,
quite likely influenced the French decisions to remain.

234 **Les travaux et les jours de la mission Sainte-Marie-du-Gabon (1845-**
     1880). Agriculture et modernisation. (The works and days of the Saint-
     Mary of Gabon mission (1845-1880). Agriculture and modernization.)
     Odette Tornezy. *Revue Française d'Histoire d'Outre-Mer*, vol. 71, no.
     3-4 (1984), p. 147-80. bibliog.

As part of their self-maintenance and attempts to improve African agriculture, the
Holy Ghost Fathers pioneered in introducing various species of vegetables and fruits
from Europe and in developing ones they encountered in tropical Africa. They were
thus able to produce a large part of their own food and to provide for their school
pupils as well as to sell commodities to the European officials and traders.

L'historicité des paroles attribuées au premier évêque du Gabon à propos du
maintien du comptoir entre 1871 et 1873. (The historicity of the words
attributed to the first bishop of Gabon concerning the maintenance of the
post between 1871 and 1873.)
See item no. 128.

Un problème d'histoire du Gabon: la sacre du Père Bichet par les Nkomi en
1897. (A problem in the history of Gabon: the consecration of Father Bichet
by the Nkomi in 1897.)
See item no. 146.

Saint Gabriel au Gabon: Ecole Montfort (1900-1948). (Saint Gabriel in
Gabon: the Ecole Montfort 1900-1948.)
See item no. 413.

Annuarium statisticum ecclesiae. (Church statistical annual.)
See item no. 528.

L'Eglise Catholique en Afrique Occidentale et Centrale. Répertoire des
missions catholiques. (The Catholic Church in Western and Central Africa.
List of the Catholic missions.)
See item no. 529.

Protestantism

235 One hundred years.
Arthur Judson Brown. New York: Revell, 1936. 1140p. bibliog.

One section of this volume (p. 196-251) contains an account of American Presbyterian activity in west and equatorial Africa, which provides the context for the work in Gabon between 1870 and 1913. An appendix contains a list of all the missionaries who served in this field.

236 Presbyterian West African missions: women as converts and agents of social change.
Penelope Campbell. *Journal of Presbyterian History*, vol. 56, no. 2 (summer 1978), p. 121-32. bibliog.

During the 1860s bible readers from the American Presbyterian mission among the Benga on the island of Corisco began to work among other Benga on the continent at Cape Esterias. In 1870 the Presbyterians assumed the work of the ABCFM of Boston in the Gabon Estuary, and then between 1875 and 1882 extended it into the lower and middle Ogooué River. The essay discusses the role of women missionaries and African converts in evangelization. It argues that women converts were important in sustaining congregations and in establishing Protestant Christianity permanently in Gabon because they were better able to conform to the strict standards of conduct required of church members. Men engaging in trade were exposed to temptations involving consumption of alcohol, non-observance of the Sabbath and sexual immorality. Important men in Gabonese society were polygynous. Women also carried the burden of educating future Christians within the family.

237 The American Presbyterian mission in Gabon: male Mpongwe converts and agents, 1870-1883.
David E. Gardinier. *American Presbyterians: Journal of Presbyterian History*, vol. 69 (spring 1991), p. 61-70. bibliog.

In 1870 the Presbyterian Board of Foreign Missions took over the work of the American Board of Commissioners of Foreign Missions in Gabon. The Presbyterians assumed direction of the schools teaching in African languages and English which had proved the main agency for educating African converts and agents of the church. They operated these schools until an increasingly nationalistic French colonial administration forced their closing in 1883 by the requirement that all instruction had to be in French. Though the Presbyterians had been able to fill their boys' schools in the Gabon Estuary with Mpongwe pupils, they could not retain very many of them in a Christian life or in mission service as teachers, catechists and elders. Mission requirements concerning monogamy, abstinence from alcoholic beverages, a strict Sabbath and not holding slaves conflicted with Mpongwe values and the circumstances of trade in the country. The one Mpongwe pastor whom the mission succeeded in ordaining and retaining in its service, the Reverend Ntâkâ Truman, had a running battle with his American colleagues over what he considered to be unjust and discriminatory financial treatment.

238 **The schools of the American Protestant mission in Gabon (1842-1870).**
David E. Gardinier. *Revue Française d'Histoire d'Outre-Mer*, vol. 75,
no. 2 (1988), p. 168-84 2 maps. bibliog.

The American Board of Commissioners for Foreign Missions of Boston, between 1842 and 1870, laid the foundations of Protestantism in the Gabon Estuary among the Mpongwe, Séké and Bakèlè. With the aid of Afro–American and West African assistants, the white missionaries opened schools to teach both boys and girls religion, numeracy and literacy in both indigenous languages and English, the regional trading language. The circumstances of trade in the Estuary society reinforced local customs such as polygyny, consumption of alcohol and Sabbath work that hindered conversions and retention of converts. Missionary unwillingness to pay Gabonese teachers and other assistants on a par with Afro–American and West African ones indirectly contributed to their departure to take up trade. ABCFM opposition to teaching agriculture and skilled trades, which might have provided alternatives to commerce, further limited Christian influences. Despite these limitations, it was the schools rather than the steady efforts at evangelization among adults that proved to be the main agency in the long term for spreading the Christian gospel among the Estuary peoples.

239 **The environment, establishment and development of Protestant missions in French Equatorial Africa.**
Benjamin A. Hamilton. PhD thesis, Grace Theological Seminary,
Goshen, Indiana, 1959. 353p. bibliog. (Available through interlibrary loan.)

Although this dissertation utilizes only secondary sources for most topics, it provides a clear and detailed account of the establishment of Protestant missions in Gabon and their development from 1842 until the eve of independence in 1960. It describes the efforts of American Protestants in the Estuary beginning in 1842 and in the Ogooué River valley from 1874; of the French Protestants who assumed their work between 1892 and 1913 as a result of official policies inimical to the Americans; and of Americans belonging to the Christian and Missionary Alliance in the N'Gounié River valley from 1934. Attention is given to the relevant international and political contexts in these various periods.

240 **Le Gabon.** (Gabon.)
Etienne Kruger. In: *Histoire des missions protestantes françaises.*
Edited by René Blanc, Jacques Blocher, Etienne Kruger. Flavion,
Belgium: Editions Le Phare, 1970, p. 157-69. map. bibliog.

This is an authoritative brief account of French Protestant missionary efforts from the 1890s to 1961. The Protestants made the most headway among the Fang people of northern Gabon, particularly in the period between the two World Wars.

241 **My Ogowe: being a narrative of daily incidents during sixteen years in equatorial Africa.**
Robert Hamill Nassau. New York: Neale, 1914. 708p. bibliog.

Nassau, who founded the first Protestant mission posts on the lower and middle Ogooué, has produced a volume of recollections that contribute much to the understanding of developments along the river from the mid-1870s through the start of the 1890s. Among the topics treated in rich detail are the planting of Christianity, including the relations between the American missionaries and the various African peoples; European economic penetration, including the role of African agents in the competition for rubber and ivory; the explorations of P. S. de Brazza; the establishment of the French administration and its interference with African trade; and the traditional life of the peoples of the Ogooué.

242 **Tales out of school.**
Robert Hamill Nassau. Philadelphia: Allen, Lane & Scott, 1911. 153p.

This work comprises ten accounts of long-time pupils in the girls' boarding school of the American Protestant mission at Baraka in the Gabon Estuary during the last half of the nineteenth century. They show conflicts that arose in the lives of these women between Christian values expressed in terms of American Calvinism and the values of Mpongwe trading society.

243 **Gabon, un réveil religieux, 1935-37.** (Gabon, a religious awakening, 1935-37.)
André Perrier. Paris: Harmattan, 1988. 240p. bibliog.

This work deals with the so-called Great Revival of the mid-1930s involving possession by the Holy Spirit. It led a French Protestant pastor and his followers to organize Pentecostal churches, today affiliated with the Assemblies of God, separate from the missions of the Paris Evangelical Missions Society.

244 **Robert Hamill Nassau, 1835-1921: Presbyterian pioneer missionary to equatorial West Africa.**
Raymond W. Teeuwissen. MTh thesis, Louisville Presbyterian Theological Seminary, Louisville, Kentucky, 1973. 212p. bibliog. (Available from University Microfilms International, Ann Arbor, Michigan, order no. 1323604.)

Nassau was a pioneering missionary among the Benga, Galoa, Bakèlè and Fang peoples between 1861 and 1898. Though a graduate of the University of Pennsylvania Medical School, Dr. Nassau was not a medical missionary. He established the first Christian mission up the Ogooué River in 1874 (relocated at Lambaréné in 1876) and a second further upstream at Talagouga in 1881. A gifted linguist and talented observer, Nassau was comparatively free of the ethnocentric bias that characterized the attitudes of his peers. His many published volumes and manuscripts form a rich source for the history of these four peoples during the late nineteenth century. His works also contribute to tropical medicine and natural science. Nassau and his sister Isabella also pioneered in the formation of African teachers, catechists and pastors. They struggled to secure a meaningful role for these agents in the face of missionary paternalism and conservatism. Nassau's close friendship with a mission-educated Mpongwe woman who cared for his motherless daughter brought him into conflict with other missionaries.

John Leighton Wilson and the Mpongwe: the 'spirit of 1776' in mid-nineteenth-century Africa.
See item no. 122.

Western Africa: its history, condition, and prospects.
See item no. 134.

Albert Schweitzer

245   Albert Schweitzer: a biography.
James Brabazon.   New York: Putnam, 1975. 509p. bibliog.

This represents the most detailed and complete biography of the missionary doctor who worked at Lambaréné between 1913 and 1917, and again from 1924 until his death in 1965. Schweitzer felt that a western-style hospital had little chance of inducing suffering Gabonese to abandon fetishers and sorcerers. Therefore, he allowed his patients to bring with them to his medical centre members of their families who prepared the patients' food and gave them moral support for getting well. Schweitzer relaxed the standards of hygiene to this end. His methods generated controversy, mainly outside Gabon, as did his views on the capacities of the Africans, which appeared racist. In Gabon itself Schweitzer was much appreciated and beloved by many whom he aided. Some of them were aware of his views but chose to overlook them. Schweitzer's experiences during a half century in the forests of Gabon contributed to the shaping of his ethical humanism (especially the idea of 'respect for life'), which though rooted in liberal Protestant traditions, rested as well on broader and older ones, including some that were African.

246   Albert Schweitzer ou la coopération avant l'heure. (Albert Schweitzer or cooperation before the hour.)
Luc Durand-Réville.   *Comptes Rendus Trimestriels des Séances de l'Académie des Sciences d'Outre-Mer*, vol. 35, no. 2 (1975), p. 307-18.

Dr. Schweitzer established a medical mission at Lambaréné in 1924, which he maintained until his death in 1965, and which he supported through tours in Europe and America speaking and playing the organ. Schweitzer was assisted by volunteers from these lands who worked for subsistence. He received no aid from mission societies nor from governments, only from individuals and groups on several continents who valued his work.

247   Albert Schweitzer: an international bibliography.
Compiled by Nancy Snell Griffith, Laura Person.   Boston: G. K. Hall, 1981. 600p.

This is a bibliography of the writings on the eminent medical missionary, including his long career in Gabon.

248   With Schweitzer in Lambaréné: Noel Gillespie's letters from Africa.
Edited by William C. Haygood.   *Wisconsin Magazine of History*, vol. 54, no. 3 (spring 1971), p. 167-203.

This article presents thirty-three letters of Noel Gillespie, who worked with Schweitzer at Lambaréné in 1923-24, his mother, Emily Rieder, and Dr. Albert Schweitzer, together with related source materials. They contribute to an understanding of the missionary doctor's vision of his work in the forests of Gabon.

Religions and Missions. Albert Schweitzer

249 **Rayonnement d'Albert Schweitzer. 34 études et 100 témoignages.**
(Influence of Albert Schweitzer. Thirty-four studies and one hundred testimonials.)
Edited by Robert Minder. Colmar, France: Alsatia, 1975. 301p.

This volume includes an essay by Minder (p. 75-95) on the reasons why Dr. Schweitzer became a medical missionary in Gabon as well as accounts by his medical associates at Lambaréné (p. 185-282). There is a bibliography of Schweitzer's publications, including those on Africa.

250 **Le docteur Albert Schweitzer et la colonisation.** (Doctor Albert Schweitzer and colonization.)
Moïse Nkoghe-Mve. *Réalités Gabonaises*, no. 38 (1977), p. 21-26.

A Gabonese evaluation of Dr. Schweitzer. Schweitzer not only treated the health problems of the Gabonese; he was their best advocate with the colonial authorities. Schweitzer believed that the interests of civilization did not coincide with those of colonization. In his opinion the Gabonese needed an improved agriculture that would produce more and better food, not employment on European terms. He sought to preserve traditional arts and crafts in order to make the people as self-sufficient as possible. He opposed the introduction of alcohol as destructive of their well-being, but tolerated polygyny until such time as an alternative system of social security could be devised.

251 **On the edge of the primeval forest and More from the primeval forest.**
Albert Schweitzer.: New York: Macmillan, 1956. 222p.

From 1913 to 1917, Dr. Albert Schweitzer, with his wife, Hélène Bresslau, served as a medical missionary at the French Protestant mission at Lambaréné on the lower Ogooué River. Because the Schweitzers, as Alsatians, had retained their German citizenship, they were eventually interned as enemy aliens and returned to Europe. Back at Lambaréné in 1924 Schweitzer built his own hospital away from mission property and earned his expenses through lectures and organ concerts in Europe and from recordings of Bach's works. Schweitzer obtained the most enthusiastic support from liberal Protestants and Unitarians who found his philosophical and theological views attractive. The methods that Schweitzer employed in treating the Gabonese, involving relaxation of hygienic standards in order to attract them away from fetishers and to his facilities, generated controversy outside Africa, as did his views on the Gabonese, which western critics saw as paternalist and racist. The Gabonese who knew of his views chose to overlook them in view of his dedication to their welfare. These two accounts by Schweitzer contain useful observations about life at Lambaréné and work at the hospital between 1913 and 1917, and from 1924 to 1927. They provide clues concerning the evolution of his views which would lead to the philosophy of respect for life in all forms.

252 **Gabon: the Albert Schweitzer Hospital.**
Andreas Steiner. *The Courier* (Brussels), (May–June 1979), p. 30-31.

A description is provided of the multi-donor project involving the European Economic Community with non-government organizations from Switzerland, France, Germany, the Netherlands and the United States to co-finance the building of a new modern Albert Schweitzer Hospital at Lambaréné.

Islam

253 **Muslims in Gabon, West Africa.**
O. H. Kasule. *Journal of the Institute of Muslim and Minority Affairs,*
vol. 6, no. 1 (1985), p. 192-206.

Whereas until the 1970s there were few Gabonese Muslims, in 1985 Islamic sources estimated 3,700. At the same time the numbers of non-Gabonese Muslims had grown from approximately 3,000 to an estimated 30,000. Islam until recently has been a religion of foreigners, mainly of the Senegalese troops imported to sustain French colonial rule from the nineteenth century and of the Hausa traders from northern Nigeria who arrived during the twentieth century. There is no evidence that either group actively sought to spread their Islamic faith to the Gabonese. Most of the 30,000 non-Gabonese Muslims are immigrant workers from the late 1960s through to the mid-1980s. In 1973, during a visit to Libya, President Albert-Bernard Bongo converted to Islam and took the name Omar. Though Bongo emphasized the personal nature of his conversion; thereafter he made official visits to Arab states and Gabon broke relations with Israel. Bongo also encouraged other prominent Gabonese to convert to Islam, which some in high places have done, including his son Alain, who became Ali Bongo. Bongo worships at a large mosque built by Morocco near his presidential palace in Libreville. Moroccans serve as his personal bodyguards. Saudi Arabia, Kuwait and Khomeini's Iran have also built mosques and madrasahs (religious schools for young people and adults) in the main towns. Among the non-Gabonese Muslims, the Mouride brotherhood has the largest following with the Tijani brotherhood second in influence.

Society and Social Issues

General

254 **Contribution à la connaissance et compréhension des populations rurales du nord-est du Gabon.** (Contribution to the understanding and comprehension of the rural populations of the north-east of Gabon.)
Laurent Biffot. Libreville: Centre National de Recherche Scientifique et Technologique, 1977. 239p. bibliog.
This is a study of the rural populations of the Ogooué-Ivindo Province, who were living mainly by subsistence agriculture without effective transportation and communication links to the outside world or very many social services.

255 **La civilisation des peuples Batéké.** (The civilization of the Batéké peoples.)
Claude Cabrol, R. Le Huart. Libreville: Multipresse; Monaco: Paul Bory, 1976. 96p. map. bibliog.
A brief study is made of the traditional life of the Téké people of the Haut-Ogooué Province, the bulk of whom live in the neighbouring Congo Republic.

256 **Notes sur les ethnies de la région du Haut-Ogooué.** (Notes on the ethnic groups of the Haut-Ogooué region.)
Doctor Miletto. *Bulletin de l'Institut d'Études Centrafricaines*, new series, no. 12 (1956), p. 19-48. maps. bibliog.
Descriptions are given of the economic and social life of the peoples of the Haut-Ogooué Province, including the Kota, Bakèlè, Mbédé, Duma and pygmies, and of the impact of the European presence upon them.

257 **La vie des pygmées dans l'Ogooué-Lolo (Lastoursville), Gabon.** (The life of the pygmies in the Ogooue-Lolo [Province], Lastoursville, Gabon.) Benjamin Moualou. *Réalités Gabonaises*, no. 35 (1970), p. 17-25.
This article describes the life of the pygmies including their manner of earning a livelihood, and the impact of modernity among them.

258 **Martin Alihanga, l'apôtre du 'communautarisme'.** (Martin Alihanga, the apostle of 'communitarianism'.) Jean-Pierre Sauvageot. *M'Bolo*, no. 14 (1985), p. 23-31.
Alihanga was born in 1930 at Franceville where his father was a traditional chief. After education in Catholic schools and seminaries, he was ordained a priest in 1960. From 1966 to 1975 he pursued graduate studies in philosophy and the social sciences in Rome, where he earned a doctorate in sociology. In his thesis he advocated what he called 'communitarianism', a social philosophy rooted in the traditional structures and values of the peoples of the Haut-Ogooué Province, but updated in the light of Christian teachings and contemporary needs. Communitarianism is the best way to promote a development that is both morally and materially sound. Since 1976 Alihanga has been teaching at the national university in Libreville and serving in administrative posts. He helped to organize the International Centre for Bantu Civilisations.

259 **Nzabi kinship. A cognitive approach.** Floyd Aaron Shank. PhD thesis, Indiana University, Bloomington, Indiana, 1974. 512p. bibliog. (Available from University Microfilms, Ann Arbor, Michigan, order no. 74-13539.)
This thesis is based on the writer's research among the Nzabi in 1969-71. The Nzabi have thirty-five public kinship categories. Every Nzabi by birth belongs to a single matrilineage but has special relations with three others. Some kinship categories derive from marriage. The study describes the possible mental patterns whereby every Nzabi knows who he is and who is not a relative and whereby it assigns individuals to any and all kinship categories of the Nzabi system.

260 **Masks and social organization among the Bakwele people of western equatorial Africa.** Leon Siroto. PhD thesis, Columbia University, New York, 1969. 341p. bibliog. (Available from University Microfilms, Ann Arbor, Michigan, order no. 7007069.)
This study deals with the special relationships between the use of masks and the dynamics of village organization among the Bakwele. The Bakwele are a Bantu-speaking people living in the rain-forest between the Dja and Ivindo Rivers in north-eastern Gabon. On the eve of European contact their compact villages consisted of small, autonomous segments of widely scattered patrisibs. A strongly developed avunculate conflicted with paternal authority and patrilocal rule, to the extent that choice of residence depended primarily upon the quest for personal advantage. The main advantages sought in village membership were wealth and leadership. In principle, the consensus of the heads of village segments determined village policy, but certain of these, who held special statuses, could markedly, although briefly, influence their peers. Limited access to wealth and leadership led to keen competition among the families composing a village. Moving to another village was a frequent tactic employed

in this quest. The impetus of competition eventually led to two masks being used extra-ritually in the quest for leadership and separate from a system of formal social control. Extra-ritual masking operated exclusively in the struggle for leadership and must therefore be regarded as political, rather than administrative. This finding is at odds with a widely accepted premise that masks invariably played administrative roles when they were used to intervene in the affairs of traditional African societies.

Women and children

261　Être ou ne pas être: quelques sociétés de femme au Gabon. (To be or not to be: some women's societies in Gabon.)
Annie Dupuis. *Objets et Mondes*, vol. 23, no. 1-2 (1983), p. 79-90. bibliog.
Traditional societies for women are examined and their evolution under the impact of recent economic and social development.

262　Quelques représentations relatives à l'enfant de la conception au sevrage chez les Nzébi du Gabon. (Some representations relative to the child from conception to weaning among the Nzabi of Gabon.)
Annie Dupuis. *Journal des Africanistes*, vol. 51, no. 1-2 (1981), p. 117-32. bibliog.
The symbolic function of the nearly constant prescriptions and proscriptions with regard to pregnancy, birth and breast-feeding on sub-Saharan Africa has never been systematically studied. Relevant discourses, if connected with institutions (e.g. marriage, kinship, women's positions), suggest that rules about the period from conception until weaning go beyond birth control. Among the Nzabi the rules seek as well to define the child's matrilineal and patrilineal identity, which is gradually formed by the time of weaning.

263　Les voies nouvelles du développement de la femme gabonaise. (The new ways of the development of the Gabonese woman.)
Isaac Nguema. *Droit et Cultures*, no. 1 (1981), p. 64-88. bibliog.
This article discusses the situation of women in the traditional society of the Ntumu Fang of the north-west. Topics include the life cycle of women, their place in family relationships and the roles of married women. The author wishes to build up traditional foundations in promoting a sound economic and social development in which women will play key roles.

264 **Initiative et pouvoir créateur de la femme. L'exemple du Gabon.**
(Initiative and creative power of woman: the example of Gabon.)
Jeanne Nzaou-Makiba.   In: *La civilisation de la femme dans la
tradition africaine.*   Edited by the Société Africaine de Culture.
Paris: Présence Africaine, 1975, p. 286-95.
The new and positive roles being played by women in a rapidly evolving Gabonese
society are examined.

Health and medicine

265 **Problèmes posés par la lutte contre la trypanosomiase au Gabon.**
(Problems posed by the fight against trypanosomiasis in Gabon.)
P. Le Bigot et al.   *Médecine d'Afrique Noire*, vol. 31, no. 1 (Jan.
1984), p. 31-40. bibliog.
This article deals with the problems of eradicating sleeping sickness, which recurred in
Gabon after elimination during the colonial period.

266 **Evolution de l'alimentation infantile au Gabon: influence de
l'lurbanisation.** (Evolution of infantile nourishment in Gabon: influence
of urbanization.)
Julien Mezu.   *Médecine d'Afrique Noire*, vol. 34 (Aug.–Sept. 1987),
p.735-742. bibliog.
Urbanization in the era of the oil boom has contributed to improved food supplies and
nutrition for city-dwellers, particularly children.

267 **Le CIRMF, phare de la recherche médicale en Afrique.** (The CIRMF
[Centre international de recherche médicale de Franceville], beacon of
medical research in Africa.)
Jean Mori.   *M'Bolo*, no. 16 (1986), p. 20-31.
A description is given of the work of the new international centre for medical research
at Franceville, funded by Elf in part; it is seeking to determine the causes of infertility
and morbidity that for decades made Gabon's rate of population increase among the
smallest in Africa.

268 **Un air du future: avenir santé.** (An air of the future: future health.)
Jean-Pierre Sauvageot.   *M'Bolo*, no. 7 (1983), p. 30-37. bibliog.
This article reviews health care and the recent improvements as a result of the
expansion of health facilities and extension of services to a larger part of the
population. The bulk of facilities and medical personnel are concentrated in the urban
areas, particularly in and around Libreville, despite government efforts to improve
health care nationwide.

269 **Aspects des médecines traditionnelles du Gabon.** (Aspects of traditional medicines of Gabon.)
Alain Wagner. Toulouse, France: Editions Universelles, 1986. 329p. bibliog.

An examination is made of various aspects of traditional medicine and healing techniques among some of Gabon's Bantu peoples.

270 **Department of Pathology, University Centre for Health Sciences, Libreville, 1978-1984.**
P. R. Walter et al. In: *Cancer Occurrence in Developing Countries.* Edited by D. M. Parkin. Lyons, France: International Agency for Research on Cancer, 1986, p. 43-46. bibliog.

This report looks at the incidence and treatment of cancer in Libreville.

The impact of colonialism on health in French Equatorial Africa, 1880-1934.
See item no. 148.

Gabon: the Albert Schweitzer Hospital.
See item no. 252.

Social security

271 **The extension of social protection in the Gabonese Republic: consolidating the development process.**
J. V. Gruat. *International Labour Review*, vol. 123, no. 4 (1984), p. 457-72.

The majority of formerly French countries in sub-Saharan Africa possess relatively well-organized social security schemes for wage earners and public employees but rarely for other groups. The numerically largest categories of the population made up of farmers, petty traders and craftsmen are still not covered in most of these countries. Gabon, however, recently made a praiseworthy stride forward by extending social security coverage (employment injuries, old age, disability, survivors, health care, family allowances, maternity) to all nationals and thus ensured them a reasonable standard of well-being.

272 **The social guarantee in the Gabonese Republic: a new kind of social protection in Africa.**
J. V. Gruat. *International Social Security Review*, vol. 38, no. 2 (1985), p. 157-71. bibliog.

Gabon's rapid economic development during the 1960s and 1970s led to the growth of a wage-earning class representing what was for Africa an exceptionally high percentage of the economically active population. These wage earners and their families were covered by a social security system that protected them against all the traditional contingencies except unemployment. By the act of January 24, 1983, the government introduced a social guarantee scheme to provide health care and family allowances, among other things, for the rest of the population, including the self-employed and the indigent. The organization and administration of this scheme required adaptations to the particular situation of Gabon where a majority of the population lives in some 1,500 villages dispersed throughout the nine provinces.

273 **Social security in Gabon.**
A. Hervo-Akendengué.   In: *African Social Security*.   Geneva: International Labour Organisation, 1967, p. 3-56. bibliog.
This article describes social security provisions in Gabon prior to its oil-based economic expansion of the late 1960s and 1970s

274 **La protection sociale dans les pays francophones d'Afrique au sud du Sahara.** (Social protection in the French-speaking countries of sub-Saharan Africa.)
Otto Kaufmann.   *Revue Juridique et Politique*, vol. 92 (Jan.–Feb. 1988), p. 61-73. bibliog.
This report provides an update on social security legislation and regulations in the late 1980s.

Politics Since 1960

Bongo regime

275 **Omar Bongo ou la racine du mal gabonais.** (Omer Bongo or the root of Gabonese evil.)
Aristote Assam.   Paris: La Pensée Universelle, 1985. 142p. bibliog.

This work provides an exposé on the misdeeds of President Bongo and his associates. It repeats some of the accusations made earlier by Pierre Péan in *Affaires africaines* (q.v.), and provides further details about some of the alleged victims of the regime within Gabon itself.

276 **Gouverner le Gabon.** (To govern Gabon.)
Albert-Bernard [Omar] Bongo.   Monaco: P. Bory, 1968. 139p.

This work records President Bongo's early ideas about governing Gabon, including some texts of speeches.

277 **Le Président Bongo, le Gabon, et le socialisme.** (President Bongo, Gabon and socialism.)
Y. N. Da Gambeg.   *Mois en Afrique*, (Mar.–Apr. 1982), p. 30-47. bibliog.

This article discusses Bongo's contacts with socialists and socialism during his student years in the Congo, where he entered the postal service in 1958. The same year he affiliated with the local socialist party, the Mouvement Socialiste Africain, led by Jacques Opangault, and socialist trade unions. The author argues that despite the appearances of neocolonialism in Bongo's regime, he is promoting economic and social development beneficial to the ordinary person in the socialist reformist tradition.

278 **Démocratie à la gabonaise.** (Democracy in the Gabonese manner.)
Marie-Françoise Janot. *Peuples Noirs, Peuples Africains*, vol. 5
(May–June 1982), p. 29-33.

In two articles entitled 'Spécial Gabon' in *Le Monde* of Paris on January 31 and
February 2, 1981, Philippe Decraene described Gabon as an 'islet of democracy' in a
sea of authoritarian regimes in Africa. The author challenges this view through a
review of the Bongo regime's handling of opponents and critics of its one-party system.
She provides details on the arrest of persons alleged to belong to the opposition party
MORENA. She claims that there are 200 political prisoners in Gabon.

279 **Le Gabon, îlot de prospérité? Réponse à Philippe Decraene du 'Monde'.**
(Gabon, islet of prosperity: reply to Philippe Decraene of 'Le Monde'.)
Marie-Françoise Janot. *Peuples Noirs, Peuples Africains*, vol. 4
(Mar.–Apr. 1981), p. 65-72.

In two articles entitled 'Spécial Gabon', in *Le Monde* of Paris on January 31 and
February 2, 1981, correspondent Decraene spoke of Gabon as an 'islet of prosperity' in
a sea of poverty in Africa. The author replies by indicating the inadequacy of the
education and health care provided to the bulk of the people under the Bongo regime.
She also challenges the rosy picture of economic benefits presented by Decraene.

280 **African patrimonial regimes in comparative perspective.**
Victor T. Levine. *Journal of Modern African Studies*, vol. 18 (Dec.
1980), p. 657-74. bibliog.

A patrimonial regime may be defined as personal rule on the basis of loyalties that do
not require any belief in the ruler's unique personal qualifications but are inextricably
linked to material incentives and rewards. Gabon under President Bongo, like the
Ivory Coast under President Houphouet-Boigny, is seen as a 'neo-patrimonial' regime
in the sense that the ruler is not linked to a traditional polity. Both states pursue
capitalist economic policies enriching a ruling class that controls the bureaucracy and
single party. If a patrimonial regime comes to be perceived as favouring too much a
certain class, ethnic group or region, and disfavouring others, it risks destabilization,
particularly if there are serious failures of leadership or regime performance.

281 **Affaires africaines.** (African affairs.)
Pierre Péan. Paris: Fayard, 1983. 340p.

This exposé deals with the inner workings of the Bongo regime and its links with
France. Despite the author's failure to control his sources on some matters, it provides
generally accurate accounts of French involvement in the affairs of Gabon during the
Fifth Republic and the inner workings of the Bongo regime. The work popularized the
expression *clan des Gabonais*, which refers to the coterie of Frenchmen and Gabonese,
including the extended families of the presidential couple, Omar and Joséphine Bongo,
who exercised power and influence while enriching themselves and their associates.
Péan alleges that members of the clan were responsible for the deaths and attempted
assassinations of presidential rivals and critics of the regime. The case which caused the
greatest sensation was the assassination of a Vietnamese house painter in southern
France on October 27, 1979, for allegedly persisting in his relationship with Madame
Bongo. Incidents relating to this affair were expunged from French police blotters and
the assassins were never apprehended or brought to justice by the officials of the
Giscard regime. The exposé also indicates that France used the Bongo regime to aid

secessionist Biafra, and to trade with the breakaway settler regime in Rhodesia and the Afrikaner National Party government in South Africa. Gabon was used as the base for mercenary forces seeking to overthrow the regimes of Ali Solih in the Comoros and Mathieu Kérékou in Benin.

282 **Le grand retour des barbouzes: le noeud de vipères au Gabon.** (The big return of the hoodlums: the nest of vipers in Gabon.)
Patrick Séry. *Peuples Noirs, Peuples Africains*, (July–Aug. 1986), p. 21-40.

This article in a sense updates some of the activities of the *clan des Gabonais* described in Pierre Péan's *Affaires africaines* (q.v.). Among those discussed are administrators Maurice Delaunay and Maurice Robert; General 'Loulou' Martin, head of the presidential guard; Georges Conan, the septuagenarian heading the Centre de Documentation (Gabon's FBI), and Jean-Pierre Rognan, director of the Gros-Bouquet prison, in which MORENA members were allegedly tortured. The article shows that the involvement of French interests dating from the Gaullist presidential era persists in the political and economic life of Gabon despite the coming to power of a Socialist–Communist coalition headed by François Mitterrand.

Le république gabonaise: treize années d'histoire. (The Gabonese Republic: thirteen years of history.)
See item no. 179.

Gabon: a neo-colonial enclave of enduring French interest.
See item no. 333.

MORENA

283 **Gabon: déni de justice au cours d'un procès.** (Gabon: denial of justice in the course of a trial.)
Amnesty International. Paris: Editions Francophones de l'Amnesty International, 1984. 112p.

In February 1982 260 persons were arrested for membership in the opposition party, Mouvement pour le Redressement National (MORENA) or participation in its activities. Thirty-seven of them were brought to trial between November 10 and 26. Thirty of the thirty-seven were Fang or Bapounou. The majority were government employees. Most of those arrested were mistreated in various ways, including being kept unclothed and not having proper food and medical care. Nearly all were beaten and some were tortured, often in the presence of high government officials. Those brought to trial were not given the opportunity for proper legal defence. The special court that tried them denied their attorneys access to data essential to their defence. The government failed to present evidence to substantiate its charge that MORENA members were planning to overthrow the regime by violent means. Nevertheless, twenty-nine of the defendants were convicted. The thirteen convicted of threatening state security as well as illegally constituting a political party and insulting the president were sentenced to twenty years of hard labour. The remaining sixteen, including journalists who had reported the events, received lesser sentences. This report, prepared by Attorney Bacre Waly N'Diaye of Senegal, noted the various injustices and concluded that the twenty-nine had committed no crimes. They had been condemned for their opinions and should be released.

284 **Gabon: les visages d'une opposition.** (Gabon: the faces of an opposition.)
  Francis Doey. *Politique Africaine*, vol. 3 (Sept. 1983), p. 13-29.
This article provides an introduction to the Mouvement pour le Redressement National (MORENA), followed by an interview with its leader, the Reverend Paul Mba-Abessole, and a copy of its programme.

285 **Pages gabonaises.** (Gabonese pages.)
  Frédéric Trautmann. *Journal des Missions Evangéliques*, vol. 159 (Apr. 1984), p. 23-38. bibliog.
This is the report of a French Protestant missionary representative on the arrest and trial of thirty-seven persons accused of belonging to the illegal opposition party, MORENA. He points out the unfairness of the procedures used to secure indictments and convictions as well as the real lack of evidence to support the government's claim that the accused were seeking a violent overthrow of the regime. This was particularly true in the case of Jean-Marc Ekoh (b. 1929), a leader of the Evangelical Church and former cabinet minister, who was sentenced to hard labour.

Reforms of 1990

286 **Le Gabon à la recherche d'un nouvel ethos politique et social.** (Gabon in search of a new political and social ethos.)
  François Gaulme. *Politique Africaine*, (Oct. 1991), p. 50-62. bibliog.
The events of 1990 and 1991 resulted in the abandonment of the single-party system established in March 1968 and the re-establishment of a multi-party system involving the restoration of democracy and the exercise of civil liberties. As a result of the elections of September–October 1990, the Parti Démocratique Gabonais (Gabonese Democratic Party) managed to retain a small majority in the National Assembly and control of the government. But its support was now concentrated among regional and local notables throughout the nine provinces, except in President Bongo's home province, the Haut-Ogooué, where it won all of the seats. Two important opposition parties emerged, the Mouvement pour le Redressement National (MORENA) (Movement for National Recovery) and the Parti Gabonais du Progrès (PGP) (Gabonese Progress Party), headed respectively by the Reverend Paul Mba-Abessolé, a Roman Catholic priest, and Maître Paul-Louis Agondjo-Okawe, head of the bar and university professor. MORENA won its largest support in the northern half of the country, particularly among the Fang people, the lower middle class, and members of Christian churches. The PGP, which had socialist and secularist orientations, won greatest support in the coastal regions and particularly among the Myènè of the Ogooué-Maritime Province. While the political changes took place peacefully for the

most part, they also involved popular demonstrations and an outburst of extended violence at Port-Gentil in May 1990 that led to French military intervention.

287   **La 'conférence nationale' gabonaise; du congrès constitutif du**
      Rassemblement Social Démocrate Gabonais (RSDG) aux assises pour la
      démocratie pluraliste. (The Gabonese 'national conference' from the
      constituent congress of the Gabonese Social and Democratic
      Assemblage (GSDA) to the assizes for pluralist democracy.)
      Charles M'Ba.   *Afrique 2000*, no. 7 (Nov. 1991), p. 75-90. bibliog.

Mounting protests resulting from economic belt-tightening influenced President Bongo to try to widen the base of support for his regime by including opposition parties, hitherto outlawed, in the national conference he summoned to discuss political reform. The conference, which met in Libreville between late March and late April 1990, established the principles for constitutional and institutional changes involving the restoration of multi-partyism and the re-establishment of the exercise of civil liberties. But the national conference was in no sense a sovereign body and Bongo and his associates were left to implement its recommendations as they saw fit. Thus Gabon has acquired a multi-party political system and a climate of free expression in speech and press but the overpowering executive of the previous quarter of a century continues to rule the country.

Constitutional and Legal Systems

288 **Les institutions constitutionnelles de la République gabonaise.** (The constitutional institutions of the Gabonese Republic.)
S. M. Ajami.   Libreville: Faculté de Droit et Sciences Economiques, 1976. 2nd ed. 118p. bibliog.

This text examines the constitutional provisions affecting the political institutions of the Gabonese Republic up to and including 1976.

289 **Les institutions constitutionnelles du présidentialisme gabonais.** (The constitutional institutions of Gabonese presidentialism.)
S. M. Ajami.   *Revue Juridique et Politique*, vol. 29 (Oct.–Nov. 1975), p. 436-66. bibliog.

This article discusses the constitutional provisions concerning the presidency within the political system.

290 **Tables des textes gabonais publiés au Ier juillet 1975 dans les journaux officiels des années 1967 à 1975.** (Tables of Gabonese texts published up to July 1, 1975, in the official journals of the years 1967 to 1975.)
Compiled by M. Guermann.   Libreville: Université Nationale Gabonaise, 1976. 102, 37p.

Indexes to laws, decrees, and regulations of the Gabonese state from 1967 to 1975 are included.

291   **Le processus de concentration des pouvoirs par le président de la**
      République au Gabon. (The process of concentration of powers by the
      president of the Gabonese Republic.)
      François Hervouet.   *Penant*, vol. 93 (Jan.–Mar. 1983), p. 5-35, and
      (Apr.–June 1983), p. 200-15. bibliog.

This is an excellent exposition and analysis of the process by which President Omar
Bongo became an all-powerful head of state, government and the single political party.
The constitutional, political and institutional dimensions are discussed with much
clarity and perspicacity.

292   **De l'histoire du droit au droit comparé: l'example du droit commercial**
      applicable au Gabon. (From the history of the law to comparative law:
      the example of commercial law applicable to Gabon.)
      Eric Lepointe.   *Penant*, vol. 101, no. 806 (June–Oct. 1991), p. 214-36;
      no. 807 (Oct.–Dec. 1991), p. 343-66.

Gabon inherited its commercial law from France. Even thirty years after independence
the law is not becoming Gabonized, that is, adapted to the evolving situation of
commerce in Gabonese society. Instead, legislators, administrators and judges treat
commercial law as if Gabon were part of France and in almost complete isolation from
Gabonese society, which lessens the usefulness of the law and leads to an uncertain
application.

293   **Essai du droit coutumier pahouin.** (Essay on Fang customary law.)
      Léon Mba.   *Bulletin de la Société des Recherches Congolaises*, no. 25
      (1938), 5-51.

This article describes Fang customary law as it was administered under French rule in
the Estuary Province between the two World Wars.

294   **Le Parti Démocratique Gabonais et l'état.** (The Gabonese Democratic
      Party and the state.)
      N'Dong Obiang.   *Penant*, vol. 93 (Apr.–June 1983), p. 131-52.
      bibliog.

This is an important article for understanding the constitutional and legal bases for the
single party's involvement in the political process in Gabon since March 1968.

295   **Répertoire alphabétique des textes législatifs et réglementaires du Gabon**
      (1961-1974). (Alphabetical list of legislative and regulatory texts of
      Gabon, 1961-1974).
      Compiled by the Centre de Recherche, d'Etude et de Documentation
      sur les Institutions et les Législations Africaines.   Dakar: CREDILA,
      1976. 192p.

This is an index to laws, decrees and regulations of the Gabonese government from
1961 to 1974.

Administration and Local Government

296 **Les communes, les assemblées départementales et provinciales gabonaises: une décentralisation territoriale effective?** (The Gabonese communes, departmental and provincial assemblies: an effective territorial decentralization?)
J. P. Kombila. *Penant*, vol. 100, no. 803 (1990),p. 236-45. bibliog.
In the last half of the 1980s the Bongo regime tried to increase popular support by activating representative bodies at the level of the provinces, departments and communes. These bodies did not function well because of the nature of a one-party regime and a tradition of centralized decision-making.

297 **L'administration gabonaise.** (Gabonese administration.)
Max Remondo. Paris: Berger-Levrault, 1974. 54p. bibliog.
This work presents a discussion of the French-derived administrative system, its structures and functioning.

298 **Le droit administratif gabonais.** (The Gabonese administrative law.)
Max Remondo. Paris: Librairie Générale de Droit et de Jurisprudence, 1987. 303p. bibliog.
This provides a detailed study of Gabonese administrative law.

Military Affairs

299   **La contribution des forces armées et de sécurité à la stabilité de l'état gabonais de 1967 à 1989.** (The contribution of the armed forces and security [forces] to the stability of the Gabonese state from 1967 to 1989.)
Dominique Bangoura.   *Cahiers de l'Institut Pan-Africain de Géopolitique*, (Dec. 1989), p. 6-38. bibliog.
A discussion is undertaken of the evolution of the armed forces and security forces under the presidency of Omar Bongo. In the aftermath of the appearance and suppression of MORENA in 1981-82, the regime increased the size of the presidential guard and upgraded its weaponry.

300   **Le capitaine Charles N'Tchoréré.** (Captain Charles N'Tchoréré.)
Louis Bigmann.   Abidjan: Nouvelles Editions Africaines, 1983. 131p. bibliog.
Charles N'Tchoréré (1896-1940), an Mpongwe from Libreville, spent a lifetime in French military service during which, in 1927, he became one of the few African commissioned officers. As a captain commanding a company during the battle of the Somme in 1940, he fought valiantly; he was killed by a German Panzer officer because he insisted on being treated as a French officer and refused to obey the order to fall in line with the black enlistees. His eldest son, Jean-Baptiste, who had followed his father's footsteps in becoming a soldier, was killed in action on the lower Somme a week later. N'Tchoréré's career and conduct show strong loyalty to France and its values of a kind that service in the colonial army often produced among its African members.

301 **La politique militaire de la France en Afrique.** (The military policy of France in Africa.)
Pascal Chaigneau. Paris: CHEAM, 1984. 147p. bibliog.
This provides a clear and concise presentation of the evolution of France's military policy in sub-Saharan Africa. Under terms of cooperation agreements made at independence and subsequently renewed, France maintains a base near Libreville and can intervene militarily in defence of the regime if requested.

302 **Cinquième République et défense de l'Afrique.** (Fifth Republic and defence of Africa.)
John Chipman. Paris: Editions Bosquet, 1986. 151p. bibliog.
This volume discusses the French African security system, its historical context and recent evolution, and Franco–African military relations.

303 **French military policy and African security.**
John Chipman. *Adelphi Papers*, no. 201 (1985),p. 1-51. bibliog.
This article describes the evolution of France's military policy, including in the early years of the Mitterrand presidency, and its impact on Gabon.

304 **Histoire militaire de l'Afrique Equatoriale Française.** (Military history of French Equatorial Africa.)
Edited by Martin J. M. Denis. Paris: Imprimerie Officielle, 1931, p. 84-124. bibliog.
This gives an official account of French military operations in Gabon, including those of the First World War.

305 **Colonial conscripts. The 'tirailleurs sénégalais' in French West Africa, 1857-1960.**
Myron Echenberg. Portsmouth, New Hampshire: Heinemann; London: James Currey, 1991. 236p. bibliog.
This work contains data on the black Africans who served in the French colonial armies, particularly in French West Africa. It includes an account of the career of Captain Charles N'Tchoréré (1897-1940), a Gabonese who became one of the few high-ranking African officers in these forces during the 1930s. N'Tchoréré was assassinated by a German officer for refusing an order to stand with black enlistees and insisting on the treatment due to a French officer. His life and career exemplify the kind of attachment to France and its culture that grew up among many African fighting men in colonial service.

306 **French militarism in Africa.**
Robin Luckham. *Review of African Political Economy*, (May 1982), p. 55-84. bibliog.
This is an excellent introduction to French military involvement in sub-Saharan Africa under French Presidents de Gaulle, Pompidou and Giscard d'Estaing.

307 **The military balance.**
London: International Institute for Strategic Studies, 1959- . annual.
The section on Gabon has detailed data on the armed forces and military equipment.

308 **La spécifité de l'armée gabonaise.** (The specificity of the Gabonese army.)
Idriss Ngari. In: *Les armées africaines.* Paris: Economica for the Institut Africain d'Etudes Stratégiques, 1986, p. 51-55. bibliog.
The Gabonese armed forces are here seen through the eyes of their commander.

309 **La coopération militaire de l'Afrique noire avec les puissances: (1) avec la France; (2) avec l'U.R.S.S. et les Etats-Unis.** (Military cooperation of Black Africa with the powers: [1] with France; [2] with the USSR and the USA.)
Romain Yakemtchouk. *Afrique contemporaine*, vol. 22 (July–Sept. 1983), p. 3-18; (Oct.–Dec. 1983), p. 3-22.
Gabon is included in this review of France's arrangements for military cooperation with its former sub-Saharan possessions. Gabon has received very limited military assistance from the United States in the training of personnel and in equipment.

Echec aux militaires au Gabon en 1964. (Failure for the military in Gabon in 1964.)
See item no. 178.

French power in Africa.
See item no. 326.

External Relations Since 1960

General

310 **The OPEC market to 1985.**
Farid Abolfathi, [et al.]. Lexington, Massachusetts; Toronto:
Lexington Books, 1977. 407p. bibliog.
This work on OPEC (Organization of Petroleum Exporting Countries) discusses the global oil market in the late 1970s and projections for the 1980s. It devotes a chapter to the place of oil production in Gabon's economy.

311 **Le Gabon à l'ONU.** (Gabon at the United Nations Organization.)
Emmanuel Mba Allo. *M'Bolo*, no. 15 (1986), p. 30-41.
This is a review of Gabon's policies on international questions expressed through the United Nations and its participation in that organization's agencies and activities.

312 **La convention de Lomé III.** (The convention of Lomé III.)
Revue du Marché Commun, (Apr. 1986), p. 183-235. bibliog.
This article discusses in detail the agreement that regulates Gabon's relations with the European Community. Included are the various benefits, privileges, and sources of aid and assistance that derive from associate status.

313 **Quatrième convention de Lomé: continuité et innovation.** (Fourth Lomé convention: continuity and innovation.)
Laurent Delahousse. *Afrique Contemporaine*, vol. 33 (July 1991),
p. 52-66. bibliog.
A discussion of the provisions of the Fourth Lomé Convention, ratified in 1990, which governs the relationship between the European Community and its associate members in Africa, the Caribbean and the Pacific.

314 **Impact of American aid and trade on resource development of Gabon.**
Lynn Harris Distelhorst. MA thesis, George Washington University,
Washington, DC, 1969. 260p. bibliog. (Available on interlibrary
loan.)
During the late 1950s and 1960s Americans began to invest in the development of
manganese, iron (which could not be brought to production) and petroleum in Gabon.
The USA became Gabon's second most important trading partner after France.

315 **The Lomé conventions: entering a second decade.**
A. Hewitt. *Journal of Common Market Studies*, vol. 23, no. 1 (1984),
p. 95-115. bibliog.
Gabon is an associate member of the European Common Market. This article
evaluates the evolution of the associates' relations with the community members.

316 **Aid from the Federal Republic of Germany to Africa.**
Rolf Hofmeier. *Journal of Modern African Studies*, vol. 24 (Dec.
1986), p. 577-602. bibliog.
As a result of the creation of the European Common Market in 1956, the Federal
Republic began to aid, assist and invest in France's territories in sub-Saharan Africa.
This process continued and expanded after their independence in 1960. German
interests were involved in the construction of the Trans-Gabon Railway.

317 **The CFA franc zone after 1973: burden or benefit for the African
members.**
Cord Jacobeit. *Afrika Spectrum*, vol. 21, no. 1 (1986), p. 257-72.
bibliog.
A discussion is made of the issues involved in the African states' membership in a
monetary union with France that offers advantages but restricts their freedom of
action.

318 **La convention de Lomé.** (The Lomé convention.)
Giorgio Maganza. Brussels: Université Libre de Bruxelles, 1990.
406p. bibliog.
This is an up-to-date study of the convention that regulates the relations between the
members of the European Community and the associate members in Africa, the
Caribbean and the Pacific. The functioning of the system is discussed up until the eve
of the negotiations for the fourth convention.

319 **Africa and the ideology of Eurafrica: neo-colonialism or pan-
Africanism?**
Guy Martin. *Journal of Modern African Studies*, vol. 20, no. 2 (June
1982), p. 221-38. bibliog.
The continued state of underdevelopment and dependency in Africa, despite the
continent's enormous wealth and tremendous economic potential, results from the
nature of the political, economic and cultural links that have tied Africa to Europe
since the fifteenth century. Trade, based on unequal exchange and specialization,

constitutes the mainstay of this relationship today as in the past. The ideology of Eurafrica, based on the two concepts of 'complementarity' and 'interdependence' appears as a convenient justification for neocolonialism and helps to explain various contractual relationships between Africa and Europe since independence. The new mechanisms of the conventions of Yaoundé and Lomé institutionalize Africa's dependency, strictly control its development and better organize its exploitation. The ideology of Eurafrica appears as the rationalization of the neoclassical theory of international development and contemporary international division of labour. Ultimately continental economic and political integration offers the best prospects for extricating Africa from the neocolonial predicament in which it presently finds itself and attaining genuine and complete independence.

320 **The franc zone: underdevelopment and dependency in francophone Africa.**
Guy Martin. *Third World Quarterly*, vol. 8 (Jan. 1986), p. 205-235. bibliog.

An analysis is made of the origin, structure and functioning of the franc zone system, and an assessment of its legal, political and economic consequences for its African member-states from the perspective of dependency theory. Through the franc zone mechanism, the African states have delegated all their financial and monetary responsibilities and, therefore, control of their economies to France. Frenchmen continue to make the important decisions on matters that should rightly be in African hands.

321 **The exclusive economic zone: state practice in the African Atlantic region.**
S. K. B. Mfodwo, [et al.]. *Ocean Development and International Law*, vol. 20, no. 5 (1989), p. 445-99. bibliog.

This study explores the implementation process of the Law of the Sea Convention relating to marine living resources in the exclusive economic zone (EEZ) of those African states facing the Atlantic Ocean. From a legal perspective it surveys the principal aspects of state practice between the African Atlantic Coastal States (AACS) and the Distant Water Fishing States (DWFS) active in this part of the Atlantic. Gabon is one of twenty-four states lying on the Atlantic coastline of Africa. The AACS are actively implementing the EEZ concept in their relations with the DWFS. The process of implementation, however, is selective so as to ensure that what passes into the new general customary law generated by their activity are the broad generalizable aspects of the treaty norm rather than the specific details of the treaty text. Thus, African Atlantic state practice with regard to the EEZ would seem to lend factual support to the increasingly dominant view that the EEZ concept, viewed as a broad principle, is now part of general customary international law.

322 **The decline of the franc zone: monetary politics in francophone Africa.**
Nicolas van de Walle. *African Affairs* (London), vol. 90, no. 4 (1991), p. 383-405. bibliog.

Between independence and the mid-1980s the countries of the franc zone enjoyed lower rates of inflation, greater economic stability and access to higher level of imports than most African states though they did not have significantly higher levels of growth. Since 1986 the economic problems of the franc zone states have worsened, especially with the oil crisis, the collapse in commodity prices, and the appreciation of the French franc in relation to the US dollar. Eight of the fourteen countries in the zone (including Gabon) have severe debt problems, with substantial payment arrears, and all but two have International Monetary Fund programmes. The regional central banks, including the Bank of the Central African States, today face crises of such dimensions that only the French Treasury's monthly infusion of capital is keeping the banking systems solvent. Political regimes long regarded as stable have been experiencing upheaval in 1990 and 1991. One-party states have made belated and ambiguous promises of political liberalization in an attempt to salvage extremely shaky regimes. In the present circumstances the various mechanisms of the franc zone allow the African regimes to postpone reforms, confident that France will bail them out. Reforms would be especially difficult to undertake because they would have to be at the expense of the urban elements and civil servants that provide the greatest support for present regimes.

Le Gabon et son ombre. (Gabon and its shadow.)
See item no. 5.

Problèmes actuels de main d'oeuvre au Gabon: conditions d'une immigration controlée. (Present manpower problems in Gabon: conditions of a controlled immigration.)
See item no. 397.

France

323 **La France face au sud: le miroir brisé.** (France faces to the south: a broken mirror.)
Jacques Adda, Marie-Claude Smouts. Paris: Karthala, 1989. 363p. bibliog.
This is a perceptive study of France's African policy in historical perspective that gives considerable attention to the period of Mitterrand and the French Left since 1981.

324 **La France et le Tiers-Monde: vingt ans de coopération bilatérale.** (France and the Third World: twenty years of bilateral cooperation.)
Patrick Cadenat. Paris: Documentation Française, Notes et Etudes Documentaires, 1983. 204p. bibliog.
This is an account of the implementation of the French policy of cooperation through bilateral agreements with African states on a variety of matters – foreign affairs, defence, strategic materials, economy, education and culture.

325 **French African policy: towards change.**
Tony Chafer. *African Affairs* (London), vol. 91, no. 1 (1992), p. 37-51. bibliog.
The deterioration of the economic situation of sub-Saharan Africa in the late 1980s led to a reassessment of the economic costs of French African policy and the political benefits that it is said to bring. It has come to be recognized that maintenance of the French presence has become a serious economic burden which France cannot continue

to bear singlehandedly. The French government is thus seeking greater help from the European Community and other western nations while private investors are shifting to more profitable markets in South-East Asia and the Maghreb. There has also been increasing questioning in France of the political benefits from propping up unpopular African regimes. The use to which French aid is being put is questioned with the conclusion that it is contributing more to unrest than to development. France is no longer treating its clients in Black Africa as a bloc. In recent years it has concentrated its activity in certain traditionally close allies, such as Gabon, Senegal and Côte d'Ivoire. France's economic role may decrease even in these countries but its military role is likely to be maintained for reasons of strategy, grandeur and the French self-image as a world power. Signs exist that France is cultivating a closer relationship with Nigeria. The franc zone is now a millstone for the French treasury because of balance of payments deficits. France is placing increased emphasis on democratic reforms as a condition of continued aid to its African clients. Political and economic union with Europe in 1993 will make it harder for France to play its traditional role in Africa, even if it wishes to do so.

326 French power in Africa.
John Chipman.   Oxford: Basil Blackwell, 1989. 289p. 3 maps. bibliog.
This represents the most comprehensive and up-to-date examination of French involvement in Africa since 1960 in historical perspective. The military, strategic, economic and diplomatic dimensions of the French presence receive particular attention. Material on Gabon is scattered throughout the various chapters. Unfortunately the work mistakenly attributes a role to Jean-Hilaire Aubame in the military coup of February 1964 which led to the short-lived provisional government that he was summoned to head.

327 The French presence in Black Africa.
Edward M. Corbett.   Washington, DC: Black Orpheus Press, 1972. 209p. bibliog.
This is a detailed examination of France's involvement in its former Black African territories in the decade after their independence. It shows the persistence of important French economic, strategic and cultural interests, generally with the support of the Gabonese ruling class.

328 France in Gabon since 1960.
David E. Gardinier.   *Proceedings of the French Colonial Historical Society*, vol. 6-7 (1982), p. 65-75. bibliog.
A review is made of continuing French involvement in Gabon during the first two decades after independence and of Gabon's relations with France under Presidents de Gaulle, Pompidou and Giscard d'Estaing. At independence Gabon lacked the means to develop further its resources in timber, manganese, uranium and petroleum. It required the assistance of expatriate personnel to assure the functioning of its government, administration, schools and economy. In these circumstances Gabon turned to France, which remained its most important source of investment capital, aid and assistance, and its chief trading partner. France also promoted the entrance of capital from its Common Market partners and the United States, generally in cooperation with French interests and never in competition with them, to develop Gabon's natural resources. France influenced the course of Gabonese history by its military intervention in February 1964 to suppress an army coup against President

Léon Mba, which permitted him to install a repressive authoritarian regime against the wishes of the people and to transfer it to his chosen successor. Gabon retained military ties with France under which French forces were based at Libreville and were ready to intervene again if requested by the government of Gabon. Gabon chose to preserve an educational system that was almost identical to that of France, and thus required a contingent of French teachers at all but the primary level to be maintained.

329 **Le Gabon de 1984 et ses relations avec la France: la prosperité et les malentendus.** (The Gabon of 1984 and its relations with France: prosperity and misunderstandings.)
François Gaulme. *Marchés tropicaux et Méditerranéens*, vol. 40 (Feb. 17, 1984), p. 359-67.
This offers a perceptive discussion of the impact of the oil boom on Gabon and of the souring of relations with France over the Mitterrand regime's refusal to muzzle the press's criticisms of the alleged misdeeds of Bongo and his associates.

330 **Les accords de coopération entre la France et les états africains et malgache d'expression française.** (The cooperation agreements between France and the African and Malagasy states of French expression.)
Maurice Ligot. Paris: Documentation Française, 1964. 187p.
This item contains the texts of the agreements that Gabon made at independence with France and the other states of former French Equatorial Africa for cooperation in such matters as foreign policy; defence and strategic materials; education and culture; monetary policy and currency; and economic, financial and technical assistance.

331 **The historical, economic, and political bases of France's African policy.**
Guy Martin. *Journal of Modern African Studies*, vol. 23, no. 2 (June 1985), p. 189-208. bibliog.
This introduction to France's African policy under Socialist President François Mitterrand shows the continuities with the earlier regimes of the Fifth Republic. The policy of *coopération* has allowed France to pursue its economic, strategic and cultural interests in its former sub-Saharan African possessions while bringing some benefits to their inhabitants.

332 **Uranium: a case-study in Franco–African relations.**
Guy Martin. *Journal of Modern African Studies*, vol. 27, no. 4 (1989), p. 625-40. bibliog.
Since the late 1950s France has had privileged access to the uranium resources of Gabon which it developed through the Compagnie des Mines d'Uranium de Franceville (COMUF). In 1989 France owned 60 per cent of COMUF's stock and the Gabonese state held 25 per cent. During the late 1980s Gabon was supplying one-sixth of France's needs in uranium, Niger two-thirds, and South Africa and Namibia one-sixth. Despite unfavourable world market conditions French interests have been undertaking exploration for additional deposits in the vicinity of Franceville and Mounana in the Haut-Ogooué Province. Through this exploration France is seeking not only to ensure its long-term needs for nuclear energy but also to prepare for the possible loss of uranium supplies from South Africa and Namibia as those states move towards black-majority rule.

333 **Gabon: a neo-colonial enclave of enduring French interest.**
Michael Charles Reed. *Journal of Modern African studies*, vol. 25,
no. 2 (1987), p. 283-320. bibliog.
A detailed account in historical perspective is given of French involvement in Gabon
during the presidency of Omar Bongo. While the focus is upon France's protection and
advancement of its economic, strategic and cultural interests, there are useful insights
concerning the country's internal political evolution and foreign relations.

334 **Dominance-dependence relationships: the case of France and Gabon.**
Joan Edelman Spero. PhD thesis, Columbia University, New York,
1973. 483p. bibliog. (Available from University Microfilms, Ann
Arbor, Michigan, order no. 74-1518.)
This thesis examines the relations between France and Gabon in terms of dominance
and dependence. In spite of Gabon's legal independence and international sovereignty,
France was able to make or to participate in a significant number of important
decisions for Gabon. These decisions concerned: economic development; military,
foreign and educational policy; and élite selection. Dominance-dependence exists not
merely as a colonial residue but as an ongoing and active interest for both parties in the
relationship. The French have multiple interests, both public and private, as well as
foreign policy concerns of major importance. France provided Gabon with the means
for economic development and political stability. The very complex means for French
dominance include transnational ties dating from the colonial period as well as
interstate ties adapted to the post-independence era. The relationship is thus not just a
colonial residue although the colonial experience is the key to understanding the
relationship. The dominance-dependence relationship is likely to persist for the
foreseeable future as a result of mutual interest as well as powerful French means for
perpetuating prerogatives in Gabonese decision-making.

335 **Francophone Africa: the enduring French connection.**
Martin Staniland. *Annals of the American Academy of Political and
Social Sciences*, vol. 489 (Jan. 1987), p. 51-62. bibliog.
This article gives a perceptive overview of France's relations with its former
possessions in Africa since their independence in 1960.

African betrayal.
See item no. 180.

French-speaking Africa since independence.
See item no. 182.

Léon Mba: the ideology of dependence.
See item no. 184.

Affaires africaines. (African affairs.)
See item no. 281.

Le grand retour des barbouzes: le noeud de vipères au Gabon. (The big return
of the hoodlums: the nest of vipers in Gabon.)
See item no. 282.

Economic development – does aid help? A case study of French development assistance to Gabon.
See item no. 362.

The rigid embrace of dependency: France and Black African education since 1960.
See item no. 418.

Africanisation, enseignement, et coopération bilatérale française.
See item no. 423.

Africa

336 **L'expulsion des Béninois du Gabon.** (The expulsion of Benin citizens from Gabon.)
Jocelyn Akoumondo.   *Peuples Noirs, Peuples Africains*, vol. 1, no. 5 (1978), p. 60-64.

Citizens of the Republic of Benin (formerly Dahomey) played an important role in the decades after the Second World War by staffing clerical and commercial jobs, in particular, for which no Gabonese were available. In the wake of accusations by President Mathieu Kérékou that Gabon was involved in a plot to overthrow him, President Bongo expelled the many thousands of workers from Benin and their families. He exempted only those who had contracts with the government.

337 **OCAM: one scene in the drama of West African development.**
Richard A. Fredland.   In: *African regional organizations.*   Edited by Domenico Mazzeo.   Cambridge, England: Cambridge University Press, 1984, p. 103-30. bibliog.

The fourteen former French territories in sub-Saharan Africa and Madagascar achieved independence in circumstances that involved the demise of the federations of French West Africa and French Equatorial Africa. France encouraged them to form new regional and intra-African organizations that would promote their mutual interests. One important organization among the francophone states, including Gabon, was the Organisation Commune Africaine et Malgache (African and Malagasy Common Organization), which was formed in 1965 to replace earlier organizations and which continued to function into the 1980s. OCAM promoted various kinds of economic and technical cooperation, including the operation of Air Afrique, as well as policy coordination. But it did not advance political unification, which was not desired by most member-states. Information is also provided on all the various ties which the francophone states developed with one another from 1957 onward.

338   **UDEAC: dream or the making of subimperial states.**
Nantang Jua.   *Afrika Spectrum*, vol. 21, no. 2 (1986), p. 211-23.
bibliog.

UDEAC (Union Douanière et Economique de l'Afrique Centrale/Central African
Customs and Economic Union) has remained moribund because the wealthiest
members, Cameroon and Gabon, have pursued autocentric development policies of
which they are the main beneficiaries. Increased trade among the members of UDEAC
has occurred mainly in manufacturing, which has benefited those two states the most
while further marginalizing such partners as the Central African Republic and Chad.
Jua interprets this situation in terms of a dependency theory that sees Cameroon and
Gabon as part of the semi-periphery of the world economic system and the other
members as part of the periphery.

339   **La Communauté Économique des États d'Afrique Centrale**
(C.E.E.A.C.): une communauté de plus. (The Economic Community of
the Central African States: one more community.)
Maurice Kamto.   *Annuaire Français de Droit International*, vol. 33
(1987), p. 833-62. bibliog.

The background is given to the creation of the Economic Community of the States of
Central Africa in 1983 and the provisions of the agreement that seeks to promote
heightened relations among them. The community includes not only the five former
French states which since 1964 had formed a customs and economic union but former
Belgian, Spanish and Portuguese territories.

340   **Islands and the delimitation of the continental shelf: a framework for**
analysis.
Donald E. Karl.   *American Journal of International Law*, vol. 8, no. 4
(Oct. 1977), p. 642-73. bibliog.

Disputes arose between Gabon and Equatorial Guinea during the early 1970s over
ownership of certain offshore islands that may be oil-bearing. This article includes a
consideration of this issue in a discussion of the principles that might be followed for
equitable solutions to such situations.

341   **Un problème en suspens: la frontière entre Gabon et Guinée**
Equatoriale. (A problem in suspension: the frontier between Gabon
and Equatorial Guinea.)
Max Liniger-Goumaz.   *Genève–Afrique*, vol. 26, no. 1 (1988), p. 113-
22.

This bibliography contains 177 articles and books dealing with long-standing boundary
dispute, particularly over offshore islands which are thought to contain oil. Included
are works discussing the early cartography of the region, the nineteenth-century
boundaries demarcated by France and Spain, and contemporary diplomacy between
Gabon and Equatorial Guinea.

342 **A review of regional economic integration in Africa with particular reference to equatorial Africa.**
N. L. Marasinghe. *International and Comparative Law Quarterly*, vol. 33, no. 1 (Jan. 1984), p. 39-56. bibliog.
A review is given of the arrangements for economic integration among the four equatorial African states and Cameroon within the overall African context.

343 **African regional organizations.**
Edited by Domenico Mazzeo. Cambridge, England: Cambridge University Press, 1985. 265p. bibliog.
Several of the chapters in this collective work have value for understanding Gabon's place within regional and international organizations that have had an impact on its economic and financial well-being or its external political ties. Among these organizations are the United Nations Economic Commission for Africa, the African Development Bank and the African Development Fund. A chapter on the Economic Community of West African States, the European Economic Community (EEC) and the Lomé Convention also has importance, for while Gabon does not belong to that community, it is an affiliate of the EEC with whom its relationship is defined by the Lomé Convention. [There are separate entries for the chapters on OCAM and UDEAC in this volume.]

344 **Les difficultés de l'intégration économique inter-régionale en Afrique noire: l'exemple de la zone UDEAC.**
(The difficulties of inter-regional economic integration in Black Africa: the example of the UDEAC zone.)
Dieudonné Mouafo. *Cahiers d'Outre-Mer*, vol. 44, no. 174 (1991), p. 167-85. map. bibliog.
In twenty-five years UDEAC has achieved a degree of economic integration through common customs regulations and use of the same currency, the CFA franc. Nevertheless much remains to be done in the domain of industrial policy as well as trade among the member-states. There is reason to be hopeful of success, for the region is potentially rich. The recent entrance of Equatorial Guinea into the union and the return of some member-states that had pulled out are clearly indicative of awareness by the younger nations that regional solidarity is very important in their struggle for economic development.

345 **Competition, conflict, and decline in the Union Douanière et Économique de l'Afrique Centrale.**
Lynn Krieger Mytelka. In: *African regional organizations*. Edited by Domenico Mazzeo. Cambridge, England: Cambridge University Press, 1984, p. 131-49. bibliog.
The four states of former French Equatorial Africa along with Cameroon formed the Union Douanière et Economique de l'Afrique Centrale (Central African Customs and Economic Union) in December 1964 to promote economic cooperation. The single tax system and the investment code which the organization adopted had the effect of promoting national development rather than interstate cooperation. As a result, only a tiny portion of the trade of the five states has been with one another, a situation that discussions among their leaders have failed to alter.

346 **A genealogy of francophone west and equatorial African regional organisations.**
Lynn Krieger Mytelka. *Journal of Modern African Studies*, vol. 12, no. 2 (1974), p. 259-320. bibliog.
Information is included on the organization of the Union Douanière Équatoriale, Union Douanière et Économique d'Afrique Centrale, and the Banque Centrale des Etats de l'Afrique Equatoriale et du Cameroun, which promote interstate cooperation.

347 **The future of the Central African Customs and Economic Union UDEAC (Union Douanière et Economique de l'Afrique Centrale.)**
Wilfred A. Ndongko. In: *The future of regionalism in Africa.* Edited by Ralph I. Onwuka, Amadu Sesay. London: Macmillan, 1985, p. 96-109. bibliog.
A discussion is presented of the integrative forces that led to the creation of UDEAC in 1964 and to its maintenance throughout the following two decades. Political considerations more than economic ones contributed to this process. At the same time considerations of national interests prevented economic integration from advancing very much.

348 **Intégration économique en Afrique Centrale avec la CEEAC (Communauté Economique des Etats de l'Afrique Centrale)?** (Economic integration in Central Africa with the Economic Community of the States of Central Africa?)
Laurent Zang. *Le Mois en Afrique* (Feb.–Mar. 1987), p. 69-99.
In 1983 Gabon along with nine other states formed the Economic Community of the States of Central Africa to eliminate barriers to trade and to promote mutually beneficial economic development. This article reviews the background to the organization of the new community and the prospects for its success.

Arab states

349 **Bibliographie.** (Bibliography.)
Bernard Founou-Tchuigoua. *Africa Development*, vol. 11, no. 2-3 (1986), p. 31-68.
This is a bibliography on the economic relations between Arab and African countries, including Gabon.

350 **Arab aid to sub-Saharan Africa.**
Robert Anton Mertz, Pamela McDonald Mertz. Grunewald, Germany, Kaiser, 1983. 287p. bibliog.
Details are given on the policies and practices of Arab states in granting aid and assistance to Black African countries, including Gabon.

351 **Arab economic aid.**
R. S. Porter. *Development Policy Review*, vol. 4 (Mar. 1986), p. 44-68. bibliog.
Gabon has been the recipient of aid from several Arab countries, including Morocco, Saudi Arabia and Kuwait. This article does not concern such aid specifically but it provides in clear form a description of the aid policies of the Arab states towards the countries of Black Africa as well as the structures and processes by which this aid has been extended.

352 **La coopération arabo–africaine. Bilan d'une décennie.** (Arab–African cooperation. Overview of a decade.)
Charbel Zarour. Paris: Harmattan, 1989. 415p. bibliog.
This volume studies the policies of the Arab states concerning aid and assistance to the countries of Black Africa, and the structures and processes by which this aid has been transmitted. President Bongo's conversion to Islam in 1973 initiated the process by which Gabon has received aid from such countries as Morocco, Saudi Arabia and Kuwait. Hoped for aid from Libya did not materialize and Gabon's relations with that country deteriorated as a result of Libyan involvement in Chad.

Economy Since 1960

353 **L'économie du Gabon. Analyse: politiques d'ajustement et d'adaptation.**
(The economy of Gabon. Analysis: policies of adjustment and
adaptation.)
Hugues-Alexandre Barro-Chambrier.   Paris: Economica, 1990. 355p.
bibliog.

An examination is made of the difficulties troubling the Gabonese economy in the era
of downturn since 1985 linked to a drop in petroleum revenues and the efforts at
restructuring under the auspices of the International Monetary Fund and the World
Bank. Gabon must undertake a profound reorientation of the political economy of
regional cooperation and a reform of individual and collective practices in order to
achieve economic well-being and financial soundness.

354 **Le Gabon.** (Gabon.)
Jacqueline Bouquerel.   Paris: Presses Universitaires de France, 1976.
2nd ed. 128p. maps. bibliog.

This now dated work nevertheless contains a good introduction to the evolution of the
Gabonese economy from the 1940s through to the early 1970s.

355 **L'évolution du commerce international des bois africains.** (The
evolution of international commerce in African woods.)
Gérard Buttoud, Amani J. Koumani.   *Afrique Contemporaine*, vol. 24
(Apr.–June 1986), p. 3-20. bibliog.

The production of woods, which was the mainstay of the country's export economy
until the development of petroleum in the 1960s and 1970s, still remains important.
But competition from less expensive South-East Asian woods and marketing practices
of questionable wisdom have hindered attempts to increase these exports.

356   **The ports and oil terminals of Nigeria, Cameroon, and Gabon.**
       Denis Fair.   *Africa Insight*, vol. 19, no. 3 (1989), p. 153-59. bibliog.

This article includes information on the port of Owendo close to Libreville on the Gabon Estuary, which is the western terminus of the Trans-Gabon Railway, and Port-Gentil at Cape Lopez. Owendo has become the point of arrival for most imports as well as the place for exporting timber and manganese. Port-Gentil is the centre for exporting petroleum and sawn wood as well as much of the unfinished *okoumé* logs. The fields of the major oil companies prior to the coming on-stream of the Rabi-Kounga field are described in detail.

357   **The banking system of Gabon and the Central Bank of Equatorial Africa and Cameroon.**
       Lorenzo Frediani.   Milan, Italy: Casse di Risparmio della Provincie Lombarde, 1974. 343p. bibliog.

The organization of Gabon's banking system reflects its French colonial past as well as continuing ties with France and other former French territories in Central Africa. Gabon has its own development bank and participates in the Central Bank of Equatorial Africa and Cameroon (later renamed the Bank of the States of Central Africa). The latter handles Gabon's relations with the franc zone. A number of French banks also have branches in Gabon.

358   **Gabon 1981: the Gabonese economy from 1970 to 1981.**
       Paris: Marchés Tropicaux et Mediterranéens, 1981. 119p. map. bibliog.

This is a translation of 'Gabon 1981: l'économie gabonaise de 1970 à 1981, un redressement indéniable, des perspectives diversifiées (*Marchés Tropicaux et Méditerranéens*, vol. 33 (1981), p. 2977-3151). It contains detailed descriptions and analyses, rich in statistical data, on Gabon's economic development, finances, trade and external economic relations during an era of rapid expansion of petroleum production that culminated in a crisis linked to unwise spending policies and a lack of financial discipline. It indicates the neglect of traditional agriculture and the creation of agro-businesses to feed the increasing urban populations.

359   **Gabon.**
       François Gaulme, Jean-François Pochon, Philippe Corsair, Hugues-Alexandre Barro-Chambrier.   *Marchés Tropicaux et Méditerranéens*, vol. 47 (Dec. 6, 1991), p. 3169-224. bibliog.

A detailed review is undertaken of the course of the economy and finances since the end of the oil boom in 1985. An introductory essay interprets the political and social evolution of Gabon during the three decades since independence. A second one examines natural resources and their utilization while a third focuses upon the secondary and tertiary sectors of the economy and the companies involved, including the parastatals. The text and many tables provide detailed statistics in support of the accounts and analyses.

360 **Les enjeux économiques du Gabon à la veille du Plan 1984-1988.** (The economic stakes of Gabon on the eve of the Plan, 1984-88.)
Pierre Jacquemot. *Afrique Contemporaine*, vol. 23 (Apr.–June 1984), p. 31-43. bibliog.

This article discusses the economic challenges facing Gabon at the height of the oil boom of 1973-85. Receipts from petroleum had become the mainstay of the economy and chief source of budgetary funds. Although oil production fell from 11,300,000 tons in 1977 to 7,800,000 tons in 1982, steady world demand and a strong dollar, the currency for the exchange of petroleum, kept income at previously high levels. But a drop in demand or prices could quickly throw the economy and finances into disarray (as happened after 1985). Gabon did not use the greatly increased revenues to create a more diversified production in order to decrease very much its dependence on petroleum. At the same time it acquired huge debts for development projects that would require large interest and principal payments in the coming years. Gabon's dependence on foreign capital, technical skill and labour made it additionally vulnerable to external conditions.

361 **Le développement économique du Gabon.** (The economic development of Gabon.)
Gaston Lotito. *Cahiers d'Outre-Mer*, vol. 23 (Oct.–Dec. 1970), p. 425-39. maps. bibliog.

Ten years after independence, Gabon's economy was making rapid progress, thanks to the exploitation of its forests and mineral resources (manganese, uranium, petroleum), which were still far from being developed fully. Nevertheless this development brought no benefits to the processing industries, the crafts sector or agriculture, this last remaining traditional and employing the majority of the population. Employees of the state and of timber or mining companies received much higher incomes than the farmers. The population was growing very slowly (half of one per cent a year) and sanitary conditions needed improvements. Local conditions favoured the establishment of large-scale industrial units for the processing of raw materials into semi-finished products.

362 **Economic development – does aid help? A case study of French development assistance to Gabon.**
Pierre-Claver Maganga-Moussavou. *African Bibliographic Center, Current Reading List Series*, vol. 11, no. 2 (1983), p. 1-243. bibliog.

This work is a translation of *L'aide publique de la France au développement du Gabon depuis l'indépendance (1960-1978)* (Paris: Publications de la Sorbonne, 1982. 303p.). It studies French public aid to Gabon from independence until the economic downturn of the late 1970s but omits much of the statistical data appended to the original French version. It is argued that French aid profited France and Frenchmen far more than Gabon and in some cases ill-served Gabon's interests. The author urges less dependence on France for aid and assistance. He favours a greater diversification of investment sources, including a larger role for the United States.

363 **Politique de développement rural en Afrique: impacts sur l'emploi et les revenus: le cas du Gabon.** (Policy of rural development in Africa: impacts on employment and revenues; case of Gabon.)
Josué Sandjiman Mamder. Addis Ababa: BIT, PECTA, 1985. 110p. bibliog.
This study examines recent efforts at rural development and their impact on employment and income.

364 **Un exemple de modelisation et de prévision en Afrique: le 'MEGA' modèle de l'économie gabonaise.** (An example of modelization and of forecast in Africa: the MEGA model of the Gabonese economy.)
Pierre-Alain Muet, Alain Fonteneau. *Observations et Diagnostics Economiques: Revue de l'OFCA*, no. 17 (Oct. 1986), p. 209-33. bibliog.
This article offers a theoretical approach to the study of the Gabonese economy in the mid-1980s.

365 **Some comments on foreign private investments and the economic and social development of Gabon.**
Y. Sabolo. *African Development*, no. 4 (1975), p. 499-534. bibliog.
An examination is made of the impact of foreign private investments in the development of Gabon's mineral and forest resources.

366 **Gabon: the economic outlook.**
Howard Schissel. *Africa Report*, vol. 30 (Jan.–Feb. 1985), p. 27-29.
This brief review of the economic evolution of Gabon from the late 1970s to the mid-1980s emphasizes the dangers of heavy dependence on petroleum revenues.

367 **Afrique et capitaux: géographie des capitaux et des investissements en Afrique tropicale d'expression française.** (Africa and capital: geography of capital and investments in francophone tropical Africa.)
Jean Suret-Canale. Paris: L'Arbe Verdoyant, 1987. 2 vols. 860p. bibliog.
This is an important reference source for French investments in tropical Africa, including Gabon, during the twentieth century.

368 **Surveys of African economies. Vol. 1 Cameroon, Chad, Congo (Brazzaville), and Gabon.**
Washington, DC: International Monetary Fund, 1968. 365p. bibliog.
In 1956 France for the first time permitted and even encouraged investors from western Europe and the United States to help to develop the mineral resources of its overseas territories in Africa. These new investments facilitated the development of petroleum, manganese and uranium in Gabon during the following decade to the point that minerals surpassed timber, cocoa and coffee as the most valuable exports and sources of government revenue. At the same time France remained Gabon's main trading partner and source of aid and assistance. This survey of the IMF provides a detailed

picture of the Gabonese economy in the mid-1960s and its evolution during the era of decolonization.

Gabon: the development of a nation.
See item no. 1.

Le Gabon. Vol. 1, Espace–histoire–société; vol. 2, Etat et développement. (Gabon. Vol. 1, Space, history, society; vol. 2, State and development.) *See* item no. 15.

Port-Gentil, centre économique du Gabon. (Port-Gentil, economic centre of Gabon.) *See* item no. 68.

Industry and Mining

369 **Industrialisation des pays d'Afrique sub-saharienne. Le cas du Gabon.**
(Industrialization of the countries of sub-Saharan Africa. The case of Gabon.)
Christine Brochet, Jacques Pierre. Paris: SEDES, Ministry of Cooperation, 1986. 31p. bibliog.
A brief introduction is given to the problems involved in the further industrialization of Gabon in both technical and economic terms.

370 **Les perspectives d l'industrie minière de l'Afrique en développement.**
(Perspectives on the mining industry in developing Africa.)
Alain-Louis Dangeard, André Papon. *Afrique Contemporaine*, vol. 23 (July–Sept. 1984), p. 3-16. bibliog.
This article reviews the possibilities of further development for the mining industries of the francophone states, including Gabon.

371 **L'impact des groupes industriels sur les pays sous-développés: le cas de Elf au Gabon.** (The impact of industrial groups on the underdeveloped countries: the case of Elf in Gabon.)
Albert Engonga-Bikora. In: *Entreprises et entrepreneurs en Afrique, xixe et xxe siècles, Vol. 2.* Paris: Harmattan, 1983, p. 507-17.
The leading company in terms of exploration and production of petroleum products in Gabon prior to the 1990s was Elf-Gabon, an affiliate of Elf-Aquitaine of France. French and Gabonese investors, including the government of Gabon, provided most of the capital for Elf-Gabon while part of Elf-Aquitaine is owned by the French state. The two companies thus played a major role in the development of Gabon's economy in which revenues from petroleum provided the main source of income from the mid-1970s.

372 **Le pétrole au Gabon, le deuxième souffle en 1990.** (Petroleum in Gabon, the second breath in 1990.)
Antoine Labey, Jean-Marie Nkouka. *Afrique Industrie, Infrastructures*, vol. 17 (July 20, 1988), p. 26-44. bibliog.

Utilization of new oilfields onshore at Rabi-Kounga, 230 miles south-east of Libreville will provide the government with new revenues and extend the oil era until at least the end of the century.

373 **Le manganèse au Gabon.** (Manganese in Gabon.)
G. Lerat. *Cahiers d'Outre-Mer*, vol. 18, no. 4 (1966), p. 354-64. bibliog.

Exploitation of manganese began in 1962 around Moanda in the Haut-Ogooué Province under the auspices of the Compagnie minière de l'Ogooué (COMILOG). United States Steel originally owned 49 per cent of the company and French interests the rest. Since the 1960s Gabon has been the fourth largest producer of manganese in the world. The reserves would last for 150 years at the rates of production of the mid-1960s. Expansion is hindered by the lack of transportation. The ore is evacuated by aerial cable that carries buckets of the metal southward to the Congo-Ocean Railway in the Congo Republic; the railway takes the ore to the port of Pointe-Noire for export to France.

374 **Les resources minières des états d'Afrique Centrale (CEEAC).** (The mining resources of the states of Central Africa, Economic Community of the States of Central Africa.)
D. Verheve. *Revue Tiers-Monde*, vol. 27 (no. 106, 1986), p. 457-65. bibliog.

This article reviews the mining resoures of the states of western equatorial Africa, including Gabon, and the economic possibilities of further exploitation.

The OPEC market of 1985.
See item no. 310.

Uranium: a case study in Franco–African relations.
See item no. 332.

The ports and oil terminals of Nigeria, Cameroon, and Gabon.
See item no. 356.

Energy

375   **A natural fossil nuclear reactor.**
Bulletin of the Atomic Scientists, vol. 33, no. 2 (Feb. 1977), p. 40-41.
This translation of a press release by the French Atomic Energy Commission explains
the discovery of the fossil remains of a prehistoric natural nuclear reactor in an open-
pit uranium mine in Gabon. The article describes the details of the process by which
this reactor operated and provides information on its discovery.

376   **The Oklo nuclear reactors: 1800 million years ago.**
Roger Naudet.   *Interdisciplinary Scientiflc Review*, (Mar. 1976), p. 72-
84. bibliog.
In the mid-1970s fossil remains of a prehistoric natural nuclear reactor were discovered
in an open-pit uranium mine in the upper Ogooué River valley. The uranium quarry at
Oklo was the site of the same self-sustaining nuclear chain reactions that have been
produced in atomic piles constructed by humankind. The discovery prompted
investigations by scientists throughout the western and communist worlds.

377   **Le phénomène d'Oklo: comptes rendus d'un colloque sur le phénomène
d'Oklo. The Oklo phenomenon: proceedings of a symposium on the Oklo
phenomenon.**
Vienna: International Atomic Energy Agency, 1975. 647p. bibliog.
Papers are included in French, English and Russian from an international symposium
on the Oklo phenomenon.

378   **Energie traditionnelle et énergie moderne dans le monde gabonais.**
(Traditional energy and modern energy in the Gabonese world.)
François Villien.   *Cahiers d'Outre-Mer*, vol. 34 (July–Sept. 1981),
p. 233-55. bibliog.

This article discusses energy sources in Gabon, past and present. Gabon has sufficient petroleum, natural gas and water power to serve its needs if properly developed and conserved.

Uranium: a case study in Franco–African relations.
See item no. 332.

Forestry

379 **Les bois du Gabon.** (The woods of Gabon.)
A. Bertin.   Paris: Larose, 1929. 306p. bibliog.
This standard older work on the woods of Gabon pays particular attention to those of
commercial and industrial potential.

380 **Okoumé et chantiers forestiers du Gabon.** (Okoumé and forest yards of
Gabon.)
Guy Lasserre.   *Cahiers d'Outre-Mer*, vol. 8, no. 30 (1956), p. 119-60.
maps. bibliog.
A detailed discussion is presented of the history of the exploitation of *okoumé*, which
is used as plywood. Okoumé was Gabon's main export until supplanted by petroleum
in the 1970s. While some Gabonese were involved in family cuttings, most production
was in the hands of French firms that used mechanization and evacuated the timber via
waterways. The article has much detail on the exploitation of okoumé in the Estuary
Province and adjacent coasts.

381 **Reforestation in the Republic of Gabon/Le reboisement en République
gabonaise.**
Faustin Legault.   *Studies in Third World Societies*, no. 13 (Sept. 1980),
p. 155-60 (English text), p. 161-67 (French text). bibliog.
This article discusses the efforts at reforestation in Gabon after the Second World War
by the French colonial administration, and after 1957 by the Gabonese authorities. The
author gives particular attention to *okoumé*.

382 **Biologie et sylviculture de l'okoumé: aucoumea klaineana Pierre.**
(Biology and sylviculture of the okoumé: aucoumea klaineana Pierre.)
J. R. Leroy-Deval.   Nogent-sur-Maine, France: Centre Technique
Forestier Tropical, 1976. 2 vols. bibliog.

This is a study of the conditions under which *okoumé*, the most important wood industrially, grows and is reforested. *Okoumé* is named after Father Théophile Klaine (1840-1911), a Holy Ghost priest, who first identified its industrial possibilities.

383 **L'homme et le développement de la fôret du Gabon dans le passé.** (Man
and the development of the forest of Gabon in the past.)
J. R. Leroy-Deval.   *Studies in Third World Societies*, no. 13 (Sept.
1980), p. 131-54. map. bibliog.

This article contains descriptions of the chief woods, including the commercially important *okoumé*, by region, and an account of human exploitation of these resources. The author urges Gabon to adopt a tropical technology of exploitation along with an appropriate tropical sylvaculture in order to reconstitute the forest sources of riches that will be indefinitely renewable through scientific management.

384 **La fôret du Gabon.** (The forest of Gabon.)
G. de Saint-Aubin.   Nogent-sur-Marne, France: Centre Technique
Forestier Tropical, 1963. 208p. bibliog.

A study is made of the forests of Gabon, along with their possible further commercial and industrial development.

The forest vegetation of Gabon/Végétation forestière du Gabon.
See item no. 35.

L'évolution du commerce international des bois africains. (The evolution of
international commerce in African woods.)
See item no. 355.

West Africa: resources management policies and the tropical forest.
See item no. 409.

La conservation des ecosystèmes forestiers du Gabon. (The conservation of
the forest ecosystems of Gabon.)
See item no. 411.

Agriculture

385   **The limits of development management: an analysis of agricultural policy implementation in Gabon.**
Howard William Anderson.   PhD thesis, Indiana University, Bloomington, Indiana, 1987. [n.p.].   (Available from University Microfilms International, Ann Arbor, Michigan, order no. DA8809808).

Despite Gabon's considerable oil and mineral resources, small population and a climate conducive to expansion of agricultural activity, the government's efforts to promote agricultural development proved ineffective and farm population declined significantly over a quarter century. The study traces the evolution of agricultural policy from the colonial era through a period of neglect (1960-74) to a period of agro-industrial expansion (1975-79). Policy is analysed from a perspective that compares the intent of formal policy goals with results obtained during implementation. An analysis was made of the Integrated Operational Zones policy (1980-85) that attempted to link industrial-scale agricultural production with the efforts of rural villagers. The study found a history of policy formulations that were never effectively implemented. Three aspects of implementation proved especially problematical: distortion in the translation of policy goals into programme objectives, ineffective administration of Agricultural Ministry operations, and failure to induce villagers' participation in project activity. The conclusion is drawn that even in a case such as Gabon's with so many positive aspects, an adequate resource base and a formal policy commitment to agriculture are necessary but not sufficient conditions for assuring agricultural development. Equally important is the ability of an African government to organize and to manage the implementation of agricultural policies.

386 **Le bananier plantain: une culture commerciale paysanne au Fernan-Vaz
(Gabon).** (The plantain banana tree: a peasant commercial cultivation
at Fernan-Vaz, Gabon.)
Yawo-Ganyo Galley. *Muntu*, no. 6 (1987), p. 153-69. bibliog.
While the countryside has been losing its population for more than a decade due to the
economic growth of the towns which irresistably attract rural young folk, the canton of
Orembo Nkomi at Fernan-Vaz has been drawing workers from the towns. They have
been attracted by the appreciable revenue available through the cultivation of the
plantain banana for urban markets. The government has provided technical support for
this enterprise, thus contributing to its success.

387 **L'organisation de l'espace agricole chez les Ntumu Beti du Woleu-Ntem.**
(The organization of agricultural space among the Ntumu-Beti of the
Woleu-N'Tem.)
Yawo-Ganyo Galley. *Muntu*, no. 3 (1985), p. 42-68. map. bibliog.
The organization of land among the Ntumi Beti people of the Woleu-N'Tem Province
has been founded on a set of strategies which ensure that the peasantry has an
adequate food production and at the same time appreciable cash revenues through
speculative cultivation. Recently, however, a combination of human and economic
factors is challenging a balance that has been precarious for some time.

388 **Production vivrière et approvisionnement urbain au Gabon.** (Food crop
production and urban provisioning in Gabon.)
Jean-Michel Lebigre. *Cahiers d'Outre-Mer*, vol. 33 (Apr.–June 1980),
p. 167-85. bibliog.
First forestry and then mining were privileged at the expense of agriculture, which as a
result preserved its archaic mode of production and its subsistence character among
widely scattered rural populations. At the same time the diffusion of cocoa and coffee
in peasant plantations remained a limited phenomenon, mainly in the north. By 1980
the rural exodus threatened to depopulate the farming villages at the very moment
when the urban growth and the rise in the standard of living linked with the expanding
petroleum output created a growing demand for foodstuffs. The country's leaders,
after completely sacrificing agriculture to industrial development for many years, now
recognize the danger of depending upon expensive food imports. A programme of
food crop projects has thus been drawn up that might permit the country rapidly to
provide for its own needs. But the creation of modern agricultural entities employing
salaried workers and the relaunching of cocoa production by overage peasant farmers
will not resolve the problem of the survival of the rural world in Gabon.

389 **Modernité tiers-mythe et bouc-hémisphere.** (Modernity, third myth, and
hemisphere scapegoat.)
Fidèle Pierre Nze-Nguema. Paris: Editions Publisud, 1989. 172p.
bibliog.
The last half of this work deals specifically with the policy of the Bongo regime
concerning agriculture. It also discusses the socio-economic consequences of the
transformation of agriculture among the Fang of the Woleu-N'Tem Province since
1920.

390 **Esquisse historique de l'agriculture en milieu forestier (Afrique Equatoriale).** (Historical outline of agriculture in a forest environment: Equatorial Africa.)
Jan Vansina. *Muntu*, no. 2 (1985), p. 5-34. bibliog.

This detailed original study provides firsthand accounts of the agricultural practices of the Bantu living in the equatorial forest during the nineteenth century. These include agricultural techniques, the organization of field work, harvesting, nutritional problems, and cultivated plants, including both these native to Africa and those imported from America and Asia. The forest agricultural system differs greatly from all neighbouring systems, largely because of the particular environment. The Bantu-speaking peoples colonized this agricultural space between 2,000 and 1,500 BC. Today's problems and their possible solution may be better understood in the light of Bantu agricultural history.

Le Gabon, vol. 2, Etat et développement. (Gabon, Vol. 2, State and development.)
See item no. 15.

Transport

391 **Les transports au Gabon. Le Transgabonais, historique des réalisations dans le temps, situation actuelle.** (Transportation in Gabon. The Trans-Gabon Railway, history of past efforts, present situation.)
Claude Cabrol. *Annales de l'Ecole Nationale d'Administration* (Libreville), vol. 2 (1978), p. 77-92. bibliog.

An account is given of the proposals to build a railway across Gabon during the French colonial period followed by a description of the construction of the Trans-Gabon Railway connecting the Gabon Estuary with the upper Ogooué River valley.

392 **Le Transgabonais.** (The Trans-Gabon Railway.)
J. E. Peter. *Afrique, Industrie, Infrastructures,* (May 1, 1975), p. 29-76. bibliog.

This article provides a detailed introduction to the construction and operation of the Trans-Gabon Railway.

393 **L'aviation au Gabon.** (Aviation in Gabon.)
J. Rocq. *Annales de l'Université Nationale du Gabon, série Lettres et Sciences Sociales,* vol. 1 (Dec. 1977), p. 88-99.

In the course of the Second World War and immediately after, Gabon acquired a network of regional airfields, mainly for passengers and small goods. But air transport did not solve the problem of evacuating the country's timber and minerals.

394 **L'aviation intérieure et l'envol du Gabon.** (The internal aviation and shipment of Gabon.)
Jean-Paul Sinsou. *Transports* (Jan. 1986), p. 27-34.

A review is undertaken of the utilization of the country's network of regional airfields for the movement of persons and goods on the eve of the opening of the Trans-Gabon Railway into the Haut-Ogooué Province.

395 **L'étonnante potentialité des transports fluvio-lagunaires par cabotage au Gabon.** (The astonishing potentiality of river-lagoon transportation by coasting trade in Gabon.)
Jean-Paul Sinsou. *Transports*, no. 322 (1987), p. 83-90. bibliog.
This article discusses the potential of waterways for moving bulk goods, in particular timber, from the interior to the Atlantic.

396 **Le transgabonais et l'économie du Gabon.** (The Trans-Gabon Railway and the economy of Gabon.)
Hugues Viel. *Marchés Tropicaux et Méditerannéens*, vol. 42 (Dec. 13, 1986), p. 3219-50. bibliog.
The role of the Trans-Gabon Railway in the present and future economic development of Gabon is discussed.

Les ports du Gabon et du Congo-Brazzaville. (The ports of Gabon and Congo-Brazzaville.)
See item no. 78.

The ports and oil terminals of Nigeria, Cameroon, and Gabon.
See item no. 356.

Labour

397 **Problèmes actuels de main d'oeuvre au Gabon: conditions d'une immigration controlée.** (Present manpower problems in Gabon: conditions of a controlled immigration.)
Claude Bouet. *Cahiers d'Outre-Mer*, vol. 31 (Oct.–Dec. 1978), p. 375-94. bibliog.
This article discusses the problems arising from the necessity to import labour (skilled from Europe and unskilled from Africa) to promote the country's economic development.

398 **Les syndicats au Gabon.** (Trade unions in Gabon.)
Laurent-Thierry Essone-Ndong. *Annales de l'Ecole Nationale d'Administration* (Libreville), vol. 3 (1979), p. 45-54. bibliog.
A historical account is given of the organization and activities of trade unions in Gabon from their legalization in 1944 up until 1979. Civil servants and salaried workers formed the core of these organizations, which under French rule were affiliated with metropolitan Communist, Socialist and Christian Democratic unions and parties. Under the presidency of Bongo, all unions were dissolved and the workers required to belong to a single organization dominated by the government. Slowdowns and wildcat strikes periodically reflected their dissatisfaction with this situation, which they were powerless to alter.

399 **Le coût de la main d'oeuvre étrangère et son incidence sur le développement économique et éducation du Gabon.** (The cost of foreign manpower and its effect on economic development and education in Gabon.)
Charles Koumba-Mombo. Master's thesis, Université Laval, Quebec, Canada, 1985. 120p. bibliog. (Available from Micromedia, Hull, Quebec, Canada).
Gabon's economic expansion during the 1970s and 1980s involved extensive use of imported labour, particularly from other African countries. This thesis studies the impact of the use of such labour on economic development and education.

400 **Les modes normaux de dissolution du contrat de travail à durée indéterminée au Gabon.** (The normal modes of dissolving a labour contract of indeterminate length in Gabon.)
J. F. Sobotchou. *Penant*, vol. 92, no. 776 (1982), p. 9-40. bibliog.
This article discusses agreements regulating terms of employment in Gabon during the era of the oil boom.

401 **Stratégies et perspectives de l'emploi au Gabon.** (Strategies and perspectives on employment in Gabon.)
Addis Ababa: BIT-PECTA, 1983. 305p. bibliog.
This study looks at employment policies and prospects in the expanding oil-based economy.

Politique de développement rural en Afrique: impacts sur l'emploi et les revenues: le cas du Gabon. (Policy of rural development in Africa: impacts on employment and revenues; case of Gabon.)
See item no. 363.

Statistics

402 **Bulletin mensuel de statistique.** (Monthly bulletin of statistics.)
     Libreville: Service de la Statistique, 1959- . monthly.
This monthly publication contains statistics on trade, production and finances.

403 **Demographic yearbook.**
     New York: United Nations, 1948- . annual.
Statistics are included on such demographic aspects of Gabon as size, distribution and trends in population, natality, foetal mortality, infant and maternal mortality, general mortality, nuptuality and divorce, and international migration.

404 **Etudes et statistiques.** (Studies and statistics.)
     Yaoundé: Banque des Etats de l'Afrique Centrale, 1956- . ten times per year.
Up-to-date statistics are provided on production, trade and finances as well as commercial operations involving France and the other states sponsoring the Bank of the States of Central Africa at Yaoundé.

405 **International Financial Statistics.**
     Washington: International Monetary Fund, 1948- . monthly.
The data are consolidated in an annual *Yearbook*.

406 **International historical statistics, 1750-1975. Africa and Asia.**
     Compiled by Brian A. Mitchell. New York University Press, 1982.
     2nd ed. 761p. bibliog.
Included are population and vital statistics, labour force, agriculture, industry, external trade, transport and communications, finance, prices, education and national accounts. (A third edition will be published in 1993 covering up to 1988: *International historical statistics, 1750-1988. Vol. 3 Australasia, Asia, and Africa.*)

125

407 **UN statistical yearbook.**
New York: United Nations, 1948- . annual.
Up-to-date economic statistics from member states are provided, including those on Gabonese production, energy, trade, transportation and communication. Also included are balance of payments, wages and prices, national accounts, finance, budget accounts, public debt and development assistance.

408 **UNESCO statistical yearbook.**
Paris: UNESCO, 1963- . annual.
Up-to-date statistics are given for education, science and technology, libraries, newspapers, films and cinema, radio broadcasting and television. Over 200 countries are represented, including Gabon.

Environment

409 **West Africa: resources management policies and the tropical forest.**
Malcolm Gillis.   In: *Public policies and the misuse of forest resources.*
Edited by R. Repetto, Malcolm Gillis.   Cambridge, England:
Cambridge University Press for the World Resources Institute, 1988,
p. 299-351. bibliog.
An examination is made of the role of public policy in deforestation in four states:
Liberia, Ivory Coast, Ghana and Gabon. The chapter provides an overview of forest
resources, deforestation and international trade in tropical hardwoods for the entire
west and equatorial African region, and on a country-by-country basis. Patterns of
property rights and foreign investment in each country are addressed, as well as the
national benefits derived from forest utilization and government receipt of timber
rents. There is a focus upon reforestation and forest concessions policies, respectively,
and upon the impact of forest-based industrialization policies. Finally, the essay
considers the impact of non-forestry policies on tropical forest utilization in each of the
four states.

410 **Conservation before the crisis – an opportunity in Gabon.**
T. O. McShane.   *Oryx*, vol. 24, no. 1 (1990), p. 9-14. bibliog.
This article examines an opportunity to practise conservation measures in order to
forestall the damage which other countries are already being faced with. Gabon has
time on its side in addressing its long-term conservation and development needs.

411 **La conservation des ecosystèmes forestiers du Gabon.** (The conservation
of the forest ecosystems of Gabon.)
Chris Wilks.   Gland, Switzerland: Union Internationale pour la
Conservation de nature, 1990. 215p. maps. bibliog.
This reference work on the forest resources of Gabon provides detailed information
about the flora and fauna, the role of the forests in the economy, and the conservation
and environmental issues.

Education

Bibliography

412 **Education in the states of equatorial Africa: a bibliographical essay.**
David E. Gardinier. *Africana Journal*, vol. 3, no. 2 (1972), p. 7-20.
This article describes the contents and discusses the themes in several hundred books, articles and reports that provide information on education in the four states of equatorial Africa between 1842 and 1972. An important part of the material on Gabon is found in publications that treat education in all of the French Congo (1886-1910) and French Equatorial Africa (1910-60) of which Gabon formed part or in all of French sub-Saharan Africa during the colonial period.

Before 1960

413 **Saint Gabriel au Gabon: Ecole Montfort (1900-1948).** (Saint Gabriel in Gabon: the Ecole Montfort, 1900-1948.)
Macaire Clémenceau. *Chronique de Saint-Gabriel*, (Oct. 1949), p. 45-73. bibliog.
From 1900 to 1918 the Brothers of St. Gabriel, a French congregation of professional teachers, operated a school in the centre of Libreville which provided a more extensive education of better quality than previously available to hundreds of Gabonese boys annually. From their ranks would come not merely better educated and more numerous teachers, brothers and priests but laymen who formed the political élite of the country during the era of decolonization.

414   **Education in French Equatorial Africa, 1842-1945.**
David E. Gardinier.   *Proceedings of the French Colonial Historical Society*, vol. 3 (1978), p. 121-37. bibliog.

Education among the indigenous peoples of Gabon, who were non-literate, was always informal. Formal education arrived in the Gabon Estuary in the early 1840s when American Protestant and French Roman Catholic missionaries established schools to educate teachers, catechists and eventually clergy as well as ordinary Christians. The colonial government aided the Catholic schools but did not attempt to regulate education until 1883 when it ordered the sole use of French as the medium of instruction. This requirement led to the transfer of the Protestant mission to the Evangelical Mission Society of Paris between 1892 and 1913. In 1907 the administration, in the wake of the separation of church and state in France, ended subsidies to the French mission schools and opened the first public school in Libreville under lay teachers. But the administration devoted such tiny sums to education prior to the Popular Front in France (1935-36) that mission schools still provided the bulk of primary and vocational education. The only post-primary education in Gabon was that provided by Christian seminaries. During the Second World War Governor-General Félix Eboué tripled the funds for education. He assigned one-third of these revenues to the mission schools, which enabled them to expand alongside the public schools and to upgrade their programmes. Though no more than one per cent of Gabon's population attended school during the colonial era, the schools educated the employees through whose assistance the colonial administration, European commerce and Christian missions were able to function.

415   **Education in French Equatorial Africa, 1945-1960.**
David E. Gardinier.   *Cultures et Développement*, vol. 16, no. 2 (1984), p. 303-34. bibliog.

France during the Fourth Republic followed an educational policy for all its territories in sub-Saharan Africa that sought to promote their advancement within a French-directed framework. The metropolitan educational system, with few adaptations to local situations, was generalized overseas. It involved primary and vocational education for the masses of people and secondary and higher education for an élite. Christian missions received important subsidies that enabled them to play an important role in the extension of educational opportunities to much larger numbers of people. At the arrival of self-government in 1957 and independence in 1960 Gabon still lacked the educated personnel to direct and to manage its government, administration, schools and economy, thus perpetuating dependence on expatriates. At the same time the entire French-derived system in which instructions was given exclusively in French was poorly adapted to promoting development and national independence.

416   **Les recommandations de la conférence de Brazzaville sur les problèmes de l'éducation.** (The recommendations of the Brazzaville Conference on the problems of education.)
David E. Gardinier.   In: *Brazzaville, janvier-février 1944. Aux sources de la décolonisation.*   Paris: Plon, 1988, p. 170-80. bibliog.

At the Brazzaville Conference of 1944 France laid plans for the reform of colonial rule in Black Africa in the aftermath of the Second World War. Under General de Gaulle's leadership it sought to promote the advancement of its overseas territories, including Gabon, within a French-directed framework that would contribute to France's recovery and renewed greatness in the world. In the field of education, the conference recommended the continuation of a French-derived education entirely in the French language but adapted to African realities. The French intended to extend primary education to all children of both sexes and to provide further instruction in technical and academic fields to the most talented. An élite would come into being that could help the French administer their respective territories. The proposals outlined at Brazzaville would form the basis of overseas educational policy of the Fourth French Republic.

417 **Vocational and technical education in French Equatorial Africa, 1842-1960.**
David E. Gardinier. *Proceedings of the French Colonial Historical Society*, vol. 8 (1982), p. 113-32. bibliog.

Until the early 1900s vocational education was provided almost exclusively by the Christian missions as part of their self-maintenance. The involvement of the colonial administration in this field resulted also from the needs of the various departments, which individually trained African personnel, often on-the-job. A few Gabonese attended formal courses in vocational and technical education organized at Brazzaville in 1935. During the Fourth Republic (1946-58) France made new efforts to provide vocational and technical education at levels comparable to those in France but adapted to local needs. Such instruction was usually considered by the Gabonese as less desirable than studies in literature and law leading to intellectual and administrative careers.

The beginnings of French Catholic evangelization in Gabon and African responses, 1844-1883.
See item no. 229.

Les Frères de Saint-Gabriel au Gabon, 1900-1918: la naissance d'une nouvelle élite africaine. (The Brothers of St. Gabriel in Gabon, 1900-1918: the birth of a new African élite.)
See item no. 230.

The American Presbyterian mission in Gabon: male Mpongwe converts and agents, 1870-1883.
See item no. 237.

The schools of the American Protestant mission in Gabon (1842-1870).
See item no. 238.

Tales out of school.
See item no. 242.

Since 1960

418 **The rigid embrace of dependency: France and Black African education since 1960.**
William Bosworth. *Contemporary French Civilization*, vol. 5 (spring 1981), p. 327-45. bibliog.

In the decades following independence Gabon retained the educational system derived from France in which French is the sole medium of instruction. This situation is described as educational dependency, a term drawn from economic dependency theory. It is argued that as long as educational dependency continues in a form in which French experts impose French values in the French language, African educational systems will remain inefficient and imbalanced, producing élites often unfit for the real tasks of national development. The French language seems destined to remain the teaching vehicle even in the richest francophone countries just so long as they lack other poles of national unity. French as the instructional medium and official national language is best justified on pragmatic grounds; it is there and for the time being there is no alternative. Members of the élite presently in power have a vested interest in maintaining a system that produced them. The educational dependency of Black Africa has taken on a life of its own, developing outside of economic reality and holding both the French and the Africans in a rigid grasp. The possibility of radical change, especially at the secondary and higher levels, in the foreseeable future, seems unlikely.

419 **Clés en mains: le lycée technique national Omar Bongo.** (Keys in hands: the Omar Bongo national technical high school.)
Moniteur Construction Afrique, (June 1979), p. 88-93.

The Bongo regime created a modern technical high school in Libreville in the late 1970s in order to prepare Gabonese for positions still occupied by expatriates in its expanding economy.

420 **Occupational andragogy and the informal working sector in Gabon.**
George William Gamerdinger. EdD thesis, Oklahoma State University, Stillwater, Oklahoma, 1981. 90p. bibliog. (Available from the University Microfilms International, Ann Arbor, Michigan, order no. DA8213025).

This study examines the processes of skill acquisition and transfer within the informal sector in Libreville. It explores the occupations, services and potential of this sector as an alternative to Gabon's technical education. It selected Gabon for study because of its rapidly expanding economy and low population level. It was learned that the informal sector's utilization of informal apprenticeship demonstrates the feasibility of learning approaches and environments outside institutional pedagogy. The use of occupational andragogy as a transfer process for skill acquisition within the informal sector merits attention for those dealing with the labour shortage.

Education. Since 1960

421 **Gabon.**
David E. Gardinier. In: *International Encyclopedia of Higher Education.* Edited by Asa Knowles. San Francisco: Jossey-Bass, 1977, p. 1789-95. bibliog.

This is a detailed account of the organization and functioning of higher education in Gabon, first in cooperation with the three other states that had formed the federation of French Equatorial Africa, and after 1970 exclusively at the national level. Gabon's institutions of higher learning were closely modelled after those of France in terms both of structures and programmes. They received significant French financial aid and staff under the *coopération* agreements made at independence and subsequently renewed. The sole use of French as the medium of instruction helped to perpetuate French cultural influence among the Gabonese élite. The bulk of the students specialized in law and economics or the humanities. Because few entered scientific and technical fields, Gabon continued to depend exclusively upon expatriates, particularly from France, to staff the higher and middle levels of government and the economy.

422 **Schooling in the states of equatorial Africa.**
David E. Gardinier. *Canadian Journal of African Studies*, vol. 8, no. 3 (1974), p. 517-38. bibliog.

Following a review of the main developments in western education in equatorial Africa during the French colonial period, there is a discussion and comparison of key aspects of education since independence in 1960. Gabon expanded opportunities in the existing system in which the instruction was given solely in French and which led to high levels of repeating of grades and dropping out. Unlike the Congo Republic and the Central African Republic, which nationalized mission schools, Gabon continued to subsidize Christian schools; these institutions enrolled one-half of primary pupils and one-third of secondary students. Gabon also provided secondary instruction for much larger numbers of students during the 1960s and early 1970s. It cooperated with the other states of equatorial Africa and France in regional higher education before organizing its own national university in 1970. Despite considerable financial sacrifices, Gabon's educational system produced disappointing results while remaining ill-adapted to promote development and national independence.

423 **Africanisation, enseignement, et coopération bilatérale française.**
(Africanization, education, and French bilateral cooperation.)
Suzie Guth. *Genève–Afrique*, vol. 29, no. 2 (1991), p. 77-85.

Between 1962 and 1982, under Gaullist and Giscardian regimes, France gradually decreased the number of *coopérants* involved in administrative and technical fields throughout Black Africa. But it increased the numbers involved in education. Thus the percentage of French personnel seconded to African governments involved in education increased from 38 per cent in 1962 to 76 per cent in 1982. Under the Mitterrand presidency, the Ministry of Cooperation has sought to diminish the role of *coopérants* in teaching and administration and to replace them by qualified Africans. It is using *coopérants* more extensively for specific projects of short-term duration. France is also directing more of its educational aid into multilateral projects instead of bilateral ones. Nevertheless the content of the educational system in the African states continues to be derived primarily from the exterior.

424 **The Africanization of the curriculum in Gabon.**
John Ogden. *French Review*, vol. 55 (May 1982), p. 855-61. bibliog.

Africanization refers to the adaptation of the subject matter, teaching methods and texts to the physical and cultural realities of the African environment. Gabon in 1974 undertook an Africanization of the curriculum in the French language and literature during the last three years of the *lycée* so as to teach French as a second language and to incorporate texts by Gabonese and other African authors. The article discusses the issues involved and the problems encountered in implementation.

425 **Rapport statistique sur la situation de l'enseignement.** (Statistical report on the situation in education.)
Libreville: Direction of Education, Bureau of Statistics, 1959- annual.

Annual report containing data on enrolments, examination results, numbers of teachers, and expenditures.

426 **Réforme et rénovation de l'enseignement au Gabon.** (Reform and renovation of education in Gabon.)
Ministry of National Education. *Recherche, Pédagogie, et Culture* (May–Aug. 1976), p. 16-24. bibliog.

A discussion, prepared by officials of the National Education Ministry, is presented of the issues involved in possible changes in the educational system derived from France in order better to serve contemporary needs.

427 **New directions in language teaching in sub-Saharan Africa: a seven-country study of current policies and programs for teaching official and national languages and adult functional literacy.**
Edmun B. Richmond. Washington, DC: University Press of America, 1983. 66p. bibliog.

A review of the teaching of French in Gabon is included.

428 **L'Université Omar Bongo.** (Omar Bongo University.)
Eduafrica, (Dec. 1986), p. 149-55.

A description is given of the programmes offered at the national university in Libreville. (Subsequently physical sciences and engineering were transferred to a new university at Masuku near Franceville.)

Literature

Bibliographies

429 **2500 titres de littérature: Afrique subsaharienne.** (2,500 titles from literature: sub-Saharan Africa.)
Notre Librairie, no. 94 (July–Sept. 1988), p. 1-198.
This was also published as a separate item (Paris: CLEF, 1988. 198p.). It includes complete bibliographical information on novels, essays, poems and plays published by writers from Gabon, as well as reference works that cite them.

430 **Lettres gabonaises: bibliographie des auteurs gabonais.** (Gabonese letters: bibliography of Gabonese authors.)
Compiled by Blaise Nicolas, Monique Costisella. Libreville: Ministry of National Education and Scientific Research & National Pedagogy Institute, 1965. 17p.
This list of Gabonese writers up to 1965 includes unpublished works available in manuscript in certain libraries.

431 **Bibliographies in African literature since 1970.**
Compiled by Yvette Scheven. *Research in African Literature*, vol. 15 (fall 1984), p. 405-19.
Some bibliographies on francophone Africa are included containing references on Gabon.

General

432 **Histoire d'un enfant trouvé.** (Story of a child found.)
Robert Zotoumbat. Yaoundé: Ed. CLE, 1971. 60p.

This partly autobiographical work gives an account of village life and of the impact of the Christian missionaries. The author was born in Gabon in August 1944 and taught in Protestant schools. In 1974 he studied in London on a government grant in order to improve his abilities to teach English.

Pierre Akendengué, musicien gabonais. (Pierre Akendengué: Gabonese musician.)
See item no. 474.

Vincent-de-Paul Nyonda: un des pères du théâtre gabonais. (Vincent-de-Paul Nyonda: one of the fathers of the Gabonese theatre.)
See item no. 476.

Traditional

433 **Introduction to a Fang oral art genre: Gabon and Cameroon meet.**
Pierre Alexandre. *Bulletin of the School of African and Oriental Studies, University of London*, vol. 37, no. 1 (1974), p. 1-7. bibliog.

In the A70 group of Bantu languages the term *mvet* is used both for a type of musical instrument and for the special genres of oral literature played or delivered to its accompaniment. Though often called a musical bow, the *mvet* is technically speaking a chordophone with resonators. It is most often made of a dry bamboo. Specialists in the *mvet* form a kind of voluntary association that has three levels of status.

434 **Fragments d'une cosmologie Banzébi.** (Fragments of a Banzabi cosmology.)
Gérard Collomb. *Journal des Africanistes*, vol. 53, no. 1-2 (1983), p. 107-18. bibliog.

Information extracted from Nzabi mythical texts collected in 1975 and presented here is fragments of ancient knowledge that subsequently melted into a syncretic cosmology containing European culture. Beyond the representations of creation and organization of the universe, the Nzabi idea of God leads the author to emphasize the problems arising, sometimes unconsciously, from the use of analytical concepts derived from western religious thought.

435 **Les sept fils de Nzébi: un mythe cosmogonique des Banzébi du Gabon.**
(The seven sons of Nzabi: a cosmogonic myth of the Banzabi of
Gabon.)
Gérard Collomb. *Journal des Africanistes*, vol. 49, no. 2 (1979), p. 89-
139. bibliog.

This mythical tale, of which several versions have been gathered from Nzabi sources, is
a text setting forth the worlds of nature and culture surrounding the necessity for
marriage outside the clan as prescribed by Nzabi society. Beyond the first level of
analysis, Collomb endeavours to prove, by establishing a relationship with the main
features of the social structure, that this tale is valued by the Nzabi society as a
justification for their social system and political organization.

436 **La littérature orale des Fang/the oral literature of the Fang.**
Elie Ekogamve. *African Arts*, vol. 2, no. 4 (summer 1969), p. 14-19,
77-78. bibliog.

An examination is made of four features of Fang oral literature: formal narration at
ceremonies by professional storytellers; the *mvet* players; simple tales told by anyone;
and proverbs. The original French text is followed by an English translation. See also
Poems from Black Africa edited by Langston Hughes (Bloomington, Indiana: Indiana
University Press, 1963. 158p.).

437 **Le mvett.** (The *mvet*).
Tsira Ndong Ntoutoume. Paris: Présence Africaine, 1970, 1975.
157p., 311p. bibliog.

The Fang epic (*mvet*) deals with the unsuccessful efforts of the people of Okü, the
mortals, to wrest the secret of immortality from the people of Engong, who are the
'people of iron'. The epic reveals both the human and superhuman dimensions of Fang
self-understanding at the mythical, historical, metaphysical, and moral levels. It gives
witness to the richness and vitality of traditional Bantu culture in northern Gabon.
Whereas the *mvet* was traditionally sung or chanted to instrumental accompaniment,
Ndong Ntoutoume here has created a written version in French. For some critics his
text reflects an effort to come to grips with the intrusion of colonial rule and western
culture into Fang life in a way that preserves the core of traditional values.

438 **Nden-Bobo, l'araignée toilière.** (Nden-Bobo, spinning spider.)
Gaspard Towo-Atangana, Françoise Towo-Atangana. *Africa*
(London), vol. 36, no. 1 (Jan. 1966), p. 37-61. bibliog.

This is a tale from the repertoire of the *bebemo-mvet* corporation, performers on the
musical bow, in southern Cameroon and Gabon among the Beti, Bulu and Fang
peoples. During the mid-1960s these musicians and storytellers still enjoyed
considerable prestige in rural areas though economic changes had reduced the supply
of new recruits. Their repertoire included epics and semi-historical legends, folk-songs
and morality plays with animal characters. The present text has as its hero the spider,
who discusses with the high god Nzame the problem of evil in the world. Although the
theme is reminiscent of the Book of Job and contains clear evidence of Roman
Catholic influence, it is not merely a recent adaptation of missionary teaching but
rather a modern presentation of a traditional subject.

439   **Contes et légendes pygmées.** (Pygmy stories and legends.)
      Henri Trilles.   Bruges, Belgium: Librairie de l'Oeuvre St. Charles,
      1935. 186p. bibliog.

This collection of stories and legends of various groups of pygmies was gathered by a
Holy Ghost Father from France long resident in Gabon.

440   **Contes gabonais.** (Gabonese stories.)
      André Raponda Walker, Roger L. Sillans.   Paris: Présence Africaine,
      1967. 384p.

This volume contains 165 orally-recounted stories of 22 of Gabon's peoples, including
from all nine provinces. They were gathered by Walker (1871-1968), Gabon's first
Catholic priest, in the course of his long ministry in different areas of the country. The
stories are presented in French translation but without commentaries or notes. There
are only brief ethnographical introductions for each of the peoples and a general essay
on the genre of oral literature to guide the reader. The stories nevertheless represent
an important means for understanding the country's traditional societies in their
complexity and diversity. Nine of the stories were excerpted in the *Anthologie de la
littérature gabonaise* (1976). (q.v.).

Anthologies

441   **Anthologie de la littérature gabonaise.** (Anthology of Gabonese
      literature.)
      Edited by the Gabonese Ministry of National Education.   Montreal:
      Editions Littéraires, 1976. 357p. bibliog.

This anthology comprises a collection of excerpts and selections from the works of
Gabonese writers.

442   **La littérature gabonaise.** (Gabonese literature.)
      Notre Librairie.   Paris: CLEF, 1991. 173pp.

This work was also published as no. 105 (April-June 1991) of the journal, *Notre
Librairie*. It provides a detailed survey of Gabonese literature in French during the
twentieth century. Genres included are traditional literature, historical texts, and
literary works. There are a bibliography of the literary works of 30 authors and
excellent brief reviews of 23 publications. Among them are the novels of Angèle
Ntyugwetondo Rawiri and Laurent Owondo, a drama of Vincent-de-Paul Nyonda, and
poems by Ndouna Dépenaud. The volume contains essays on these and other writers,
thematic essays, and excerpts from various works. There are data on depositories and
research centres as well as journals published in Gabon, such as the *Revue gabonaise
des sciences de l'Homme* (Libreville, 1988-   ). Also of interest is Chinweizu's *Voices
from twentieth century Africa: griots and towncriers* (London: Faber, 1988. 424p.)

443 **Ecrivains, artistes et artisans gabonais.** (Gabonese writers, artists and artisans.)
Edited by Henry Walker-Deemin. Monaco: Paul Bory for the Institut Pédagogique National, 1970. 94p. bibliog.

This anthology contains literary excerpts and photographs, along with biographical information about Gabon's early writers, artists and artisans.

Criticism

444 **Laurent Owondo's 'Au bout du silence' or the age when the masks give up their secrets.**
Jacques Bourgeacq. *Research in African Literatures*, vol. 22, no. 2 (summer 1991), p. 71-81. bibliog.

Owondo's novel is difficult to understand because he has written in a poetic, allegorical style without providing the explanations from Gabonese magical-religious thought that would enlighten his readers. This article draws upon various ethnographic studies to provide the necessary understandings of these elements to appreciate a beautifully written story of a young man's struggle for self-understanding in terms of the ancestral cosmic vision. Influences from Bwiti and Ombwiri, in particular, are noted. The bibliography includes a review of the novel by Kenneth Harrow in *World Literature Today*, vol. 61, no. 1 (1987), p. 143.

445 **'La mort de Guykafi' de Vincent-de-Paul Nyonda ou les méfaits du tribalisme.** (*The Death of Guykafi* of Vincent-de-Paul Nyonda or the ravages of tribalism.)
Guy Daninos. *Culture Française*, no. 3-4 (1982)–no. 1 (1983), p. 79-82.

This offers a critical discussion of *La Mort de Guykafi* (Paris: Harmattan, 1981), a drama by Vincent-de-Paul Nyonda (b. 1918). The story deals with a powerful warrior, Guykafi, who kidnaps a seductive maiden only to learn that in his absence from home his own wife has yielded to a seducer. In keeping with tribal custom Guykafi kills his unfaithful wife but in turn is killed by the brothers of the maiden he violated. This panorama of love, marriage, infidelity, honour, war, tribalism, and death teaches much about the values of traditional society in a manner that intermingles imagination and realism.

446 **L'aide au Tiers Monde vue dans 'Elonga'.** (Aid to the Third World seen in 'Elonga'.)
Jérôme Ndzoungou. *Présence Africaine*, no. 1-2 (1985), p. 241-47.

This article discusses the ideas of Angèle Ntyugwetondo Rawiri in her novel *Elonga* (Paris: Editaf, 1980), about aid from western countries to African ones. *Elonga* emphasises that Western nations must not impose their model as the goal for African countries while the latter must be willing to accept change originating from the exterior.

447   **La romancière africaine face à la réalité socio-politique: l'exemple
d'Elonga de N. Rawiri.** (The African novelist faces socio-political
reality: the example of *Elonga* of N. Rawiri.)
Femi Ojo-Ade.   *Conjonction: Revue Franco-Haitienne*, no. 165 (1985),
p. 61-86. bibliog.

This is a critique of *Elonga*, the second of the three novels of Angèle Ntyugwetondo
Rawiri (b. 1954). *Elonga* means 'hell' in Myènè. The work deals with the effects of
fetishism upon a young person of mixed race who has returned to the country of his
Gabonese mother.

448   **La littérature gabonaise: Paul-Vincent Pounah à la recherche de la
poésie perdue.** (Gabonese literature: Paul-Vincent Pounah and the
search for lost poetry.)
Jean-Pierre Sauvageot.   *M'Bolo*, no. 1 (1980), p. 22-31. bibliog.

Pounah (b. 1914) was educated in Catholic mission schools and had a long and
distinguished career as a civil servant, retiring as head of the official news agency, the
Agence Gabonaise de Presse, in 1971. He has published several works on the history
and culture of the Galwa people of the Lambaréné area, including *Notre passé* ([Our
past] Paris: Société d'Impressions Techniques, 1970); *Carrefour de la discussion*
([Crossroads of the discussion] Coulonges sur l'Antize, France: Imprimerie Reynaud,
1971); and *La recherche du Gabon traditionnel: hier Edongo, aujourd'hui Galwa* ([In
search of traditional Gabon Edongo yesterday, Galwa today] Paris: Imprimerie
Loriou, 1975).

449   **Ntyugwetondo Rawiri, romancière gabonaise.** (Ntyugwetondo Rawiri,
Gabonese novelist.)
Jean-Pierre Sauvageot.   *M'Bolo*, no. 10 (1984), p. 20-29.

Gabon's first woman novelist was born at Port-Gentil in 1954 of Galwa parents. Her
father, Georges Rawiri, was a prominent politician and deputy prime minister under
the Bongo regime (until 1990). Angèle Ntyugwetondo Rawiri received her secondary
and higher education in France where she specialized in commercial translation from
English. Her first novel *G'amarakano au carrefour* ([American at the crossroads] Paris:
ABC, 1983), concerns the clash between an older generation's desire to safeguard
traditional values and a young girl's desire for material goods and pleasures.

450   **Mythe et dualité dans 'Au bout du silence'.** (Myth and duality in *Au
bout du silence*.)
André Hountondji Tolofon.   *African Littéraire*, no. 83-84 (1988),
p. 50-53.

This article discusses Laurent Owondo's use of myth and duality in his novel *Au bout
du silence* ([At the end of silence] Paris: Hatier, 1985). In the novel the hero, Anka,
achieves inner peace and self-understanding as a result of the struggle to acquire a
proper knowledge of the deeper meanings in the myths and symbols of traditional
Mpongwe society. Life in the modern African city, Little Venice, heightens his
awareness of his need to penetrate the mysteries of the ancestral way of life,
represented by his recently deceased grandfather, Chief Rediwa. Guided by the
feminine figure, Shadow, Anka comes to perceive the fundamental truths of traditional
society, which are expressed in terms of ambivalence and contrast.

The Arts

General

451 Pépin Antonio, Ernest Walker-Onewin, Christian Ndong Menzamet, David Nal-Vad.
Basile Allainmat-Mahine. *Revue Africaine* (Paris), no. 5 (June–Aug. 1992), p. 5-14.
An English text provides biographical sketches and photographs of contemporary sculptors and painters, all of whom were born in the mid- and late 1950s.

452 The exposition and imposition of order: artistic expression in Fang culture.
James W. Fernandez. In: *The traditional artist in African societies.* Edited by Warren d'Azevedo. Bloomington, Indiana: Indiana University Press, 1973, p. 194-220. bibliog.
Traditionally Fang society was highly egalitarian and loosely structured. The introduction of western culture under French colonial rule promoted social disorientation and cultural disintegration in Fang society. The author discusses the role of the artist in imposing order on a society in flux, using as his examples the carver, the troubadour, the chief judge of disputes (*palabras*) and the Bwiti cult leader.

453 Principles of opposition and vitality in Fang aesthetics.
James W. Fernandez. *Journal of Aesthetics and Art Criticism*, vol. 25, no. 1 (fall 1966), p. 53-64. bibliog.
Traditional Fang culture used the balance of opposite elements to express vitality. In both aesthetics and social structure the Fang aimed not to resolve opposition and to create identity but to preserve a balanced opposition. To the degree that western influence has upset this arrangement through acculturation, some of the vitality of Fang arts has been diminished.

454 **Gabonese artists' panorama.**
Revue Africaine (Paris), no. 5 (June–Aug. 1992), p. 24-30.
Biographical data and photographs of the works of twenty-six contemporary Gabonese artists, mainly sculptors and painters, are presented in this new Parisian quarterly.

455 **République gabonaise. Premier festival culturel national. Colloque sur le thème: culture et développement.** (Gabonese Republic: first national cultural festival. Colloquium on the theme: culture and development.)
Libreville: Ministry of Culture and the arts, 1975. 80p. bibliog.
These essays on ethnic differentiation and national unity in the face of development, literature, cinema, plastic arts and the theatre in Gabon were presented during a colloquium in the capital, March 19-26, 1974. The essay on cinema lists several films that Gabonese have produced.

456 **L'art sacré du Bwiti.** (The sacred art of the Bwiti.)
Stanislaw Świderski. *M'Bolo*, no. 24 (1989), p. 37-43.
A beautifully illustrated article indicates that Bwiti incorporated both African influences in sculpture and Christian influences in painting while retaining use of the sacred harp and masks. There is an English text in the unpaginated appendix.

Sculpture and masks

457 **Zur Kunst in Gabon: Stilkritische untersuckungen an Masken und Plastiken des Ogowe-Gebietes.** (On art in Gabon: research into the style of masks and sculptures from the Ogooué region.)
Ingeborg Bolz. *Ethnologica*, no. 3 (1966), p. 85-221. bibliog.
The art of the Bakwele, Fang and Kota peoples is known through European museums and published works. The *mbulu-ngulu*, that is, the brass-covered heads which accompanied the containers of the skull and bones of the ancestors of the Kota, are classified into six types while attention is drawn to the round heads of the same people. Bakwele art is not well documented so that more pieces collected during the 1920s must be studied before the style can be defined.

458 **The segmentation of form in Pahouin reliquary figures.**
Francine Deewilla Farr. Master's thesis, University of California at Los Angeles, 1983. 72p. bibliog. (Available on interlibrary loan).
The works of the Fang are included in this brief but detailed discussion of Pahouin figures.

459   **Fang reliquary art: its qualities and quantities.**
      James W. Fernandez, Renate L. Fernandez.   *Cahiers d'Études*
      Africaines, vol. 15, no. 4 (1975), p. 723-46.

This review essay responds to the views expressed by Louis Perrois in *Statuaire Fan,*
Gabon (Paris: ORSTOM, 1972), which was based on a study of 272 Fang reliquary
carvings. The Fernandez couple challenge certain of his findings and then discuss what
the statues reveal about Fang views of the supernatural and Fang culture in general. In
their view Fang reliquary figures, among their other purposes, were intended to inspire
caution in those uninitiated into the ancestor cult (*bieri*). The steady gaze of the eyes,
often accentuated by metallic discs, arrests the viewer. The locking of the arms across
the chest or their symmetrical extension towards the belly, the squareness of the
presentation, the crouch of the legs – all suggest unambiguous power in alert repose.
'Hieratic meditation' is a term often used to describe the posture of these figures but
they impose themselves more forcefully than such a passive description.

460   **Two masks from French Equatorial Africa.**
      H. U. Hall.   *Museum Journal, University of Pennsylvania*, (Dec.
      1927), p. 381-409. bibliog.

A description is given of masks from the peoples of the N'Gounié River valley.

461   **Masques du Gabon.** (Masks of Gabon.)
      Libreville: Ministry of Culture, Arts, and Popular Education for the
      National Museum of Arts and Traditions of Gabon, 1988. 92p.

This attractively illustrated catalogue depicts masks of various Gabonese peoples from
the collection of the National Museum of Arts and Traditions in Libreville.

462   **Ancestral art from Gabon: from the collection of the Barbier–Mueller**
      Museum.
      Louis Perrois.   Dallas, Texas: Museum of Art, 1986. 238p.

This is an annotated catalogue of Gabonese art.

463   **Aspects de la sculpture traditionnelle du Gabon.** (Aspects of traditional
      sculpture in Gabon.)
      Louis Perrois.   *Anthropos*, vol. 63-64, no. 5-6 (1968-69), p. 869-88.
      map. bibliog.

The art of Gabon has close links with traditional religion and social structure.
Traditionally ancestral figurines were used to preserve and reinforce the basic
organisation of the kinship group while masks were means of controlling social life.
The artist was a specialist in his village. Though in his work he represented a
traditionally and locally inspired art style, he did not copy from other works. As a rule
his skill and profession were passed on in the same family. Stylistic classifications
roughly followed tribal boundaries. While the figurines represented essentially a
unique type with its morphological variations, the masks expressed a greater
diversification of style and function. The well-known Mpongwe mask with its
mongoloid features appears to be an indigenous creation aiming at an idealist
representation of beauty. The conquests and migrations of the nineteenth century,

social mobility, and the effects of colonialism and religious disintegration brought about by the Christian missions have contributed to the destruction of traditional art in Gabon.

464 **Bakota funerary arts figures.**
Ladislas Segy. *Zaire*, vol. 6 (May 1952), p. 451-60. bibliog.
Bakota funerary figures show a tendency to abstraction in which the human body is portrayed without regard for the visual reality. The figures are two-dimensional sculptures carved from wood about an inch thick and then covered with sheets or strips of hammered metal. This distinctive art form does not seem to be influenced by neighbours nor does it influence their art. The Kota carvers do not attempt to represent the physical reality of the dead person but his spirit. The carvings that result from this conception often show great inventiveness and vivid improvisation.

465 **The face of the Bwiti.**
Leon Siroto. *African Arts*, vol. 1, no. 3 (spring 1968), p. 86-89, 96.
This article describes the process by which the source of some Osseyba figures was found. The association of these figures with the Bwiti cult among the Mahongwe and Shaké peoples, and the rites and function of the cult are explained.

Masks and social organization among the Bakwele people of western equatorial Africa.
See item no. 260.

Wood and metal working

466 **Technologies traditionnelles bantu: méthodes et rituel de la construction d'une pirogue et de ses apparaux au cap Santa Clara au Gabon.**
(Traditional Bantu technologies: the method and ritual for construction of a dugout canoe and its equipment at Cape Santa Clara in Gabon.)
Basile Allainmat-Mahine. *Muntu*, no. 3 (1985), p. 101-19.
The author has based his article on a meeting with a builder of dugout canoes who is a Benga living on Cape Santa Clara. The builder is also a respected traditional spiritual chief. Building such a canoe thus becomes a complex operation in which technology and metaphysics are intimately blended. The author has illustrated the work of the builder through a series of detailed drawings and diagrams.

467 **Quelques aspects techniques de la forge dans le bassin de l'Ogooué, Gabon.** (Some aspects of the forge in the Ogooué basin, Gabon.)
Gérard Collomb. *Anthropos*, vol. 76, no. 1-2 (1981), p. 50-66. map. bibliog.
In the Ogooué basin iron is produced solely by specialists and then only among certain peoples. In pre-colonial times there were many more blacksmiths than today. In fact, every village had some. This study of the course of the art of blacksmithing or iron-working describes both the tools and techniques used to produce the best results.

Architecture

468 **Fang architectonics.**
James W. Fernandez. Philadelphia, Pennsylvania: Institute for the Study of Human Issues, 1977. 41p.
The science of architecture as practised by the Fang is studied, including structural design and implementation.

469 **L'architecture au Gabon.** (Architecture in Gabon.)
Bonaventure Mvé-Ondo. *M'Bolo*, no. 13 (1985), p. 26-35.
This article gives a brief introduction to the traditional architectural styles of Gabon's indigenous peoples.

Music

470 **African music: a bibliographical guide to the traditional popular, art, and liturgical musics of sub-Saharan Africa.**
Compiled by John Gray. Westport, Connecticut: Greenwood, 1991. 499p.
This guide contains references on music and musicians in Gabon, including by ethnic group, as well as discography.

471 **Music: Akendengué in town.**
West Africa, (June 18, 1984), p. 1264-65.
This account of the London appearances of the Gabonese musician and composer, Pierre Akendengué, provides details on his life and career. He showed great versatility through the great variety of African musical forms and instruments that he employed in his review. He impressed his audiences by singing and telling stories of great dignity and beauty about his homeland.

472   **Gabon.**
   Pierre Sallée.   In: *New Grove dictionary of music and musicians, Vol.*
   7.   Edited by Stanley Sadie.   London: Macmillan, 1980, p. 49-54.
   map. bibliog.

The traditional music of Gabon's Bantu peoples resembles that of the other Bantu populations of the southern half of Africa in its forms and genres. Vocal music is frequently accompanied by string instruments, wooden flutes, xylophones and drums. Among the most notable instruments are the eight-string harp of the Bakèlè, the mouth-resonated musical bow of the Mitsogho and Myènè, and the *mvet* of the Fang. In the last named, a calabash provides the sounding chamber for the strings, which are plucked to accompany recitation of the epic of the same name. The Bantu peoples possess songs and chants in fixed form as well as traditional themes for vocal and instrumental improvisation, which are used to accompany religious rituals and social events of various kinds. The Bwiti cult, both in its older form among the Mitsogho and its contemporary form among the Fang, has liturgical ceremonies involving music and dance. The vocal music of the pygmies has features in common with that of other hunting and food-gathering peoples in Africa, including the use of a pentatonic tonal system incorporating tetratonic forms and of a yodelling technique with polyphonic imitation.

473   **Un musicien gabonais célèbre Rempano Mathurin. Sa place dans la**
   musique traditionnelle Nkomi. (A celebrated Gabonese musician,
   Rempano Mathurin. His place in traditional Nkomi music.)
   Pierre Sallée.   Libreville: ORSTOM, 1966. 43p. bibliog.

This is an account of a performer of traditional Nkomi music in the Ogooué-Maritime Province and his role in transmitting the artistic legacy of his people.

474   **Pierre Akendengué, musicien gabonais.** (Pierre Akendengué, Gabonese
   musician.)
   Nungu Tei Wadda.   *Agecop-Liaison*, (May–June 1983), p. 20-22.
   bibliog.

The musician and composer Pierre Akendengué (b. 1943) was born on the island of Awuta off the coast from Port-Gentil. His experiences of its forested environment, creatures and people have inspired many of the songs that he has composed during the last three decades. At first he recorded his own compositions in Nkomi and French by singing them to his own guitar accompaniment. Thereafter he set to music poems about everyday life by fellow countryman P. E. Mondjegou. As a result of further study, he sought to utilize traditional Gabonese musical forms involving choruses, vocal soloists, instrumentalists and dancers. During the late 1970s and 1980s he presented spectacles at Lagos and Paris featuring his compositions for these ensembles. Music for Akendengué came to be an assertion of the dignity of the African, the revaluation of his cultural patrimony, and the cornerstone of his identity. In France Akendengué also pursued university studies in psychology, sociology and educational sciences.

La harpe sacrée dans les cultes syncrétiques au Gabon. (The sacred harp in the syncretic cults of Gabon.)
See item no. 219.

Introduction to a Fang oral art genre: Gabon and Cameroon meet.
See item no. 433.
Le mvett. (The *mvet.*)
See item no. 437.

Theatre and film

475 **Cinéma au Gabon.** (Cinema in Gabon.)
Victor Bachy. Brussels: OCIC, 1986. 156p. bibliog.

This work presents a detailed history of film-making in Gabon. As early as 1936 French companies began to make films, mainly documentaries, in Gabon. After independence, Gabon's first professionally trained actor, Philippe Mory (or Maury) (b. 1932), who had won acclaim for his role in Parisian films, organized the Compagnie Cinématographique du Gabon (1962). In collaboration with a French company, he wrote and produced *La Cage*, which earned much praise at the Cannes Film Festival in 1963. During the following years, Mory, Pierre-Marie Ndong, Louis Mébalé, and Simon Augé produced films privately, including some for local television after 1963. Ndong's television drama, *Carrefour humain* (1969) dealt with the problem of the social integration of persons of mixed race (*métis*). President Bongo, installed a cinema seating 400 persons in his new palace, and in 1975 established the Centre National du Cinéma with Mory as director, a position he held until 1985. However, Bongo devoted far more resources to Les Films Gabonais, a company which he founded. It produced two films based on plays on social themes by his wife Joséphine, *Obali* (1976) and *Ayouma* (1977), as well as a third written by the president himself, *Demain, un jour nouveau* (1978). Gabonese film-making thus tended to become an enterprise supported and supervised by the Bongo couple. The volume contains summaries of the plots of the main films produced by Gabonese, biographies of film makers, and photographs of the producers and of scenes from the films.

476 **Vincent-de-Paul Nyonda: un des pères du théâtre gabonais.** (Vincent-de-Paul Nyonda: one of the fathers of the Gabonese theatre.)
Jean-Pierre Sauvageot. *M'Bolo*, no. 8 (1983), p. 49-53.

A discussion of the life and career of one of Gabon's first dramatists, whose works have been presented throughout Francophone Africa and in Paris. See also item no. 445.

Libraries, Archives and Research

Gabon

477 **Le CICIBA, pour rassembler et exalter le génie bantu.** (The ICBACI, in order to gather together and exalt the Bantu genius.)
Pierre Amrouche. *Géopolitique Africaine*, (Mar. 1986), p. 139-46.
A discussion of the founding and development of the International Centre of Banto Civilizations, which is located in Libreville. The centre seeks to raise the profile of Bantu culture, and publishes the quarterly journal *Mutu*.

478 **International guide to African studies research.**
Compiled by Philip Baker. London: Hans Zell, 1987. 264p.
Information about four research institutions in Gabon is included on p. 55.

479 **Archival resources in Gabon.**
Henry H. Bucher. *History in Africa*, vol. 1 (1974), p. 159-60.
At independence, French administrative records were removed to the depository of the French National Archives at Aix-en-Provence. The centralized Gabonese National Archives and Library in Libreville nevertheless contain much copied material from European depositories as well as Gabonese records. The library of the Chamber of Commerce has a collection of old books and maps while the libraries of ORSTOM and the National Museum have more recent published works.

480 **The Robert Hamill Nassau Collection in Gabon's National Archives: a bibliographical essay.**
Henry H. Bucher. *Journal des Africanistes*, vol. 47, no. 1 (1977), p. 186-95. bibliog.

This is a description of the complete published works and microfilmed manuscripts of Dr. Nassau, a prominent American Presbyterian missionary and extraordinary individual who made contributions to ethnography, linguistics, tropical medicine and natural science. The collection was deposited in the National Archives of Gabon in 1976 as a gift from American Presbyterians. Nassau worked among the Benga at Corisco and at Benita in Equatorial Guinea from 1861 to 1871; at Kangwe near Lambaréné among the Galoa and Bakèlè from 1874 to 1880; at Talagouga above N'Djolé among the Fang and Bakèlè from 1881 to 1891; and at Baraka near Libreville among the Mpongwe from 1893 to 1898.

481 **La recherche en sciences sociales au Gabon.** (Social science research in Gabon.)
Jean Ferdinand Mbah. Paris: Harmattan, 1987. 189p. bibliog.

The young Gabonese social anthropologist, Jules Mbah, has reviewed the major published research on the impact of the West upon Gabonese societies, particularly under French colonial rule. He has focused on the processes of transformation: material (modes of production, organization of space); social (relations of classes and generations); ideological (practices, representations, values and symbols). Of particular interest is his discussion of the mechanisms of capitalist domination that throw light on the social and political dimensions of the strategies of the various agents. This work may be read with profit in conjunction with that of Pourtier (see item no. 15).

482 **Le Centre International des Civilisations Bantu (CICIBA).** (The International Centre of Bantu Civilizations, ICBACI.)
Louis Perrois. *Afrique Contemporaine*, vol. 26, no. 1 (1987), p. 52-54.

An account of the activities of the CICIBA. See also Amrouche's article, *Le CICIBA, pour rassembler et exalter le génie banto* (q.v.).

Traditions orales et archives au Gabon. (Oral traditions and archives in Gabon.)
See item no. 106.

Western Europe

483 **Materials for West African history in French archives.**
Compiled by Patricia Carson. London: Althone Press, 1963. 170p.
This volume includes materials on Gabon.

484   **Resources for the history of Gabon in French missionary archives in**
       Rome.
       David E. Gardinier.   *History in Africa*, vol. 8 (1981), p. 323-25.
This article discusses the records of the Immaculate Conception Sisters of Castres,
France, who worked with women and girls from 1849 in the Gabon Estuary and
elsewhere, and of the Brothers of St. Gabriel, who ran boys' schools at Libreville and
Lambaréné beginning in 1900.

485   **Resources in Paris missionary archives and libraries for the history of**
       Gabon.
       David E. Gardinier.   *History in Africa*, vol. 7 (1980), p. 159-60.
A description is given of the records of the Holy Ghost Fathers (Spiritans), who first
arrived in the Gabon Estuary in 1844 and who later spread throughout the country,
and of the Evangelical Missions Society of Paris, who took over Protestant work
between 1892 and 1913 and then expanded into new areas of the north. Also included
are the relevant materials in the Paris branch of the Oeuvres Pontificales et
Missionnaires of Lyons, who aided the Catholic missions financially.

486   **The SCOLMA directory of libraries and special collections on Africa in**
       the United Kingdom and western Europe.
       Edited by Tom French.   Oxford: Zell, 1992. 5th ed. 240p.
This is a guide to collections having materials on former French Africa, including
Gabon.

487   **Le centre des archives d'outre-mer d'Aix-en-Provence.** (The centre of
       the overseas archives of Aix-en-Provence.)
       Jean-François Maurel.   *Afrique Contemporaine*, vol. 27, no. 1 (1989),
       p. 60-63.
In 1986 the overseas section of the French National Archives, which contained the
records of the Ministry of the Colonies/Overseas Ministry from the 1890s to 1960, was
transferred from Paris to Aix. Already in Aix were the archives of French Equatorial
Africa, which had been transferred there from Brazzaville in the early 1960s. Maurel
describes the centre which holds these two major collections.

488   **Sources d'information sur l'Afrique francophone et Madagascar:**
       institutions, répertoires, bibliographies. (Sources of information on
       French-speaking Black Africa and Madagascar: Institutions, lists,
       bibliographies)
       Compiled by Laurence Porgès.   Paris: Ministry of Cooperation and
       Documentation Française, 1988. 389p.
This work includes descriptions of institutions, lists or indexes, and bibliographies that
are sources of information on Africa. Material on Gabon is found in entries on all of
francophone Africa and central or equatorial Africa as well as on Gabon specifically.

489 **Répertoire des thèses africanistes françaises.** (List of French Africanist theses.)
Paris: Centres d'Etudes Africaines, CARDAN, Ecole des Hautes Etudes en Sciences Sociales, 1977-   . annual.

This annual publication lists theses, including ones on Gabon, completed in French universities.

490 **Sources de l'histoire de l'Afrique au sud du Sahara dans les archives et bibliothèques françaises.** (Sources for the history of sub-Saharan Africa in French archives and libraries.)
Interdocumentation Co.   Switzerland: Zug, A. G. 1971, 1976. 2 vols.

These archival guides were prepared under the auspices of the International Council for Archives (UNESCO). The first volume includes archives and the second libraries. The volumes are 959p. and 930p. in length.

491 **United Kingdom publications and theses on Africa.**
Standing Confrence on Library Materials on Africa.   Cambridge, England: Heffer, 1963-   . irregular.

This is a guide to research and publications in the United Kingdom.

492 **French Colonial Africa: a guide to official sources.**
Gloria D. Westfall.   London: Hans Zell Publishers, 1992. 226p.

This volume provides the most up-to-date, complete, and useful guide for the official sources for the colonial period in Equatorial Africa. Included in this excellent reference work are detailed descriptions of: the guides and bibliographies for the official sources on the period of French colonial rule in Africa; the archival holdings in France and the African states (including Gabon) and the inventories to them; the publications of the central administration; semi-official publications; and the publications of colonial governments. Also of interest is Edwin K. Welsch's *Research resources France: libraries and archives of France* (New York: Council for European Studies, 1979. 146p.).

USA and Canada

493 **African studies information resources directory.**
Compiled and edited by Jean E. Meeh Gosebrink.   Oxford: Hans Zell, 1986. 572p. bibliog.

This is an invaluable reference guide to the archives, libraries and research centres in the United States containing materials on Africa. There is an index of their location by states.

494 **American and Canadian doctoral dissertations and master's theses on Africa, 1947-1987.**
Compiled by Joseph J. Lauer, Gregory V. Larkin, Alfred Kagan.
Atlanta, Georgia: African Studies Association, 1987. 377p.

This compilation is particularly useful because it lists Canadian master's theses in French that are usually not included in the abstracts published by University Microfilms International.

495 **Guide to federal archives and manuscripts in the United States relating to Africa.**
Edited by Aloha P. South.   Waltham, Massachusetts: Crossroads, 1977. 556p. bibliog.

This volume describes the contents of the holdings of the US Congress, executive departments, special commissions and boards.

496 **Guide to non-federal archives and manuscripts in the United States relating to Africa.**
Edited by Aloha P. South.   London; New York: Hans Zell, 1989. 2 vols. 1250p. bibliog.

A description is given of the contents of 500 Africana archival collections and the guides available for their use.

Periodicals and Media

General

497 **Africa Confidential.**
   London: Miramoor, 1960. fortnightly.
This periodical contains news items and articles on Gabon and on French involvement in sub-Saharan Africa. 'Confidential' in the title refers to the fact that these writings are unsigned.

498 **Africa Research Bulletin. Series A. Political, social, cultural. Series B. Economic, financial, technical.**
   Exeter, England: Economist Intelligence Unit, 1964- . monthly.
This is a press digest of the most important developments in Africa, including Gabon. The digests generally include verbatim translations of such important publications as *Marchés Tropicaux et Méditerranéens*, *Bulletin de l'Afrique Noire*, *Le Monde* and *Jeune Afrique* as well as items from *West Africa* and *Africa Confidential* (q.q.v.).

499 **Afrique Contemporaine.** (Contemporary Africa.)
   Paris: Documentation Française, 1959- . quarterly.
In addition to occasional articles and news items on Gabon, this periodical regularly features a chronology of important events and reviews of books.

500 **Bulletin de l'Afrique Noire.** (Bulletin of Black Africa.)
   Paris: Ediafric, 1957- . weekly.
This provides reliable economic and financial news concerning Gabon. Cabinet changes are also listed.

501 **Bulletin de l'Institut d'Études Centrafricains.** (Bulletin of the Institute of Central African Studies.)
Brazzaville: Institut d'Etudes Centrafricaines, Imprimerie Officielle, 1945- . quarterly.
This journal includes articles on the history and anthropology of Gabon.

502 **Bulletin Quotidien d'Afrique.** (Daily Bulletin of Africa.)
Paris: Agence France-Presse, 1960- . daily.
The daily news bulletin of the official French news agency has generally accurate and reliable news of events in Gabon.

503 **Jeune Afrique.** (Young Africa.)
Paris: Jeune Afrique, 1960- . weekly.
This review, with many African correspondents, focuses mainly on political events. It frequently contains interpretive articles dealing with the long-term implications of particular happenings as in the case of the upheaval of 1990-91.

504 **Marchés Tropicaux et Méditerranéens.** (Tropical and Mediterranean Markets.)
Paris: René Moreux, 1945- . weekly.
Since the late 1970s this weekly has been the most important French source for reliable economic and financial news concerning Gabon. In addition to a weekly news section, there are periodically some interpretive articles and occasionally a cluster of articles dealing with trends in historical perspective.

505 **Le Monde.** (The World.)
Paris: Le Monde, 1944- . daily.
This Parisian daily provides the most complete and reliable press coverage on events in Gabon and relations with France.

506 **Muntu.** (Man.)
Libreville: International Centre of Bantu Civilisations, 1985-
quarterly.
This publication is particularly concerned with the Bantu peoples of Gabon and western equatorial Africa, their history and culture.

507 **Quarterly Economic Review of Congo, Gabon, Equatorial Guinea.**
London: Economist Intelligence Unit, 1984- . quarterly.
This detailed survey of economic and political news is sometimes weak in terms of the context for developments. Between 1960 and 1983 Gabon was included in a quarterly economic review grouping larger numbers of countries.

508 **Répertoire de l'information en Afrique et dans l'Océan Indien.** (List of information [sources] in Africa and the Indian Ocean.)
Paris: Radio France Internationale, 1989. 245p.
This work provides a list of media sources, including Gabon.

509 **La radio en Afrique noire.** (The radio in Black Africa.)
A. J. Tudesq. Paris: Pedone, 1983. 312p. bibliog.
Gabon has a national radio station broadcasting in French and local stations in French and indigenous languages. Gabon is also the site of the pan-African radio station, Africa. no. 1.

510 **West Africa.**
London: West Africa Publishers, 1917- . weekly.
Brief but reliable news items from Gabon are included.

Gabon

511 **Annales de l'Université Nationale du Gabon, série Lettres et Sciences Sociales.** (Annals of the National University of Gabon, Letters and Social Sciences series.)
Libreville: National University of Gabon, 1977- . irregular.
This publication contains articles, primarily on Gabon, by university faculty members.

512 **Annales de l'Université Nationale du Gabon, série Sciences.** (Annals of the National University of Gabon, Sciences series.)
Libreville: National University, 1977- . irregular.
This journal has articles on the physical and natural sciences in Gabon.

513 **Journal Officiel.** (Official Journal.)
Libreville: Imprimerie Nationale, 1959- . semi-monthly.
This contains texts of laws, decrees, administrative regulations and appointments to government employment.

514 **M'Bolo.**
Libreville: Air Gabon, 1980- . irregular.
This publication of the national airline has contained articles on Gabonese personalities with information found nowhere else. General articles on the country's history and culture are clearly written and of a very high standard.

515 **Africa no. 1.**
Jean Mori. *M'Bolo*, no. 17 (1986), p. 35-43.
In 1978 in cooperation with France, Gabon built Africa no. 1, a pan-African or international radio station broadcasting in the French language. The four transmitters of 500 Kw each at Moyabi in the Haut-Ogooué Province allow the broadcasts to be heard as far away as Senegal. Africa no. 1 broadcasts programmes from Radio France International, Swiss radio and Japanese radio as well as its own programmes.

516 **Réalités Gabonaises: Revue Pédagogique et Culturelle du Gabon.**
(Gabonese Realities: Pedagogical and Cultural Review of Gabon.)
Libreville: Ministry of National Education, 1959- . semi-monthly.
This pedagogical and cultural review for school teachers contains many brief articles on Gabonese history and culture by the teachers themselves and by Gabonese scholars.

517 **L'Union: Quotidien Gabonais d'Information.** (Union: Gabonese Information Daily.)
Libreville: Multipresse, 1974- . daily.
This daily expresses the viewpoint of the Bongo regime on events in Gabon and elsewhere. It contains useful economic and financial news as well as information about the activities of the Parti Démocratique Gabonais, the country's ruling political party.

General Reference Works

518 **Africa south of the Sahara.**
London: Europe Publications, 1971- . annual.
This annual directory repeats much of the material of previous years in its chapter on Gabon while updating it so that the reader obtains a good perspective on politics, external relations, economic trends and social affairs in the decades since independence in 1960. There are statistics, a bibliography, and a directory of practical information on ministries and businesss.

519 **Année africaine.** (African year.)
Paris: Pedone, 1963- . annual.
General articles are included on France in Africa and a section on developments in Gabon.

520 **Année politique africaine.** (African political year.)
Dakar: Sociéte Africaine d'Edition, 1966- . annual.
This contains general articles on French relations with Africa and a section on political developments in Gabon.

521 **Annuaire du Tiers-Monde.** (Third World annual.)
Paris: Berger-Levrault, 1976- . annual.
This publication provides an annual survey of events in Gabon plus articles on French relations with the franocphone states and Third World issues.

522 **African boundaries. A legal and diplomatic encyclopedia.**
Compiled by Ian Brownlie. London: C. Hurst, 1979. 1355p. bibliog.
This volume contains the texts of the international agreements that established Gabon's boundaries in the nineteenth and early twentieth centuries.

156

523   **Congo, Gabon, Equatorial Guinea. Country report.**
      London: Economist Intelligence Unit, 1985- . annual.
This is an annual composite of economic and political news from Gabon with statistics.
Sometimes the context for the data is incomplete or inadequate.

524   **Place names of Africa, 1935-1986: a political gazetteer.**
      Compiled by Eugene C. Kirchherr.   Metuchen, New Jersey; London:
      Scarecrow Press, 1987. 136p.
This political gazetteer includes names from Gabon.

525   **Africa contemporary record.**
      Edited by Colin Legum (1968-88), Mario Doro (1989- . New York;
      London: Africana Publishing, 1968/69- . annual.
This offers a reliable review of contemporary happenings throughout the continent of
Africa. In addition to general essays, including one on France in Africa that generally
touches upon Gabon, there are documents and statistics on economic, social, regional,
constitutional and international issues. An individual country report on Gabon
summarizes political events, external relations, economic matters and the social
situation. The author of this report starting with 1989-90 is David E. Gardinier.

526   **Official standard names approved by the United States Board of**
      Geographic Names.
      Washington, DC: Government Printing Office, 1962. 113p.
This is a guide to the official spelling of names from Gabon.

Directories

527 **Annuaire national officiel de la République gabonaise.** (Official national yearbook of the Gabonese Republic.)
Libreville: Agence Havas Gabon, 1973- . annual.
This publication contains addresses of governmental departments, foreign embassies and businesses. There are biographies of the careers of the top office-holders, including the president, vice-president and cabinet members.

528 **Annuarium statisticum ecclesiae.** (Church statistical annual.)
Rome: Secretaria Status Rationarum Generale Ecclesiae, 1987. 439p.
Statistics are included on the Roman Catholic Church in Gabon by diocese, parish, religious congregation and school.

529 **L'Eglise Catholique en Afrique Occidentale et Centrale: répertoire des missions catholiques.** (The Catholic Church in Western and Central Africa. List of Catholic Missions.)
Paris: ONCP-RF, 1989. 1100p.
This work lists the parishes within the four dioceses of Gabon and the numbers of clergy, religious and sisters serving in them by religious congregation. There is also information on other church institutions, including schools and health care facilities.

530 **Les élites gabonaises.** (Gabonese élites.)
Paris: Ediafric, 1988. 3rd ed. 200p.
Biographical data are supplied on Gabon's politicians and high civil servants, provided by themselves. An earlier edition of this work was published in 1977.

Bibliographies

531   **Africa south of the Sahara: index to periodical literature, 1900-1970.**
   Compiled by African Section, US Library of Congress.   Boston: G. K.
   Hall, 1971. 4 vols.

A supplement to this item was published in 1973. All of the periodicals and articles are found in the Library of Congress in Washington, DC.

532   **Bibliographie des travaux en langue française sur l'Afrique au sud du**
   Sahara. (Bibliography of works in the French language on sub-Saharan
   Africa.)
   Paris: Ecole des Hautes Etudes en Sciences Sociales, Centre des Etudes
   africaines, CARDAN, 1977-   . annual.

Chapters in collective works are included as well as books and articles.

533   **Africa bibliography.**
   Edited by Hector Blackhurst.   Manchester, England; New York:
   Manchester University Press, 1983-   . annual.

In addition to books and articles, chapters in collective works are included. There are also subject and author indexes.

534   **Bibliographie de l'Afrique Equatoriale Française.** (Bibliography of
   French Equatorial Africa.)
   Georges Bruel.   Paris: Larose, 1914. 326p.

This represents the standard work on publications on Gabon prior to the First World War.

535 **Ouvrages sur le Gabon.** (Works on Gabon.)
Annie Cros.   Libreville: Centre Culturel Saint-Exupéry, 1978. 81p.
This is a bibliography that is particularly useful for the natural and physical sciences up to 1978.

536 **Current Bibliography of African Affairs.**
Washington, DC: African Bibliographic Center, new series, 1968-
quarterly.
This bibliography on current affairs often lists materials not found elsewhere.

537 **Afrika index to continental periodical literature.**
Compiled by Colin, Darch, O. C. Mascarenhas.   Oxford, Hans Zell,
1976- . annual.
This constitutes an index to articles published in Africa.

538 **Connaissance du Gabon: guide bibliographique.** (Knowledge of Gabon: bibliographical guide.)
Compiled by L. Olenka Darkowska-Nidzgoroka.   Libreville:
Université du Gabon, 1978. 151p.
This bibliography was compiled for the users of the library of the National University.

539 **Bibliography of Africana bibliographies, 1965-1975.**
Compiled by David L. Easterbrook.   *Africana Journal*, vol. 7, no. 2
(1976), p. 101-48.
This article has some bibliographies containing references to Gabon. A supplement for 1975-76 was contained in *Ibid.*, vol. 8, no. 3 (1977), p. 232-42.

540 **Le Gabon: répertoire bibliographique relatif aux sciences humaines.**
(Gabon: bibliographical list relative to the human sciences.)
Paris: BDPA, 1962. 44p.
This older bibliography is strong for works published after 1945 and before independence.

541 **Africa.**
Compiled by David E. Gardinier.   In: *Recently Published Articles.*
Washington, DC: American Historical Association, 1976-90. three
times per year.
This is a bibliography of articles of interest to historians drawn mainly from the humanities and social sciences but including some titles in archaeology, biology and the fine arts. From 1964 to 1975 the bibliography was published as a part of the *American Historical Review.*

542 **French colonial rule in Africa [1914-62]: A bibliographical essay.**
David E. Gardinier. In: *France and Britain in Africa: imperial rivalry and colonial rule.* Edited by Prosser Gifford, Wm. Roger Louis.
New Haven, Connecticut: Yale University Press, 1971, p. 787-902.
This is a historiographical essay and a bibliography on French colonial rule that contains many references to Gabon in and of itself, as a part of French Equatorial Africa, and as part of the French Empire and Union.

543 **International African Bibliography.**
London: Mansell, 1971- . quarterly.
This represents the most complete bibliography for the humanities and social sciences in Gabon in terms of non-French publications. It has an author index and subject categories in the entries themselves.

544 **Liste bibliographique des travaux des chercheurs et techniciens ORSTOM en République gabonaise, de 1949 à 1977.** (Bibliographical list of the works of ORSTOM's researchers and technicians in the Gabonese Republic from 1949 to 1977.)
Libreville: Mission ORSTOM, 1978. 73p.
This is a bibliography of French-sponsored research publications.

545 **Bibliographies for African studies, 1970-1986.**
Compiled and edited by Yvette Scheven. London: Hans Zell, 1988. 615p.
A very useful bibliography of bibliographies for francophone Africa and Gabon.

546 **U.S. imprints on subSaharan Africa: a guide to publications catalogued at the Library of Congress.**
Washington, DC: Library of Congress, 1985- . annual.
A list of works on Africa published in the United States and deposited, as required by law, in the Library of Congress.

547 **French-speaking Central Africa: a guide to official publications in American libraries.**
Compiled by Julian W. Witherell. Washington, DC: Library of Congress, 1973. 314p.
Publications on Gabon are included in this bibliography.

548 **Official publications of French Equatorial Africa, French Cameroons and Togo, 1946-1958.**
Compiled by Julian W. Witherell. Washington, DC: Library of Congress, 1964. 78p.
The items included were published during the Fourth French Republic when Gabon was an overseas territory as well as still a territory of the federation of French Equatorial Africa.

549 **The United States and Africa: guide to U.S. official documents and government sponsored publications on Africa, 1785-1975.**
Edited by Julian W. Witherell. Washington, DC: Library of Congress, 1978. 949p.
Materials on French Equatorial Africa and Gabon are included.

Bibliographical essay: decolonization in French, Belgian, and Portuguese Africa.
See item no. 169.

Decolonization in French, Belgian, Portuguese, and Italian Africa: bibliography.
See item no. 170.

2500 titres de littérature: Afrique subsaharienne.
See item no. 429.

Bibliographies in African literature since 1970.
See item no. 431.

African music: a bibliographical guide to the traditional, popular art, and liturgical musics of sub-Saharan Africa.
See item no. 470.

Indexes

There follow three separate indexes: authors (personal and corporate); titles; and subjects. Title entries are italicized and refer either to the main titles, or to other works cited in the annotations. The numbers refer to bibliographic entries, not to pages.

Index of Authors

A

Abolfathi, Farid 310
Adda, Jacques 323
Adloff, Richard 7
African Section, US
    Library of Congress
    531
Ageron, Robert 164
Aicardi de Saint-Paul,
    Marc 1
Akélaguélo, Aganga 99
Ajami, S. M. 288-89
Akoumondo, Jocelyn 336
Allainmat-Mahine, Basile
    451, 466
Allard, Giles O. 23
Alexander, Caroline 79
Alexandre, Pierre 433
Alihanga, Martin 100
Allo, Emmanuel Mba 311
Ambouroué-Avaro,
    Joseph 101
Amnesty International 283
Amrouche, Pierre 477
Anderson, Howard
    William 385
Assam, Aristote 275
Aubreville, A. 28
Austen, Ralph A. 135
Azevedo, Warren d' 452

B

Bachy, Victor 475
Baker, Philip 478
Balandier, Georges 80, 136
Ballard, John A. 162-63
Bangoura, Dominique 299
Barbier-Decrozes,
    Madeleine 37
Barret, Jacques 19
Barnes, James F. 2
Barnes, R. F. W. 38
Barro-Chambrier, Hugues-
    Alexandre 353, 359
Bernard, Pierre A. 50
Bernault-Boswell,
    Florence 164
Bertin, A. 379
Best, Jacob 198
Biffot, Laurent 254
Bigmann, Louis 300
Bikoro, Blandine Engonga
    206
Binet, Jacques 207
Birmingham, David 67,
    102
Biteghe, Moise N'sole 178
Blackhurst, Hector 533
Blanc, René 240
Blanchon, Jean A. 191
Blocher, Jacques 240
Boltenhagen, Eugène 24
Bolz, Ingeborg 457
Bongo, Omar 276

Borella, François 165
Bosman, William 81
Bosworth, William 418
Bouche, Denise 226
Bouet, Claude 11, 397
Bouquerel, Jacqueline 68,
    354
Bourgeacq, Jacques 444
Bowdich, Thomas Edward
    82
Brabazon, James 245
Brasseur, Paule 227-28
Brochet, Christine 369
Brown, Arthur Judson 235
Brownlie, Ian 522
Bruel, Georges 534
Brunschwig, Henri 137
Bucher, Henry H. 83, 92,
    103–04, 122-25, 479-80
Buttoud, Gérard 355

C

Cabrol, Claude 255, 391
Cadenat, Patrick 324
Caldwell, John C. 189
Campbell, Penelope 236
Carpenter, Allen 8
Carson, Patricia 483
Carter, Gwendolyn 163
Chafer, Tony 325
Chaigneau, Pascal 301

165

Index of Titles

Index of Subjects

A

ABCFM Mission 88, 236-39, 242
Adjumba language 197
Administration 1, 297-98
Adouma 56
Africa No. 1 515
Agondjo-Okawe, Paul-Louis 286-87
Agriculture 15, 254, 385-90
Air Afrique 37
Akendengué, Pierre 47, 474
Alar ayong 168
Alihanga, Martin 258
Animals 37-46
Antonio, Pépin 451
Apindji 220-21
Archaeology 52-68
  in Estuary 52
  in Haut-Ogooué 52, 54-57, 62
  in N'Gounié 54-56, 62
  in Woleu-N'Tem 52
Architecture 468-69
Armed forces 299, 307–08
Atlases 19
Aubame, Jean-Hilaire 4, 161-62, 164, 178, 180, 183, 326
Aviation 393-94
Awandji 143, 150
Ayouné, Jean-Rémy 161

B

Babuissi 153
Bakale, P. 210
Bakèlé people 105, 111, 137, 238, 244, 256, 472, 480
  language 198
Bakota 75, 256, 457, 464
Bakouélé 260, 457
Banks 346, 357, 404

Bantu expansion 52, 61, 63, 66-67
Bantu languages 194, 199
Bapounou 153, 283
  language 191
Benga 229, 236, 244, 480
Benin 281, 336
Bessieux, Jean-Rémy 128, 233
Bichet, Marie-Georges 146
Birds 47
Bloc Démocratique Gabonais 162
Boganda, Barthélémy 167
Bongo, Ali 253
Bongo, Josephine 281
Bongo, Omar 178, 253, 275-82, 286-87, 329, 333, 398
Bonnel de Mézières 149
Bosman, William 81
Boundaries 15, 149, 522
Bowdich, Thomas 82, 88
Brazil 23, 123
Brazza, Pierre S. de 84, 91, 151, 241
Brazzaville Conference 161, 416
Brothers of St. Gabriel 230, 232, 413, 484
Bwiti 207–09, 211-13, 215-16, 218-21, 224, 444, 452, 456, 465

C

Cameroon 154-55, 168
Cancer 270
Canoe-making 466
Cape Santa Clara 466
Cape Esterias 236
Catholic Church 231, 422, 528-29
Catholic missions (see History)
CEEAC 339, 348, 374

Chimpanzee 46
Christian and Missionary Alliance Mission 239
CICIBA 258, 477, 482
Cinema 455, 475
CIRMF 267
Clémenceau, Macaire 232
Climates 16, 57
Cocobeach 156
COMILOG 373
COMUF 332
Conan, Georges 281-82
Concessionary companies 139-40, 142, 144
Congo Republic 71, 153, 373
Constitution 1, 287-91, 294
Copper 57, 59
Cottes 149
Crampel 149

D

De Gaulle, Charles 161, 177-78, 180
Decolonization 7, 125, 171, 173-77
Delaunay, Maurice 281-82
Denis, King 131
Drugs 207, 209, 215
Du Bellay, M.-T. Griffon 88
Du Chaillu, Paul B. 83, 88-90
Dutch 81, 96, 108, 112, 118

E

Eboué, Félix 161, 414
Economic development 361-63, 365
Economy 1-3, 5, 15, 353-68
Education 161, 203, 229-30, 237-38, 242, 412-28
Ekoh, Jean-Marc 285

175

Map of Gabon

This map shows the administrative districts and major towns.

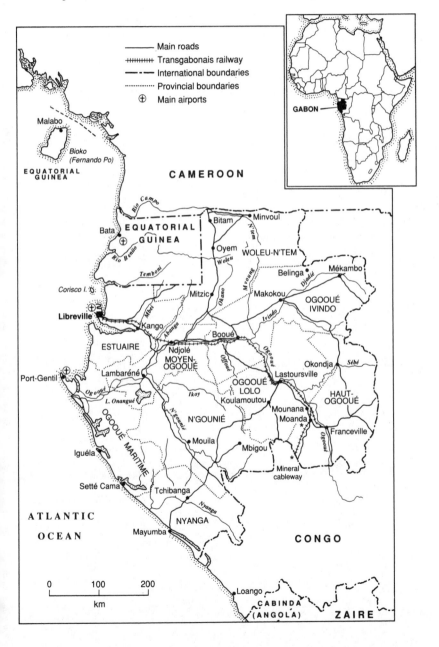